SAMANTABHADRA'S PRAYER

Volume I
With Commentaries
by Nagarjuna and Tony Duff

BY TONY DUFF
PADMA KARPO TRANSLATION COMMITTEE

Copyright © 2015 Tony Duff. All rights reserved. No portion of this book may be reproduced in any form or by any means, electronic or mechanical, including photography, recording, or by any information storage or retrieval system or technologies now known or later developed, without permission in writing from the publisher.

First edition, July 2015
ISBN paper book: 978-9937-572-60-6
ISBN e-book: 978-9937-572-61-3

Janson typeface with diacritical marks
designed and created by Tony Duff

Produced, Printed, and Published by
Padma Karpo Translation Committee
P.O. Box 4957
Kathmandu
NEPAL

Committee members for this book: translation and composition, Lama Tony Duff; sutra translation Tamás Agócs; cover design, George Romvari of Purica.

Web-site and e-mail contact through:
http://www.pktc.org/pktc
or search Padma Karpo Translation Committee on the web.

CONTENTS

VOLUME I

Introduction v
   1. The Importance of Samantabhadra's Prayer x
      1. It is one of the Five Important Prayers of the Great
         Vehicle Tradition x
      2. The Prayer's Place in Tibetan Buddhist Practice
         with a Note on its use in Dzogchen Practice in
         East Tibet xii
   2. The Origin of Samantabhadra's Prayer xiii
   3. The Prayer is an Extract xiv
      1. What are the Extracts like? xiv
      2. Problems with the Extracts xv
      3. Fixing Problems xv
   4. Explanations of the Prayer xv
      1. Indian Commentaries xvi
      2. The First Tibetan Commentary on the Prayer .. xvii
      3. Later Tibetan Commentaries on the Prayer xviii
      4. A Recent but Very Useful Tibetan Commentary .. xx
      5. A Western Commentary xxi
   5. Translating the Prayer into English xxii
      1. In General xxii
      2. Specific Issues xxiii

CONTENTS

    6. Arrangement of the Materials xxvi
    7. Gender Issues xxvii
    8. Sanskrit xxviii
    9. Supports for Study xxviii
    10. Tibetan Texts xxix
    11. Make a Practice Text xxix

FROM THE GAṆḌAVYŪHA SUTRA: SUDHANA MEETS WITH
THE BODHISATVA SAMANTABHADRA AND
SAMANTABHADRA EXPRESSES THE PRAYER 1

SAMANTABHADRA'S PRAYER AS ARRANGED FOR USE BY
    TIBETANS 33

SAMANTABHADRA'S PRAYER AS ARRANGED FOR USE BY
    NON-TIBETANS 35

A THOROUGH EXPLANATION OF SAMANTABHADRA'S
    PRAYER BY TONY DUFF 39

AN EXPLANATION OF SAMANTABHADRA'S PRAYER BY
    NOBLE NĀGĀRJUNA 169

GLOSSARY OF TERMS 230
SUPPORTS FOR STUDY 245
INDEX 251

VOLUME II

A TIBETAN COMMENTARY TO SAMANTABHADRA'S PRAYER
    BY ONTRUL TENPA'I WANGCHUK

INTRODUCTION

This book is volume one in a series of books that offers, for the first time in the English language, a comprehensive guide to the prayer known as "Samantabhadra's Prayer". Note that the content of each volume, including this introduction, is exactly the same except for the commentaries that explain the prayer. This has been done so that each volume would be a complete resource, with only the explanations given in the commentaries changing. Note also that in the Tibetan tradition there are two prayers with the name "Samantabhadra's Prayer". The prayer in this series is the prayer from the Great Vehicle sutras that sets out the excellent conduct of a bodhisatva, not the prayer that explains profound Great Completion.

Samantabhadra's Prayer has been widely used by Great Vehicle Buddhists in Asia for millennia and is known to have been recited daily in Tibet by a significant portion of the Buddhist population. In recent times Western followers of Tibetan Buddhism have begun to recite translations of the prayer into English. As one of the Westerners who took up daily recital of the prayer, I sometimes recited the Tibetan text of the prayer and sometimes recited one of the translations that had been made into English. With that, I began to notice what seemed to be significant discrepancies between the existing English translations and the Tibetan text of the prayer.

During a stay in a monastery in Tibet in 2011, I was required to join a week-long all-day recitation of the prayer. Each day I saw discrepancies between the existing English translations—which I had with me—and the Tibetan version of the prayer and each day asked the head scholar of the monastery about them. His answers revealed a very high level of problems with the existing English translations. The existing translations missed many subtle but important points, had the meaning back to front or twisted around in many places, had outright mis-translations of words, had many places where the grammar had simply been ignored, and more. By the end of the week, I felt compelled to make a new English translation that would accurately reflect the wording and meaning of the prayer as understood by the tradition. I envisaged a publication that would put the new translation together with extensive explanations that would verify every wording and meaning of the prayer.

As I undertook the work, I found that there were complications surrounding the prayer, which I will now describe.

I started by assembling several Tibetan texts of the prayer and nearly twenty commentaries to it. Commentaries to it had been written in India well before the great translation of Buddhist texts into Tibetan language and several of them had been translated into Tibetan language at the time of the great translations. I obtained copies of all of them and also obtained a copy of the first commentary to the prayer written in Tibetan language, which had been written by one of the greatest of all Tibetan translators, Yeshe De, in conjunction with the Indian masters who were advising him and others during the great translations.

The first complication that I discovered was that Yeshe De's explanations of the prayer were entirely consistent with the explanations given by Indian masters in their commentaries but that, after some centuries had passed, the Tibetan "experts" writing commentaries had become so sure of their Tibetan explanations that they had stopped looking at the Indian commentaries and Yeshe De's Tibetan commentary and had started propagating their own, mistaken understandings. These misunderstandings were then passed on, everyone apparently believing what the teacher told them and no-one stopping to research the matter properly. It is obvious from looking at commentaries written over the last few centuries that their mistaken explanations have become entrenched in Tibetan explanations of the prayer. Worse, I found that those very mistakes were present in the existing English translations—the mistakes had simply been copied across from the Tibetan mistaken explanations, without further research. All in all, I found that it cannot be assumed that Tibetan commentaries of the last several centuries are correct, even if a Tibetan teacher says so. With that, I found that we non-Tibetans have to rely on Indian commentaries and Yeshe De's first Tibetan commentary to find the earliest accepted understanding of the prayer.

Next, I found that the Tibetan texts of the prayer had problems. I for one had assumed from looking at Tibetan texts of the prayer that the prayer was a standalone piece of literature formally written with a title, and so on, because the Tibetan framework that is used to package the prayer strongly conveys that sense. However, it is not a standalone prayer, rather, it is part of a sutra and the entire sutra has to be read and understood if the prayer and its wording is to be properly understood. I also found that the Tibetan framework used to package the prayer after extracting it from the sutra conveys several other things about the prayer that are not true. In short, the Tibetan framework used to package the prayer is not suitable for presenting the prayer and it is not all right to translate it from the Tibetan and use it as the framework for a translation of the prayer into other languages such as English. As a result, I had to explain all of this and make a new framework for use with translations of the prayer that would present the prayer properly.

There are other problems too, but you can begin to understand from the above why it is not a simple task to make a reliable translation of Samantabhadra's Prayer into English. Simply taking a copy of the prayer in Tibetan and translating it into English, even if done with the help of a learned Tibetan, will almost certainly result in mistakes—a reliable translation of the prayer requires much research and that has, at very least, to include a careful reading of the original sutra containing the prayer as well as multiple Indian commentaries and Yeshe De's commentary. Then, simply translating the Tibetan framework for the prayer and using that to present the prayer in English is not workable because of the faults with the Tibetan framework—a suitable framework requires the preparation of a new framework. Then, simply translating a Tibetan commentary to the prayer to explain it will probably result in mistaken explanations of the prayer in several places—to have a commentary that provides correct information requires the provision at least of an Indian commentary, an appropriate Tibetan commentary with annotations, and a commentary written directly in English. The latter is essential because the Indian and Tibetan commentaries will not cover points that need to be explained for an English translation. All of the above is what has gone into the volumes that comprise this series of books and why they form the first comprehensive and reliable presentation of Samantabhadra's Prayer to become available in English.

There is another problem, which also has to be clearly stated. The existing English translations are mistaken but, worse than that, have been used as a basis for translations of the prayer into other European languages. I know of German, French, and Russian translations made from the existing English ones and I suspect that there are more. All of these translations have been made with the assumption that the English translations are correct and will therefore provide a good basis for a translation of the prayer into another European language. Unfortunately the translators were wrong and all of these translations made from the existing English translations simply perpetuate all the mistakes of the English translations. The extent of the problem can be seen when the four or so Russian translations that are floating around the internet are considered. All of them were made on the basis of the mistaken English translations, with no reference to the original Tibetan at all. I have verified with a Russian translator that they do perpetuate all the mistakes in the English translations from which they have made. One of them trumpets its superiority over the other Russian translations by saying: "We compared four different English translations [which they listed] and made up our own version which therefore is superior to all the other existing Russian translations". In fact, their translation is even worse than the others! The translators involved did not even consider the fact that the English translations might be mistaken, let alone that blithely combining them without even looking at the Tibetan could only lead to even more mistakes!

All in all, in the two and a half thousand years since the prayer was expressed, many things have happened that conspired to cover the prayer's actual meaning. I have spoken openly about these factors that have hindered the arrival of a reliable translation of the prayer into the English and other European languages. However, this was not intended as and should not be taken as a personal attack on the Tibetan experts who have propagated mistaken explanations of the prayer. Nor was it intended as and nor should it be taken as a personal attack on the translators whose translations into English, and other European languages have been mistaken in many ways. There are various reasons why these things have happened. One worth mention is the fault of long-standing spiritual traditions in general that the people in them, in their desire to maintain the purity of the transmission, tend to blindly believe whatever the teacher or tradition says and pass that on without further investigation. That happened in Tibet where it sometimes caused significant problems with the correct transmission of meaning and it has now carried over to non-Tibetans who are trying to follow the Tibetan Buddhist ways. In this case, it has caused corruption in the presentation and explanation of the prayer of Samantabhadra. Personally, I would prefer not to talk about these problems at all, but there are people out there who want to have a reliable translation of the prayer and explanations of it so that they can use it with confidence in their own practice. For their sakes, all of this had to be explained.

1. The Importance of Samantabhadra's Prayer

1.1. It is One of the Five Important Prayers of the Great Vehicle Tradition

The Mahāyāna or Great Vehicle tradition as it came into Tibet identified five prayers as the most important ones for its followers to recite: Samantabhadra's Prayer, Mañjushrī's Prayer, Maitreya's Prayer, the Sukhāvatī Prayer, and the chapter of prayers in Shāntideva's famous guide to the conduct of a bodhisatva, *Entering the Bodhisatva's Conduct*[1]. A short description of each follows.

Samantabhadra and Mañjushrī were the two most senior bodhisatva sons of Shākyamuni Buddha. Both had completed the tenth bodhisatva level and were in line to become buddhas in the future. Samantabhadra, though regarded as the foremost bodhisatva of the time had been predicted to become a buddha in the far distant future[2] whereas Mañjushrī had been predicted to become a buddha in this era called "The Good Aeon" in which one thousand and two buddhas will appear. Regardless of the closeness or distance of their attainment of buddhahood, these two bodhisatvas were the most advanced of Shākyamuni Buddha's bodhisatva disciples, so the prayers composed by them are particularly valuable to us who follow in their footsteps.

Maitreya's Prayer is a potent summary of the bodhisatva path and how to follow it. The prayer is generally assumed to have been composed by Maitreya who the Buddha predicted as the fifth buddha of this era, the next buddha after himself. In fact, it was

---

[1] This is the correct spelling, not "bodhisattva". See "bodhisatva" in the glossary for more information.

[2] This Samantabhadra is frequently referred to as the "bodhisatva Samantabhadra" in order to distinguish him from the primal guardian Samantabhadra of the Nyingma tantras.

composed by a previous being in the string of lives of Maitreya at a time many universes ago when that being for the first time aroused the intent to become a buddha. Padma Karpo Translation Committee has published a book containing Maitreya's Prayer, the full story of how it came about, and a commentary that clarifies its meaning.[3]

The Sukhāvatī Prayer—which is actually any of several prayers having a common purpose—has become important because it is said to create the causes for an easy exit from samsara or cyclic existence. This type of prayer creates the causes needed to leave the intermediary state following death and be born in the pure realm called Sukhāvatī of the buddha Amitābha, and so permanently escape from cyclic existence. The importance of such a prayer can be seen in the fact that Samantabhadra's Prayer includes a section which is essentially a short Sukhāvatī prayer.

The chapter of prayers in Shāntideva's *Entering the Bodhisatva's Conduct* is a distillation of prayers found in the sutras. It is so well arranged and complete that it has become popular as a liturgy for performing extensive bodhisatva prayers and also for making an extensive dedication of merit.

Samantabhadra's Prayer is regarded as the foremost of all these five major prayers and also the foremost of prayers in this era on the excellent conduct of a bodhisatva. Being foremost in those two ways is said to be a direct result of its author, Samantabhadra, being the foremost of all Shākyamuni Buddha's bodhisatva sons[4] and, in particular, the one most capable at composing prayers of aspiration for the excellent conduct of a bodhisatva. This is not mere platitude, for Samantabhadra himself says in his prayer that the prayer is "the

---

[3] *Maitreya's Sutras and Prayer with Commentary by Padma Karpo*. Publication details of all cited books are found in the supports for study section at the end of the book.

[4] See the section in this introduction about gender terminology.

best of acquisitions" for anyone in this life and that its superior qualities are due to his being the one most knowledgeable of the bodhisatva's conduct and also most capable of creating prayers of aspiration for that conduct. The commentaries to the prayer in this series explain more about this when commenting on the relevant verse towards the end of the prayer. In short, because Samantabhadra was the best in many ways at the various aspects of the Great Vehicle he had the skills needed to express what is unanimously considered to be the best of prayers of the Great Vehicle and the best of prayers on the excellent conduct of a bodhisatva.

1.2. The Prayer's Place in Tibetan Buddhist Practice with a Note on its use in Dzogchen Practice in East Tibet

Because Samantabhadra's Prayer is considered to be the best of prayers in those ways, it is very popular amongst all Tibetan practitioners—lay people, monastics, and yogins alike—and is equally popular amongst followers of all four Tibetan schools. Many Tibetans make a point of including it in their daily prayers and many also make a point of reciting large numbers of the prayer at various times during their lives.

The prayer is not only of general interest because of being regarded as the greatest of prayers in the Great Vehicle tradition, but also has a place of special importance within the various traditions of Dzogchen teachings that flourished in East Tibet during the last two and a half centuries. The Dzogchen teaching says that the approach a Dzogchen practitioner must take is described in the adage "Devotion to the guru above and compassion for sentient beings below". Thus a Dzogchen practitioner should do the core practices, which depend on devotion to guru above, and spend the rest of his time working intently on the bodhisatva's path. Therefore, Dzogchen lineages give even more importance than usual to Śhāntideva's *Entering the Bodhisatva's Conduct* and Samantabhadra's Prayer. For example, there is the Dzogchen master Ontrul Tenpa'i Wangchuk who was regarded as one of the greatest Dzogchen masters alive in east Tibet until he passed away while this book was being written. His monastery in east Tibet is famous in throughout the region for its intensives in which Samantabhadra's Prayer is recited all day for several days at a time by the whole monastery—yogins, monks, nuns, and lay people alike. In that practice, the assembly does not merely recite the prayer but recites it within the context of an extensive liturgy that neatly and beautifully wraps the recitation of the prayer into a full day of complete Great Vehicle practice. I have, as mentioned earlier, done one of these intensives. At the time, Ontrul Tenpa'i Wangchuk encouraged me to translate the liturgy into English and it is my hope to bring the tradition of day-long recitations of Samantabhadra's Prayer, done with the liturgy, to the West.

2. The Origin of Samantabhadra's Prayer

It is often thought that Samantabhadra's Prayer is a standalone prayer made for general use, but that is not so. It is the conclusion, composed in verse, to a teaching on the conduct of a bodhisatva that was given to a young bodhisatva named Sudhana when he encountered the tenth-level bodhisatva Samantabhadra. The entire story with the teaching and concluding verses was written down in detail in the last chapter of a large sutra of the Great Vehicle named the *Gaṇḍavyūha Sutra*, which in turn is the last sutra of an extremely large collection of Great Vehicle sutras called the *Avataṃsaka Sutra*.

In order to understand the verses and to be able to recite them while realizing the full significance of their words, it is essential to have read that chapter and some explanation at least of its very profound meaning. To assist with that, we have translated the chapter into English in this book and provided a brief explanation of it in the commentary to the prayer by myself.

It has to be emphasized that knowing the story of the verses is essential to being able to understand and use the verses as a prayer. When the verses are recited without having read and thought about the story behind them, an important part of their meaning, and with that their potency, is lost. For example, Samantabhadra frequently speaks of beyond-ordinary levels of experience in the verses and these are not mere concepts that he is adding to embellish them but are direct expressions of his own, master of the tenth bodhisatva level, state of being. Therefore, someone who first reads and thinks about the story behind the verses will understand the intent of the verses and will also have opened the door to connecting directly with that state of being, making the recitation of the verses as a prayer more potent in every way. You are urged to go now to that chapter on page 1 and read it in conjunction with the English explanation of it in the author's thorough explanation of Samantabhadra's Prayer on page 45.

3. The Prayer is an Extract

The sutra with the meeting of Sudhana and Samantabhadra plus the verses is too long to use for recitation. However, the concluding verses are very suited to the purpose. Therefore, at some point in ancient India the verses alone were extracted from the sutra and written down separately for use as a prayer for recitation. The same thing was done later on in Tibet.

3.1. What are the Extracts Like?

Indian Buddhists extracted the verses from the sutra and wrote them down in a very simple format—they wrote the name "Samantabhadra's Prayer" followed by the verses. Later, when the Tibetans first translated the sutra, they did the same, using the same simple arrangement as the Indians. However, the Tibetans later shifted to a complicated arrangement that packed the verses into a framework that had been royally decreed as the framework for holding all such translations. That arrangement of the verses within that framework has been in use for over one thousand years. It has sometimes been corrupted during that time, but the basic and most commonly seen form of it can be seen, translated into English, on page 33.

3.2. Problems with the Extracts

The extracts just described are convenient for personal use. However, there is nothing about them that says that the verses in them are an integral and important part of something larger. Instead, the extracts lead people to believe that the verses are a standalone prayer with no relation to anything else. Then those people never know about the all-important context of the verses, with the result that their full import is lost.

The complicated Tibetan arrangement has that and several other problems with it. Most translations of the prayer into English have simply translated the entire Tibetan extract, carrying all of these problems into English. Therefore, if you are using one of those English translations, it is important to know about these problems. Rather than clutter the introduction with all of the details, they have been laid out clearly in the author's complete explanation of the prayer on page 49.

3.3. Fixing the Problems

It is not hard to fix the problems with the problematic Tibetan arrangement. All that is needed is to make a revised framework that correctly informs the reader of the original context of the prayer and provides the reader with other, correct information. I have made such a framework for English, but the same framework could and I hope will be used for other languages. It can be seen on page 35.

4. Explanations of the Prayer

In the short space of sixty-two four-line verses, the prayer covers many of the key points of the Great Vehicle teaching. As a result, there are many places where the literal meaning of the words might seem obvious but their full import can only be known through a careful explanation of the relevant points of the Great Vehicle teaching. Moreover, there are many places where the prayer is so terse that even the literal meaning cannot be known without further explanation. And still further, there are many places where the Sanskrit syntax of the original prayer has to be correctly understood in order to understand the syntax of the prayer and also to see the fullness of the meaning cleverly woven into the expression of the prayer. Finally, there are points of grammar in the composition of the prayer which need to be clarified. Altogether, the prayer needs a significant amount of explanation to be correctly understood, so, what explanations are available to us?

4.1. Indian Commentaries

The earliest explanations that I have seen are in commentaries composed by Indian masters, starting with Nāgārjuna. Several of them were translated and preserved by the Tibetans in their *Translated Treatises*[5] at the time of the great translations in Tibet. The earliest is an oral teaching given by master Nāgārjuna [100 C.E.][6] that was recorded in writing by one of his students. After that there were commentaries composed in writing by the masters Śhākyamitra, a heart disciple of Nāgārjuna, Vasubhandu [375–430], Dignāga [480–540], and Bhadravaha.

I read all of those Indian commentaries. It was obvious from doing so that there was a strong commentarial tradition in India on which these masters agreed. Moreover, bearing in mind that the original Sanskrit language of the prayer was the native language of these masters, it was clear that they knew the points in the prayer where the language of the prayer had to be explained. These points made all the commentaries of special value not only for understanding the prayer but for translating it too.

---

[5] For *Translated Treatises*, see the glossary.

[6] There are questions about the dates of Nāgārjuna. However, his commentary seems to have preceded all the others, and the earliest date given for him, the one given here, seems to be appropriate.

I found that master Nāgārjuna's commentary was especially useful. His explanations not only had the mark of an expert who could explain the meaning of the words according to the Great Vehicle tradition but also had the mark of a supreme expert who, knowing the points at which misunderstanding could arise, made a point of definitively stating the meaning at those points. I found his commentary to be essential reading for obtaining an accurate understanding of what the verses of the prayer actually say. Additionally, I found it to be the best basis for translators needing a commentary that would elucidate every aspect of the prayer according to the language in which it was originally composed—its literal meaning, syntax, and grammar.

These Indian commentaries, and especially Nāgārjuna's commentary, were the basis for the official translation of the prayer into the Tibetan language and, having read them, I am sure must also be the basis for translations into languages other than Tibetan.

4.2. The First Tibetan Commentary on the Prayer

The first Tibetan commentary to the verses was composed by the great translator Yeshe De. He was the chief translator of many sutras, including the *Gaṇḍavyūha Sutra* containing the verses of Samantabhadra's Prayer, at the time of the great translations in Tibet. It is important to note that he was considered to be one of the three greatest translators during that period and was famed for his vast knowledge of scripture, Sanskrit, and how to translate Sanskrit into Tibetan.

In order to translate Samantabhadra's Prayer from Sanskrit into Tibetan, he relied on the Indian commentaries mentioned just above and also received explanations in person from the Indian masters who were advising him at the time. He incorporated all of this knowledge into one of the largest Tibetan commentaries on the prayer that has ever been written. I found that his commentary agreed with the Indian commentaries and also included many explanations of how the Sanskrit should be understood in Tibetan. As expected, his commentary had the same uncluttered style as the Indian commentaries in which there is simply commentary on the verses and none of the artificiality seen in later Tibetan commentaries that comes with explaining the Tibetan framework for the extracted verses.

Yeshe De's commentary also has to be set, together with Nāgārjuna's commentary and other Indian commentaries, as the basis for translations of the prayer from Tibetan into languages other than Tibetan.

4.3. Later Tibetan Commentaries on the Prayer

As time went by, a number of commentaries to the prayer were written by Tibetan experts. Unfortunately, several centuries ago—I have not been able to pin down exactly when, but four hundred or more years ago—it seems that these "experts" stopped going back to the Indian commentaries and to Yeshe De's commentary written based on the explanations of Indian experts. As a result, mistakes began to arise in the Tibetan way of explaining and hence commenting on the verses.

The Tibetan commentaries most commonly mentioned or used these days are now discussed. There is a commentary by each of two of the hierarchs of the Jonang lineage—the famous Tāranātha [1575–1634] and Tobbar Ozer—but both commentaries impose a structure on the prayer which is not found in any other commentary and which has been called into question by other Tibetan masters.

Followers of Kagyu and Nyingma schools of Tibetan Buddhism often rely on the commentary of Karma Chagmey Raga Asyas [1613–1679], a great Kagyu master who had close ties to the Nyingma tradition. His commentary is short and sometimes a little unclear because of its brevity. Nevertheless, it has been popular because it is easy to read. With his commentary, we can see that, by the seventeenth century C.E., mis-understandings of Sanskrit syntax and grammar have crept into commentaries on the prayer. From that time on, we find that all Tibetan commentaries on the prayer simply repeat the mistakes.

Tibetans generally accept that Lochen Dharmaśhrī[7] of Mindroling monastery [1654–1717] was one of the greatest Tibetan translators in more recent times. He was reputed to have a vast knowledge of Sanskrit and his translations and statements about translations are generally regarded as infallible. Therefore, it was very surprising to find that his commentary on Samantabhadra's Prayer also shows the failure to understand Sanskrit syntax that was mentioned in an earlier section, making his commentary less than reliable.

Shortly after Lochen Dharmaśhrī wrote his commentary, the exceptionally knowledgeable Gelugpa master Changkya Rolpa'i Dorje [1717–1786] wrote a commentary to the prayer. His commentary is especially favoured by followers of the Gelugpa school.

A small commentary written in recent times by a Tibetan hermit who was a follower of the Khyentse lineage has to be mentioned because it was translated into English then widely distributed amongst Western practitioners who have been using it since then. This is really unfortunate because the Tibetan commentary is mistaken in many places and the translation into English not only embodies those mistakes but also has many other mistakes in it. The commentary was published in the early 1980's under the name of the Marpa Translation Committee, with the name of Elizabeth Callahan mentioned as the translator of the commentary. A copy of the prayer based on this translation has been widely distributed in the West. It is one of the English translations that I found to have significant problems. Unfortunately, it has been used as a basis for translations into other European languages, thereby propagating the errors.

---

[7] "Lochen" means "great translator".

My conclusion is the later Tibetan commentaries do not have anything special to commend them over the commentaries of the Indian masters and Yeshe De. At very least, these later Tibetan commentaries have to be read and their content understood in relation to those earlier commentaries.

4.4. A Recent but Very Useful Tibetan Commentary

For the sake of completeness, a Tibetan commentary needs to be included in this series. I chose a very recent one by the great Tibetan master Ontrul Tenpa'i Wangchuk who was mentioned earlier in this commentary. Tenpa'i Wangchuk was an unusually good scholar and a great Dzogchen master. His commentary to the prayer was given as an oral teaching to the lay men and women yogis living in his encampment that was then written down and included in his collected works.

His commentary has two distinct features that make it a particularly useful resource for the reader. Firstly, it is far more detailed and hence longer than any of the other commentaries mentioned so far. It goes through the meaning of the words of the verses in great detail, giving explanations that leave nothing un-examined. Secondly, it stays focussed on explaining the prayer in a very practical way and does not go off into scholarly investigations. It is unique in that last respect, being the only commentary to the prayer that I know of that shows the prayer in a very practical light. English-speaking practitioners who recite the prayer regularly will find it to be a treasure-trove of instruction.

His commentary is what is called a "bitwise" commentary; it quotes a word or a phrase or perhaps a chunk of the prayer then explains that "bit" of the prayer. A bit-wise commentary allows the exact meaning of the words of the prayer to be easily understood and in a way that allows no room for doubt. The "bits" of the prayer being commented on are marked off in the Tibetan text and that has been carried over into the English translation by marking them off in bold italics. In e-book versions, they are additionally given a different colour from the rest of the text, making them even easier to see.

The lineage of the commentary also is very interesting. It comes from the masters of the relatively-recent Longchen Nyingthig lineage of the Dzogchen teaching, a lineage that began in the late 1700's with Jigmey Lingpa and flourished greatly in Eastern Tibet. One of the early masters of the system was the very learned and highly accomplished Dza Patrul [1808-1887] who spent most of his life at Dzogchen Monastery in East Tibet. Dza Patrul gave oral instructions on the prayer that were preserved in a verbal transmission and not committed to paper until Adzom Gyalsay [1842–1924] recorded them in writing. From there, the oral tradition for this commentary came down from Adzom Gyalsay to Lodro Gyatso of Dzogchen Monastery [?–2003]—a master who died a few years before this book was written and who at the time of his passing showed all the signs of having achieved buddhahood in his very life. It was given to him to his heart disciple, Ontrul Tenpa'i Wangchuk who passed away while this book was being written.

Ontrul Tenpa'i Wangchuk was an extraordinary scholar as well as great master of Dzogchen, and his commentaries in general have become famous amongst Tibetans around the world for their in-depth yet very practical style. As a matter of good fortune, while receiving his complete teachings in Tibet in 2011, I received the complete reading transmission for this commentary together with all of his other works and was then encouraged by him to translate all of them.

4.5. A Western Commentary

There is a mass of detail that comes from that reading all those Indian and Tibetan commentaries that has to be drawn together in place. As well as that, there are many points of English grammar, syntax, and meaning connected with the prayer that are not covered in the Indian and Tibetan commentaries and could only be covered in a commentary written directly in English. Therefore, I wrote a very extensive commentary that brought all of this information together in one place. You will find that it will clarify many points about the prayer.

5. Translating the Prayer into English

5.1. In general

The best way to translate the prayer would be to do what the Tibetans did—to translate the entire *Gaṇḍavyūha Sutra* or at least its chapter with the entire story of Sudhana's meeting with Samantabhadra and then simply extract the verses into a suitable framework for the prayer. Translating the entire sutra was more than could be done here, so it was decided to translate the entire chapter with the story of the meeting.

An original Sanskrit version would be the best source for such a translation but is not available, so I had to rely on the translations that had been made into Tibetan or Chinese. The Chinese version of the sutra has already been translated into English by Thomas Cleary, but the Tibetan version is closer to the original Sanskrit for linguistic reasons and hence better suited as a basis for translation into other languages, therefore I used that.

The Tibetan translation of the *Gaṇḍavyūha Sutra* is preserved in *The Translated Word*. There are seven major editions of *The Translated Word* of which the Derge edition is, for various reasons, regarded as excellent, so I settled on that. In particular, I used a recently-published comparative edition of *The Translated Word*, one that presents the Derge edition but with every difference between it and the other six editions carefully noted. I found that there were differences in the Tibetan wording of the verses between the seven editions, most of which were slight and did not end up affecting the meaning as it would be translated into English, but a few of which were major and could not be reconciled. After looking at the differences involved, I saw that to make a critical edition of the prayer in English would result in an extremely complex translation that would not be usable by practitioners who are, in the end, the audience for whom this book and its translations are intended. Therefore the Derge edition's reading of the prayer was set as the basis for the translation into English.

The chapter to be translated is, starting at the beginning of the meeting between Sudhana and Samantabhadra and going down to the beginning of the verses at the very end of the sutra, straightforward if one is well-versed in the Great Vehicle sutras. However, the verses need explanation and I have stated above which sources are best for those explanations.

5.2. Specific Issues

This section presents some specific issues related to the translation of the verses of the prayer.

5.2.1. Added verses

The official Tibetan translation of the verses of the prayer found in all editions of the *Translated Word* is comprised of sixty-two verses. However, it is probable that the sixty-first and sixty-second verses were not part of the original but were added in India before the sutra came to Tibet. The earlier Indian commentaries do not mention the sixty-first and sixty-second two verses, for example, Nāgārjuna's commentary abruptly ends following the explanation of the sixtieth verse. Then, Yeshe De says that the Indian masters advising him acknowledged that the sixty-first and second stanzas were probably Indian additions, but in the end advised him to keep the two verses in the official translation of the prayer into Tibetan. Thus, the actual number of stanzas in the original prayer cannot be known with certainty, but there is a strong probability that the sixty-first and sixty-second stanzas are not part of the original.

On top of that, when the Tibetans extracted the sixty-two verses from the sutra in the *Translated Word* into their framework as described earlier, they added a verse composed by the great Tibetan translator Vairochana to the end of the official translation. Thus, the Tibetan texts of the prayer came to have sixty-three verses. You can see this verse in the Tibetan framework on page 33. It is not part of the prayer and should not be made part of English translations of the prayer.

5.2.2. Misunderstandings of Sanskrit syntax

Having read all the Indian commentaries and then Yeshe De's commentary, I believe that Yeshe De translated the prayer into Tibetan well. His commentary, as can be seen from reading the available Indian commentaries translated into Tibetan, presents the Indian understanding of the syntax of the prayer as originally written in Sanskrit. However, some centuries ago, Tibetans experts began to write commentaries in which they incorrectly explained some places in the prayer due to incorrectly understanding certain Sanskrit constructions that had been correctly translated by Yeshe De into Tibetan. All currently-available English translations and translations into other European languages that I know of have inherited this type of mistake.

A clear example of this type of mistake can be seen in the explanation of the very first words of the first stanza of the prayer given in Tibetan commentaries of the last several centuries. A full explanation of this appears on page 58 in my own commentary to the prayer. Other mistakes of this type have appeared in Tibetan commentaries and they too are fully explained in my own commentary.

5.2.3. Misunderstandings of words

From the foregoing, we know that this is a prayer spoken by a master of the tenth bodhisatva level, which means that it was spoken by someone with an amazing capacity for expressing the teaching in words. The prayer is a masterpiece of composition and, with that, has an exceptional level of meaning packed into a very short space. As a result, it is very easy to mistake the meaning of the words of the prayer.

Tibetan commentaries mostly explain the words of the prayer correctly, though later ones sometimes have mistakes at that level. Existing English translations on the other hand, because it seems of lack of familiarity with the vocabulary, with the details of the vast teachings of the Great Vehicle, and especially with the details of Tibetan grammar, have many mistakes.

5.2.4. Discrepancies between wordings of the verses

It would have been very nice if the verses as they appear in the sutra and in the arrangements for its use as a prayer and in the commentaries on the verses all used exactly the same wording of the verses, but they do not. The differences are often small and in many cases do not change the rendering in English. However, sometimes it is not so.

As mentioned above, I first produced a translation of the verses into English based on the official Tibetan translation as it appears in the Derge edition of *The Translated Word*. That is the version intended for readers to use as the basis for keeping, reciting, and teaching the prayer. After that, rather than try to force that to be consistent with what is in the commentaries and the texts of the prayer, I simply translated them as is.

This lack of consistency can be very frustrating to all of us who would like to see an exact match between the verses as they appear in the sutra, in the commentaries, and texts of the prayer. However, we have reached a time when we have to accept that translations of our beloved Buddhist literature cannot always be done perfectly. It is a sign of our degenerate times.

6. Arrangement of the Materials

There is a deliberate order to the various materials presented in the books comprising this series. This introduction comes first to lay the ground. Then the main part of each book begins with the complete record of Sudhana and Samantabhadra's meeting as found in the *Gaṇḍavyūha Sutra*. It is placed first because, as explained earlier, Samantabhadra's Prayer is an integral part of the sutra and the sutra must be read first to gain a proper understanding of the verses that form Samantabhadra's Prayer.

The sutra with the verses of the prayer is followed by the framework used to contain the verses when they have been extracted from the sutra for use as a prayer. First there is the Tibetan framework then there is the new framework I have made in order to overcome the many problems with the Tibetan framework. Both have been explained in this introduction and further explanations of them are available in my own commentary in volume one.

Once the original form of the prayer then the frameworks used to contain it have been seen and understood, the reader needs to have clear explanations of the many difficult points of the prayer. Therefore, each volume then contains one or more commentaries to explain the prayer thoroughly. At the moment there are three commentaries in two volumes of the series—one each by an Indian, Tibetan, and English-speaking expert. Of them, my commentary written directly in English is placed first in volume one because it gives most clarification of the prayer. The terse Indian commentary by Nāgārjuna follows it. Then the very long and highly practical Tibetan commentary by Tenpa'i Wangchuk appears in the second volume. The commentaries can be read alone but reading them in conjunction with one another brings significant rewards.

7. Gender Issues

The ideas about human gender in ancient India and Tibet were very different from today's Western ideas of it. However, that does not give us the right to blithely change the wording of texts written in those cultures and times to suit ourselves. This book translates materials from those cultures and times and in doing so presents what those materials are saying, not someone's opinion—often emotionally charged—about what they should say.

If those who do not like this approach were to take the time to study in depth the meanings transmitted with for example wordings like "bodhisatva sons" or "sons of the conqueror", they would find that this is not mere exclusion of women, but that the words support an enormous amount of carefully thought out teaching. For example, the bodhisatva teachings speak of buddha "sons" because they are the ones who carry on the line of the tathāgatas. There is a thread to that that runs through the entirety of the Buddha's teaching and is lost if the translation is changed. If you have a extensive knowledge of the Buddha's teachings, you will understand this point and have no trouble with it, regardless of your status as man or woman. This use of "sons" is not intended to exclude women and in fact, because of its usage, both men and women are included.

I could write here extensively on this point but I see little value to it. The fact is that the materials being translated use gender terms and it is not my job or anyone else's job to change them and lose important threads of meaning in the process. Of course, if you use the prayer for recitation and want to change the gender wording to suit yourself, you are free to go ahead and do so. It seems to me that that is the correct solution to what has become a problem for some people, not the solution of insisting that translators change the wording of ancient texts to suit others' emotional needs.

8. Sanskrit

Sanskrit terms are an important aspect of a technical book like this. They are properly rendered into English with diacritical marks. For the sake of precision, diacritical marks have been used with them throughout this book.

The IATS system of transliteration of Sanskrit, which is the one generally in use in academic circles is hard for non-scholars to read. Therefore, we have modified that system slightly to make the transliterated Sanskrit more readable even when the meaning of the diacritical marks is not understood. This same approach seems to becoming commonplace amongst translators of Tibetan Buddhism. In it:

ś is written the way it sounds, as śh ;
ṣ is written similarly as ṣh ; and
ṛ is written similarly as ṛi ;
ṅ is written similarly as ng ;
ca is written as cha;
cha is written as chha.

The other letters for transliteration are used in the same way as they are used in the IATS scheme. In general, if you do not understand the system, simply read the letters as though they did not have the diacritical marks and, with our modified system, you will have a good approximation to the actual pronunciation.

9. Supports for Study

Padma Karpo Translation Committee has amassed a range of materials to help those who are studying this and related topics. In particular several books on sutras have been published, all of which support each other and each of which clarifies another important aspect of the Buddhist teaching. Please see the chapter Supports for Study at the end of the book for the details.

10. Tibetan Texts

We make a point of publishing the Tibetan texts together with the English translations where possible. Space considerations meant that it was not possible with this book. However, a complete set of the Tibetan texts for this book have been made available for free in digital format on our PKTC web-site.

11. Make a Practice Text

If you would like a text of the prayer for practice, you could make a copy of the framework for the prayer on page 35, then copy the prayer out of the sutra and add it into the framework at the place marked in the framework. The prayer in the sutra starts on page 23. There will also be a free edition of the prayer set up as a practice text for recitation on our PKTC web-site.

Tony Duff,
Swayambunath,
Nepal,
June, 2015

From the Great Vehicle Gandavyuha Sutra:

Sudhana's Meeting with the Bodhisatva Samantabhadra Culminating in Samantabhdra's Prayer

What follows is taken from the final section of the last chapter of the Great Vehicle *Gaṇḍavyūha Sutra*. In it, Sudhana meets with the great bodhisatva Samantabhadra who teaches him then sums up all that has happened in the meeting by expressing it clearly in verse.

The translation was made from the *Gaṇḍvyūha Sutra* as found in a reprint of the blocks of the Derge Black edition of *The Translated Word* published in Chengdu, China in the 1990's. A scanned copy of the reprint downloaded from the Tibetan Buddhist Resource Center, TBRC Volume Number 923, TBRC Work Number 22084 was used. Page and line numbers are incorporated into the English text for the use of those who want to follow the Tibetan.

───── ◆◆◆ ─────

The twenty-second bundle.[8]

689.2 Then, the merchant's son Sudhana—who had respectfully apprenticed with spiritual friends as numerous as the extremely subtle atoms of a great third-order thousandfold world realm; who possessed a mind in which the accumulations for all-knowingness had been gathered; who had engaged in, by keeping in harmony with, the oral instructions and teachings of all spiritual friends; who had gone with the same thought to the feet of all spiritual friends; who possessed a mind which understood that all spiritual friends are, because they are to be pleased, not to be displeased; who had followed the ocean-like oral instruction and teaching of all spiritual

---

[8] Sanskrit texts were written on palm leaves which were then stitched together in bundles. The original Sanskrit edition of the *Gaṇḍvyūha Sutra* that was used as a basis for the Tibetan translation came in a set of twenty-two bundles. Translations of sutras into Tibetan usually recorded the number of each Sanskrit bundle, as was done here.

friends; who possessed an essence which was genuinely arisen from the ocean-like thought of great compassion; who had completely brightened all migrators with a cloud of the varieties of great loving kindness; who possessed a body in which a force of great joy had been highly developed; who lived in utter peace within the vast complete emancipation of a bodhisatva; who possessed the eye of giving due to giving that strongly came forth from every possible door; who had utterly completed a careful development of the ocean-like good qualities of all tathāgatas; who had entered into the path which is the one that all tathāgatas admire; who had completely developed the force of perseverance needed for the accumulation of all-knowingness; who possessed a mind that had been thoroughly processed using the minds and thoughts of all bodhisatvas; who had engaged in a stream one after another all of the tathāgatas of the three times[9]; **690** who had mastered the ocean-like modes of dharma of all the buddhas; who had followed the ocean-like wheels of all the tathāgatas; who possessed a domain such that he could wholly show his image in all the world's birthplaces; who had entered into the ocean of varieties of prayer of all bodhisatvas; who had utterly entered into the bodhisatva conduct for all aeons; who had utterly gained the appearance of the objects of all-knowingness; who had completely developed all of the bodhisatva faculties; who had utterly gained the appearances of the path of all-knowingness; who had appearances without obscuration in all directions; who possessed a mind which had utterly entered all modes of dharmadhātus; who had utterly accomplished appearance in all modes of fields; who had gone into, in a way without discordance with their mindstreams, working for the sake of all the infinite sentient beings; who had completely destroyed all the mountains of abysmal obscuration; who had followed the dharma which is without obscuration; who had thoroughly assessed in utter peace the bodhisatva's complete

---

[9] This refers to what is spoken of later in the prayer, a bodhisatva's development of the capacity to step through the buddha-fields of all of the buddhas, one after another, meeting the buddhas of all of those fields, one after another.

emancipation having an essence of dharmadhātu present as the ground of all levels; who had sought out the domain of all tathāgatas; and who had been blessed by all tathāgatas—completely assessed[10] and became present in the domain of the bodhisatva Samantabhadra.

Then, having heard the name of the bodhisatva mahāsatva Samantabhadra, heard of his bodhisatva conduct, heard of his special prayers, heard of his special engagement in and remaining within the entire accomplishment of accumulation, heard of his special path of attainment and occurrence, **691** heard of the mindstream connected with the mode of Samantabhadra's level, heard of the accumulation connected with the level, heard of the force connected with the gaining of the level, heard of his wholly treading upon the level, heard of his abiding on the level, heard of his treading upon it by casting off the previous level, heard of the level's domain, heard of the level's blessing, and heard of his truly abiding on the level, he was glad at the prospect and eager to see the bodhisatva Samantabhadra w—his mind of extreme openness like the expanse of space was elevated above all clinging, and the perception of a field was something he had meditated on in the extreme, and his mind of true transcendence over all possibility of being affected had a domain which was without obscuration for all dharmas, and his mind of being without impediment extensively filled all the direction-oceans, and his mind of being without obscuration entirely trod the objects of all-knowingness, and his mind of extreme complete purity had entirely purified the core, the enlightenment ornament, by vipaśhyanā, and his mind of having made extreme classifications had entered the dharma ocean of all the buddhas, and his mind of extreme vastness was to thoroughly ripen sentient beings of all makeups, and his mind of extensively filling and highly distinguishing taming was doing the entire purification of all buddha-fields, and his mind of measurelessness was going forth as an image into the

---

[10] "Completely assessed" means that he had entered into Samantabhadra's domain, carefully taken note of all of its particulars and was, in that way, fully present there.

maṇḍala of the retinue of every buddha, and his mind which because of remaining throughout all aeons had no end and was without final limit was not fearful of the strength of all the tathāgatas, and because of the final limit of the unmixed buddha-dharmas he was one who had the core enlightenment present as the vajra holy core. He was seated on a lotus seat a mound of all kinds of jewels, with the tathāgata's seat, a lion-throne, in view directly ahead of him.

Then, the merchant's son Sudhana, **692** because of being moist with roots of virtue from the past that came from diligently pursuing intentions and ideas of that sort, having the blessing of all tathāgatas, and having a karmic lot of roots of virtue from the past consistent with that of the bodhisatva Samantabhadra, ten portents arose indicating that he would see the bodhisatva Samantabhadra. What were the ten? They were as follows. All buddha-fields became complete purity through the complete purity of the core of all tathāgatas, the enlightenment ornament. All buddha-fields became complete purity through all unfree states and bad migrations and paths to bad migrations being completely removed. All buddha-fields became complete purity, as with a lotus-grove's ornament, through the complete purity of a buddha-field. All buddha-fields became complete purity through making all sentient beings' body and mind glad and content. All buddha-fields became complete purity through ever remaining in the nature of all jewels. All buddha-fields became complete purity through sentient beings of all makeups always remaining in being utterly ornamented by the excellent marks and signs. All buddha-fields became complete purity through always remaining in being totally covered by clouds that adorn and move about. All buddha-fields became complete purity through sentient beings of all makeups always remaining in the possession of minds of mutual loving kindness, mutual benefit, and mutual being without malicious mind. All buddha-fields became complete purity through always remaining in being ornamented by the core, the enlightenment ornament. All buddha-fields became complete purity through all sentient beings always remaining in diligently thinking of the recollection of buddha. **693** Those were the ten portents that arose indicating that he would see the bodhisatva mahāsatva Samantabhadra.

Furthermore, ten great appearance portents arose indicating that he would see the bodhisatva mahāsatva Samantabhadra. What were the ten? They were as follows. From the extremely subtle atoms of all world realms and moreover from each extremely subtle atom, many nets of light-rays of all the tathāgatas became completely apparent. From the extremely subtle atoms of all world realms, moreover from each extremely subtle atom, many light mandalas of all the buddhas issued forth—in one colour, in various colours, and in many hundreds of thousands of colours, extensively filling all dharmadhātus. From the extremely subtle atoms of all world realms, moreover from each extremely subtle atom, clouds of all kinds of jewels showing up many shapes of all the tathāgatas issued forth, extensively filling all dharmadhātus. From the extremely subtle atoms of all world realms, moreover from each extremely subtle atom, many clouds of wheels and mandalas of the radiant light of all the tathāgatas issued forth, extensively filling all dharmadhātus. From the extremely subtle atoms of all world realms, moreover from each extremely subtle atom, many clouds of aromatic substances, flowers, garlands, ointments, and incenses issued forth, resounding with thunder of all the clouds of the ocean-like dharmas of the good qualities of the bodhisatva Samantabhadra and extensively filling all dharmadhātus of the ten directions. **694** From the extremely subtle atoms of all world realms, moreover from each extremely subtle atom, many clouds of suns and moons and stars issued forth, utterly giving off the light of bodhisatva Samantabhadra and extensively filling all dharmadhātus. From the extremely subtle atoms of all world realms, moreover from each extremely subtle atom, many clouds of oil-lamps present as all the shapes of bodies issued forth, utterly illuminating like the light-rays of a buddha and extensively filling all dharmadhātus. From the extremely subtle atoms of all world realms, moreover from each extremely subtle atom, many clouds of precious gem-forms, appearing as the bodies of all the tathāgatas, issued forth, extensively filling all world realms of the ten directions. From the extremely subtle atoms of all world realms, moreover from each extremely subtle atom, many clouds of light-forms appearing in the shape of the bodies of all the tathāgatas issued forth; a rain of clouds of the blessings and prayers of all buddhas strongly fell and all dharmadhatus were extensively filled. From the extremely subtle atoms of all world realms, moreover from each extremely subtle atom, a cloud ocean with all the types of forms of bodies of bodhisatvas appearing as colour images, and they, possessing the yogas for rescuing all beings, performing many completions of the dharma thoughts of all sentient beings, issued forth, extensively filling all dharmadhātus. Those were the ten great appearance portents that arose indicating that he would see the bodhisatva mahāsatva Samantabhadra. **695**

Then, the merchant's son Sudhana having seen those ten appearances which were portents, the occasion during which he would see the bodhisatva Samantabhadra began—his own roots of virtue had supported it; all of the tathāgatas had blessed it; the appearance of the dharma of all the tathāgatas actually occurred; the conduct of bodhisatva Samantabhadra became manifest; the bodhisatva Samantabhadra, through the blessing contained in his prayer, blessed it; in the domain of all tathāgatas, it was truly admired; the strength and force of extreme certainty about the tremendous domain of a bodhisatva was utterly gained; he was thinking that if he saw the bodhisatva Samantabhadra, it would be equivalent to attaining all-knowingness; the faculty for being able to see the bodhisatva Samantabhadra became manifest; a great force of perseverance for being able to see the bodhisatva Samantabhadra was gained; a yoga of irreversible perseverance in seeking out the bodhisatva Samantabhadra came into his possession; with a bodhisatva-body that could tread everywhere by a sphere of sense faculties manifest throughout all directions and concomitant total viewing and a mind to follow after bodhisatva Samantabhadra who was present at the feet of all buddhas without exception he was truly given to the observation of all tathāgatas, and he was minding not to separate from seeking observation of the bodhisatva Samantabhadra, and with his eye of wisdom having at core the idea that he should observe the bodhisatva Samantabhada he had entered the path of the bodhisatva Samantabhadra, **696** and he had an intention vast as the expanse of space, and a special intention of wielding the vajra of great compassion, and aspired to follow after the bodhisatva Samantabhadra, and was blessed until the end of the final aeon of the future, and had a completely pure ability to tread everywhere[11], and went into conduct the same as the bodhisatva Samantabhadra's conduct, and came to dwell in the wisdom of abiding on the level of the bodhisatva Samantabhadra, and came into the possession of truly abiding in the place of all tathāgatas. He saw the bodhisatva Samantabhadra—who had attained sameness with all the tathāgatas, had gone to three times sameness, had come into possession of an inconceivable place, had a domain he could not be deprived of, had come to possess a place of boundless wisdom, would be fully viewed by all bodhisatvas, could not be overcome by anyone in the world, would be followed by all the retinue-maṇḍalas, and come into possession of a truly elevated body—he saw him seated in direct view of the bhagavan tathāgata Vairochana in the maṇḍala-ocean of the bodhisatva retinue, totally surrounded by a bodhisatva assembly, seated in front of the bodhisatva saṅgha, and sitting on a precious lion-throne with heart of a great lotus.

He saw many clouds of light-rays numbering the extremely subtle atoms of all buddha fields issue forth from every one of the hairs from all his hair-pores which then utterly illuminated all the world realms infinite as the dharmadhātu reaching to the limits of space then were pacifying the suffering of sentient beings. **697** He saw maṇḍalas of light, many clouds having a variety of colours, numbering the extremely subtle atoms of all buddha fields issue forth from his body, which were vastly increasing the force of all bodhisatvas' joy and admiration. He saw many rains present in a variety of colours of clouds of aromatic substance-radiant-light, strongly issue

---

[11] ... meaning that his capacity for treading through aeons of time to their limit and through buddha-fields with their buddhas and bodhisatva sons to their limit was truly perfected ...

forth from his crown, his two shoulder bumps, and all of his hairs, which extensively filled the retinue-mandalas of all the tathāgatas, strongly coming down. He saw many rains, numerous as the extremely subtle atoms of all buddha-fields, of clouds of all kinds of flowers strongly issue forth from each and every hair from all his hair-pores, which extensively filled the retinue-maṇḍalas of all the tathāgatas, strongly pouring down. He saw many clouds of trees of various aromatic substances, numerous as the extremely subtle atoms of all buddha-fields, strongly issue forth from each and every hair from all his hair-pores, which extensively filled all dharmadhātus infinite as the limits of the expanses of space, adorned them with the ornament of clouds of trees of aromatic substances which utterly sent out a rain of an inexhaustible store of aromatic substances, powders, and incense and extensively filled the retinue-mandalas of all the tathāgatas, strongly pouring down. He saw many clouds of various clothes strongly issue forth from each and every hair from all his hair-pores, totally clothing and so adorning all dharmadhātus, infinite as the limits of the expanse of space. He saw a rain of clouds of shawls of various silks, of clouds of various garlands, and of clouds of various pearls, and clouds of wish-fulfilling precious gems **698** numerous as the extremely subtle atoms of all buddha-fields strongly issue forth from each and every hair from all his hair-pores, which extensively filled the retinue-maṇḍalas of all the tathāgatas, strongly pouring down. He saw clouds of jewel trees numerous as the extremely subtle atoms of all buddha-fields strongly issue forth from each and every hair from all his hair-pores for the purpose of completely fulfilling the thoughts of all sentient beings extensively fill all dharmadhātus infinite as the limits of the expanse of space, then ornament them with ornamentation radiated from the precious trees in the form of a store of jewels, making a great rain of jewels strongly fall in the retinue-mandalas of all the tathāgatas. He saw clouds of the strata of the form-realm gods numerous as the extremely subtle atoms of all buddha-fields strongly issue forth from each and every hair from all his hair-pores, giving genuine commendation to the bodhisatvas and extensively filling all buddha-fields. He saw many clouds of manifestations of all the strata of gods belonging to the continuum of Brahma strongly issue from each and every hair from all his hair-pores, supplicating the manifest-buddha tathāgatas to turn the wheel of dharma. He saw many clouds of bodies of the Indra gods belonging to all the desire-realms issue forth from each and every hair from all his hair-pores, truly holding many dharma-wheels of all the tathāgatas. He saw clouds of buddha-fields similar to all the buddha-fields belonging to the three times **699** numerous as the extremely subtle atoms of all buddha-fields issue forth from each and every hair from all his hair-pores in each and every single moment of mind, which extensively filled all dharmadhātus infinite as the limits of space, turning into homes, shelters, and supports for sentient beings without home, shelter, or support. He saw clouds of completely pure buddha-fields, entirely filled with all the risen buddhas and retinue-maṇḍalas of bodhisatvas, numerous as the extremely subtle atoms of all buddha-fields strongly issue forth from each and every hair from all his hair-pores in every single moment of mind, which extensively filled all dharmadhātus infinite as the limits of space then produced entirely pure, tremendous intentions of sentient beings. He saw many clouds of completely purified totally afflicted buddha-fields numerous as the extremely subtle atoms of all buddha-fields strongly issue forth from each and every hair from all his hair-pores in every single moment of mind which, having extensively filled all the dharmadhātus infinite as the limits of the expanse of space, were accomplishing the complete purity of each totally afflicted sentient being. He saw many clouds of completely purified totally afflicted buddha-fields numerous as the extremely subtle atoms of all buddha-fields strongly issue forth from all his hairs from each hair-pore in every single moment of mind, extensively fill all dharmadhātus infinite as the limits of the expanse of space, accomplishing complete purity for the afflicted sentient beings as one. He saw clouds of bodies of all sentient beings numerous as the extremely subtle atoms of all buddha-fields strongly issue forth from each and every hair from all his hair-pores, **700** which extensively filled all sentient beings' makeups infinite as the expanse of space then were following after the conduct of all sentient beings and were thoroughly ripening all sentient beings into unsurpassed, truly complete enlightenment. He saw clouds of bodies of bodhisatvas numerous as the extremely subtle atoms of all world realms strongly issue forth from each and every hair from all his e hair-pores in every moment of mind, which extensively filled all dharmadhātus infinite as the expanse of space and then, in order to increase the roots of virtue of all sentient beings, were expressing many names of all buddhas. He saw clouds of bodies of bodhisatvas numerous as the extremely subtle atoms of all buddha-fields strongly issue forth from each and every hair from all his hair-pores, which extensively filled all dharmadhātus infinite as the expanse of space and then in all the infinite buddha fields' regions produced the accomplishment of all roots of virtue, from the initial generation of arousal of the mind to its full uptake, of all bodhisatvas. He saw clouds of bodhisatvas numerous as the extremely subtle atoms of all buddha-fields strongly issue forth from each and every hair from all his hair-pores who then in all the buddha-fields in order to produce the completely purity of bodhisatva Samantabhadra's conduct audibly expressed all the ocean-like prayers of the bodhisatva. He saw, for the sake of the thoughts of all sentient beings being fulfilled, a rain of clouds of bodhisatva Samantabhadra's conduct **701** that was increasing the force of their joy by truly causing them truly to arise in all-knowingness, numerous as the extremely subtle atoms of all buddha-fields, strongly issue forth from each and every hair from all his hair-pores, then strongly pour down. He saw clouds of beings who were becoming manifest complete buddhas showing becoming a manifest complete buddha in all the buddha-fields who were developing great clouds of the dharma causing arising in all-knowingness numerous as the extremely subtle atoms of all buddha-fields strongly issue forth.

Then the merchant's son Sudhana, due to having seen that kind of object of the miraculous display of the bodhisatva Samantabhadra, delightedly rejoiced, and, being gratified and pleased, was content and happy in mind. Then, as he paid even more attention to bodhisatva Samantabhadra's body, in each of the bodhisatva Samantabhadra's limbs, each section of his limbs, each of part of his body, each section of each part of his body, each area of his limbs, each section of each area of his limbs, each body, each section of body, each hair-pore, each section of each hair-pore, he saw in the manner of a reflection this great third-order thousand-fold world system together with its air aggregate, water aggregate, earth aggregate, fire aggregate, oceans, continents, rivers, precious mountains, Mount Sumeru, surrounds[12], villages and cities, lands and places and realms and king's places, forests, houses, **702** groups of beings, sentient being hell-worlds, animal birth-places, Lord of Death worlds, asura worlds, nāga worlds, garuḍa worlds, human worlds, god worlds, Brahmā worlds, desire-realm places, form-realm places, formless realm places, bases, supports, shapes, clouds, lightning, stars, solar days, half-months, full-months, seasons, years, intermediate aeons, aeons, and he saw all this as in the manner of a reflected image. Exactly as he saw this one so he also saw all of the world realms of the eastern directions. And exactly as he saw the ones in the eastern direction, so he also saw in the manner of a reflection all the world realms of all directions—the southern direction, the western direction, the northern direction, the north-eastern intermediate direction, the south-eastern intermediate direction, the south-western intermediate direction, the north-western intermediate direction, and the below and above directions—together with their risen buddhas and together with their retinue-maṇḍalas of bodhisatvas. He saw all, however many they are, one after another, the world systems to the earliest limit in the past before this Endurance World[13] from each of the marks of a great man of the bodhisatva Samantabhadra, together with **703** the risen buddhas, together with all retinue-mandalas of bodhisatvas, sentient beings, houses, solar days, and aeons. He also saw in the same way all the infinite buddha-fields till the latest limit in the future. Just as he saw one after another the world realms to the earliest and latest limits of the

---

[12] The surrounds of Mt. Meru are the seven rings of oceans containing the continents, the seven rings of iron mountains, and so on.

[13] For Endurance World, see the glossary.

past and future of this world realm, so he also saw all one after another of the world realms to the earliest and latest limits of the past and future of all the world realms of the ten directions for each body of Samantabhadra and each of his marks of a great man and from each hair pore down to each smallest section with none of the details of one another mixed up.

Moreover, how bodhisatva Samantabhadra was seen sitting on a precious lion-throne having the heart of a great lotus in the direct view of the bhagavan tathāgata Vairochana and fully showing this kind of play, he likewise also was seen in the eastern direction, sitting in the world realm Padmaśrī of the tathāgata Bhadraśrī, fully showing this same play. Just as in the east, likewise the bodhisatva Samantabhadra was also seen sitting on a precious lion-throne having the heart of a great lotus at the feet of all the tathāgatas of all world realms in all cardinal and intermediate directions, and fully showing this same play. **704** How he was seen sitting on a lion-throne having the heart of a great lotus at the feet of all tathāgatas of all the world realms of the ten directions and fully showing this same play, likewise, the bodhisatva Samantabhadra was seen in the extremely subtle atoms of all the buddha-fields of all ten directions, in the dharmadhātu-like vastnesses of the retinue-maṇḍalas of the buddhas of each of the extremely subtle atoms, sitting on a precious lion throne having the heart of a great lotus at the feet of all tathāgatas and fully showing this same play.

Each of those bodies moreover was seen to have strongly shown all the references that have arisen in the three times as references whose form was in the manner of a reflected image. They were seen to have strongly shown the references of all fields, all sentient beings, and all risen buddhas and all retinue-mandalas of bodhisatvas in the manner of a reflected image. He heard the sounds of all sentient beings, the voices of all buddhas, all special miracles of entirely teaching the dharma-wheels and oral instructions of all tathāgatas, all the bodhisatvas' authentic gatherings[14], and the plays of all buddhas. Having seen and heard in that way those sorts of play of the bodhisatva Samantabhadra, he gained ten types of living in the pāramitā of wisdom. What were the ten? They were as follows. **705** He gained the living in the pāramitā of wisdom in which he could extensively fill all buddha-fields with his body in one moment of mind. He gained the living in the pāramitā of wisdom in which there was no difference in going before the feet of all the tathāgatas. He gained the living in the pāramitā of wisdom in which he would make offerings to and honour all the tathāgatas. He gained the living in the pāramitā of wisdom in which he could utterly take up the entire petitioning of all and moreover each one of all the tathāgatas. He gained the living in the pāramitā of wisdom in which he could definitely comprehend the dharma-wheel of all tathāgatas. He gained the living in the pāramitā of wisdom in which he could perform a buddha's inconceivable transformations. He gained the living in the pāramitā of wisdom in which, having had inexhaustible individual authentic knowledge blessed to the aeon of the latest limit of the future, he could teach to the extreme one word of dharma. He gained the living in the pāramitā of wisdom in which he could utterly know in direct perception all dharma oceans. He gained the living in the pāramitā of wisdom of all the oceans of modes of dharmadhatu. He gained the living in the pāramitā of wisdom in which he could entirely accomplish the ideas of all sentient beings. **706** He gained the living in the pāramitā of wisdom in which he could, in one instant, utterly know in direct perception the conduct of bodhisatva Samantabhadra.

Then the bodhisatva Samantabhadra extended his right hand and placed it on the crown of the merchant's son Sudhana who now possessed those ways of living in the perfection of wisdom. Immediately the bodhisatva Samantabhadra had like that placed his hand on the merchant's son Sudhana's crown, he indeed entered into doors

---

[14] The gatherings are the four ways of gathering disciples explained in the Prajñāpāramitā sutras.

of samādhi numbering the extremely subtle atoms in all buddha-fields, and moreover, he also, through each of those samādhis, entered world realms numbering the extremely subtle atoms of the buddha-fields that had previously been unseen. His all-knowingness accumulation also became an accumulation in the amount of the extremely subtle atoms of all buddha-fields. His all-knowingness dharma accumulation rose also to the amount of the extremely subtle atoms of all buddha-fields. The great utterly staying in all-knowingness became elevated also by the amount of extremely subtle atoms of all buddha-fields. Prayer oceans became entered also in the amount of the extremely subtle atoms of all buddha-fields. The path on which one arises in all-knowingness rose also by the amount of extremely subtle atoms of all buddha-fields. The bodhisatva conduct became utterly entered also in the amount of the extremely subtle atoms of all buddha-fields. The intensity of the force for all-knowingness was increased also by the number of extremely subtle atoms of all buddha-fields. The appearances of the wisdom of all buddhas became utterly illuminated also by the number of extremely subtle atoms of all buddha-fields. **707**

Just as here in this Endurance World Samantabhadra sitting in direct view of the bhagavan tathāgata Vairochana extended his right hand and placed it on the crown of the merchant's son Sudhana, so the bodhisatva Samantabhadra sitting at the feet of the tathāgata of every world realm also extended his right hand and placed it on the crown of merchant's son Sudhana. Likewise, the bodhisatva Samantabhadra sitting at the feet of every tathāgata of the world realms contained within the extremely subtle atoms of the world realms of every one of all the cardinal and intermediate directions also extended his right hand and placed it on the crown of the merchant's son Sudhana. In the same way as the merchant's son Sudhana entered many dharma-gates on being touched by the hand of the bodhisatva Samantabhadra sitting at the feet of the bhagavan Vairochana, so the merchant's son Sudhanas who were contacted by the many clouds of hands reaching across from all the bodies of Samantabhadra also entered many dharma-doors in various ways.

Then, the bodhisatva mahāsatva Samantabhadra said this to the merchant's son Sudhana:

"Son of the family, did you just now see the transformations I made?"

He said:

"Noble one! What I saw was as much as I saw of an inconceivable complete emancipation; if a tathāgata were to know it **708** that would be the amount to be known."

He said:

"Son of the family, I strongly desired the mind of all-knowingness and worked at it for aeons numbering the extremely subtle atoms of the inexpressible buddha-fields, and in each of those great aeons, moreover, I was thoroughly purifying enlightenment mind[15] and I respectfully apprenticed myself to tathāgatas numerous as the extremely subtle atoms of those inexpressibly inexpressible buddha-fields. In each of those great aeons moreover, I was entirely collecting the merit of all-knowingness, was connecting with every type of great offering and giving, was becoming highly renowned in all worlds, and made the offering too of provisions for all sentient beings. In each of those great aeons, I was strongly aspiring for the dharma of all-knowingness and performed giving, great giving, and extremely great giving as much as the extremely subtle atoms of the inexpressibly inexpressible buddha-fields. In each of those great aeons, moreover, by placing no value on body and life but setting the buddha-dharma as that to be cherished, I gave up an inexpressibly inexpressible many bodies. I also gave up great kingdoms. I also gave up my cities, villages, lands, countries, realms, and royal seats. I also gave up retinues whose beauty and delight were not easy to let go of. I also gave up my sons, daughters, and wives. I also gave up my bodies and flesh. I also gave the blood from my bodies to those who requested it. I also gave my bones and marrow. **709** I also gave

---

[15] For enlightenment mind, see the glossary.

up my legs and arms. I also gave up my limbs and their parts. I also gave up my nose and ears. I also gave up my eyes. I also gave up my tongue-faculty from my own mouths. In each of those aeons, moreover, I had been strongly aspiring for a head[16] of all-knowingness that would be above and superior to the whole world and gave away my own head in an amount numbering the extremely subtle atoms of the inexpressibly inexpressible buddha-fields. Just as in each great aeon, likewise in each great aeon ocean, and in each of the aeon oceans derived from the numbering of extremely subtle atoms of inexpressibly inexpressible buddha-fields, I had moreover become an excellent faculty of and rendered service to tathāgatas numerous as the extremely subtle atoms of the inexpressibly inexpressible buddha-fields. I honoured them. I bowed to them. I offered clothing, food, bedding, medicine for sickness, and utensils. I went forth into the teaching of those tathāgatas and also fully entered all of the oral instructions of buddhas. I took ownership of their teachings, too.

"Son of the family! Throughout the aeon-oceans of that number moreover, I do not remember even a few times having aroused a mind not in harmony with the mind to be aroused for the tathāgata's teaching. Throughout the aeon-oceans of that number, I do not remember even a few times having aroused an angry mind, or a self-grasping mind, or a mind protective of and owning a self, **710** or a mind making a division between self and other, or a mind to leave the path of enlightenment, or a mind wearied by remaining in samsara, or a disheartened mind, or a mind of stupefied by obscuration. To the contrary, in order to accumulate the accumulation of all-knowingness, I always aroused the enlightenment mind, wisdom which cannot be affected by other and which possesses a core which is difficult to cross.

---

[16] This is a metaphor for "peak" but is used to tie it to the giving up of physical heads.

"Son of the family, it is thus. If I were to show you the perfections of my past yogas—the yoga of having entirely purified a buddha-field and thereby utterly gained the mind of great compassion, the yogas of having entirely protected sentient beings, working to thoroughly ripen them, and having thoroughly trained them, the yogas of offering to and respectfully apprenticing to the buddhas, the yogas of being respectful to the guru for the sake of seeking out the holy dharma, the yogas of having given up my body for the sake of owning the holy dharma, and the yogas of having given up my own life for the sake of guarding the holy dharma—it would take all of the aeon-oceans to do so.

"Son of the family! I, with even just a few words or letters from that number of dharma-oceans strived to protect all sentient beings, strived to know for certain my own mindstream, strived to actually hear dharma taught by others, strived to express all appearances of worldly wisdom, strived to utterly express all beyond-the-world wisdom, **711** strived to generate samsaric happiness for all sentient beings, and strived to truly commend the good qualities of all tathāgatas. By that, I have given up the sovereignty of a wheel-wielding king because of which no purchasing has been done, that is, by having given up on all material goods there has been nothing left unpurchased. Like that if I were to show you all the perfections of my own past yogas, it would take aeon-oceans numerous as the extremely subtle atoms of the inexpressibly inexpressible buddha-fields.

"Son of the family! In that way, I, by the strength of accumulations of that sort, the strength of accumulated causal roots of virtue, the strength of vast intent, the strength of being assiduous at good qualities, the strength of mastering all dharmas as they truly are, the strength of the eye of prajñā, the strength of tathāgata blessing, the strength of great prayers, the strength of great compassion, the strength of the extra-perceptions that come with having been thoroughly processed, the strength of being taken on by spiritual friends, have gained a entirely pure body of dharma that is not different in the three times. This unsurpassed body of form which is elevated over all worlds, references the types of thoughts just exactly as they are of all migrators, conforms with all of them, alights in all buddha-fields, utterly stays in all of them, shows all transformations in all aspects, has also been entirely purified into one that delights the minds of all migrators. **712**

"Son of the family! Behold this body I have gained which is perfect, which was accomplished during infinite aeon-oceans, which is difficult to come by and difficult to see in many hundreds of thousands of quadrillions of aeons!

"Son of the family! If I am not even heard of by sentient beings who have not created roots of virtue, then why mention their seeing me?!

"Son of the family! There are sentient beings who merely by hearing my name become irreversible from unsurpassed, truly complete enlightenment. There are also those who by merely seeing, merely escorting, merely touching, merely following me, merely seeing me in a dream, or merely hearing my name in a dream become irreversible from unsurpassed, truly complete enlightenment. Some sentient beings will become thoroughly ripened if they remember me for a day. Some will become thoroughly ripened if they recall me for seven days, some for half a month, some for one month, some for one year, some for one hundred years, some for one aeon, some for one hundred aeons, some for aeons as numerous as the extremely subtle atoms of the inexpressibly inexpressible buddha-fields. Some will become thoroughly ripened if they recall me for a lifetime. Some will become thoroughly ripened because of a string of lives numerous as the extremely subtle atoms of the inexpressibly inexpressible buddha-fields. Some sentient beings will become thoroughly ripened by seeing my light. **713** Some will become thoroughly ripened by seeing my emitted light rays, some by movement of the field, some by being shown my form-body, and some by having been pleased. Son of the family! By types of method like that numerous as the extremely subtle atoms of a buddha-field sentient beings will become irreversible from unsurpassed, truly complete enlightenment.

"Son of the family! Sentient beings who hear of my entirely pure buddha-field will be born in an entirely pure buddha-field. Ones who see my entirely pure body will be born in a body like mine. Therefore, son of the family, behold my complete purity body!"

Then, the merchant's son Sudhana put his attention onto the body of bodhisatva Samantabhadra and saw each hair-pore entirely filled with buddhas of inexpressibly inexpressible buddha-field oceans. In each of those field-oceans, moreover, he saw many tathāgatas present, totally surrounded by their retinue-oceans of bodhisatvas. All of those field oceans, moreover, he saw having various grounds, various shapes, various ornaments, various surrounds, various clouds, various skies covering them, various buddhas arising, and voices of various dharma-wheels. Exactly as with each hair-pore, likewise in all hair-pores without exception and all the excellent marks and all the illustrative signs and all limbs and their parts, he saw from each and every field ocean clouds of manifested buddha-bodies numerous as the extremely subtle atoms of all buddha-fields extensively fill all the world realms in the ten directions **714** then do the deed of thoroughly ripening sentient beings into unsurpassed, truly complete enlightenment.

Then, the merchant's son Sudhana, having been taught by the oral instructions and teachings of the bodhisatva Samantabhadra, entered into all the world realms included within the body of bodhisatva Samantabhadra, where he became active in thoroughly ripening sentient beings.

In that way, the merchant's son Sudhana went before spiritual friends numbering the extremely subtle atoms of the buddha-fields where, by seeing and respectfully apprenticing to them, he accumulated wisdom appearances and roots of virtue. However, they did not come close to being even one hundredth part of the roots of virtue he accumulated by seeing the bodhisatva Samantabhadra. They were not even a thousandth part, nor even a hundred-thousandth part, nor even a one-hundred billionth part of them; they could not come up to a fraction of a number or count or example or cause of them.

There were, from the first time he had aroused the mind and fully taken it up until the time he saw the bodhisatva Samantabhadra, the entrances he had made into however many, one after another, buddha field oceans. Going from those up to the number of extremely subtle atoms in the inexpressibly inexpressible buddha-fields, he entered in one instant of mind into many one after another buddha-field oceans in each of the hair pores of the bodhisatva Samantabhadra. And, moreover, exactly as in each hair-pore, likewise in all hair-pores without exception, he trod in each moment of mind through world realms numbering the extremely subtle atoms of inexpressibly inexpressible world realms, blessing them to the aeon of the latest limit of the future, entering the world realms by extensively filling them, **715** but never finished passing one after another through field-oceans; he did not arrive at a finish of the mass of field-oceans, the specifics of field-oceans, the whole of field-oceans, the production of field-oceans, the perishing of field-oceans, the classifying of field-oceans, the passing one after another through buddhas-risen oceans, the bodies of buddhas-risen oceans, the specifics of buddhas-risen oceans, the whole of buddhas-risen oceans, the arising of buddhas-risen oceans, the perishing of buddhas-risen oceans, the classifying of buddhas-risen oceans, the maṇḍala-oceans of bodhisatva retinues, the passing one after another through maṇḍala-oceans of bodhisatva retinues, the bodies of maṇḍala-oceans of bodhisatva retinues, the specifics of maṇḍala-oceans of bodhisatva-retinues, the whole of maṇḍala-oceans of bodhisatva retinues, the arising of maṇḍala-oceans of bodhisatva retinues, the destruction of maṇḍala-oceans of bodhisatva retinues, entering into the makeups of sentient beings, entering moment by moment into knowing the faculties of sentient beings, mastering of knowledge of the faculties of sentient beings, the thorough ripening and taming of sentient beings, completely abiding in profound bodhisatva's transformation, or wholly treading the bodhisatva levels.

He lived in some fields for aeons. He acted in some fields for aeons as many as inexpressibly inexpressible buddha fields and without moving from them. **716** In each moment of mind, moreover, he was entering field oceans without edge or centre and also, for the sentient beings there, was thoroughly ripening them into unsurpassed, truly complete enlightenment. He came in that way up to the limit of seeing sameness with the conduct and prayer oceans of bodhisatva Samantabhadra. He gained, following him, sameness with the tathāgatas, sameness with extensively filling all fields with bodies, sameness with extensively filling conduct to completion, sameness with extensively filling by showing the transformation of becoming a manifest complete buddha, sameness with turning the dharma wheel, sameness with the complete purity of individual authentic knowing, sameness with expressing the voice, sameness with the yoga of all the ocean-like aspects of voice, sameness in strengths and fearlessness, sameness with living as a buddha, sameness with great loving kindness and great compassion, and sameness in the inconceivable transformations belonging to a bodhisatva's complete emancipations.

Then, the bodhisatva mahāsatva Samantabhadra who had trod those aeons and infinite aeons and world realms one after another numbering the extremely subtle atoms of the inexpressible buddha-fields made, in order to express clearly what he had shown, this prayer in melodious verse:

However many they are, all the lions of men gone
In the three times in the worlds of the ten directions,
I prostrate to all of them without exception,
With admiring body, speech, and mind.

Through the forces of excellent conduct prayer
All conquerors are seen in direct perception by mind;
Through utterly bowing with bodies many as the field atoms,
I utterly prostrate to all the conquerors.

On a single atom buddhas many as atoms
Are seated at the centre of buddha sons;
I imagine in that way that all the dharmadhātus
Without exception are filled with conquerors.

Those oceans of unending commendation
Have using all sounds of the ocean of aspects of the voice
The good qualities of all the conquerors utterly expressed
And I praise all of the ones gone to bliss.

I will make offerings to those conquerors
With the finest flowers, finest garlands,
Small cymbals, ointments, supreme parasols,
Supreme oil lamps, and finest incense.

I will make offerings to those conquerors
With the finest clothes, supreme scents,
And mixed powders equal to Mt. Meru,
And all with the best of excellent displays.

The offerings which are unsurpassed, vaster,
Those are also imagined for all the conquerors.
Through the forces of faith in excellent conduct
I will prostrate and offer to all the conquerors.

Under the influence of desire, anger, and delusion
And through body, speech, and likewise mind,
The evils I have done whichever they might be,
I lay all of them aside, each one individually.

I rejoice in all merits whoever has them,
Those of all the conquerors of the ten directions and
The buddha sons, of the pratyekabuddhas, of those
In training and not in training, and of all migrators.

Ones who are lamps of the worlds of the ten directions
Have become buddhas at the enlightenment stage and gained the
    undefiled state;
I urge all of those guardians
To turn the unsurpassed wheel.

I also will supplicate with palms joined together those
Who have asserted they will show passage into nirvana
To stay for aeons as many as the field atoms
In order to bring benefit and ease to all migrators.

I dedicate every trifle of virtue that
I have accumulated in prostrating, offering,
Laying aside, rejoicing, urging, and supplicating
For the purpose of enlightenment.

May I offer to the past buddhas and the ones
Who are seated in the worlds of the ten directions.
Those whoever have not descended, most quickly completing
    your intentions
Descend to buddhahood at the enlightenment stage!

May the fields which exist in the ten directions,
However many they are, be vast and wholly pure.
May they be utterly filled with conquerors gone
Before the leading bodhi tree and with buddha sons.

May the sentient beings of the ten directions,
However many, always be free of sickness and have ease.
May all migrators' objectives of dharma be with
Harmony and their hopes also be accomplished.

While I perform the conducts of enlightenment
May I remember my births in all migrations.
At death transfers and births in all successive lives
May I always become ordained.

May I train following all the conquerors,
Working to wholly complete the excellent conduct
And doing the stainless, totally pure discipline conduct
In a way that is always uncorrupted and faultless.

I will teach dharma in all languages—
In gods, nāgas, and yakṣhas' languages,
In khumbandha and mens' languages and
In all migrators' languages many as there are.

Gentled, I'll be most diligent at the pāramitās;
I will never forget enlightenment mind.
May the evils become obscurations
Without exception be totally cleansed.

May I be free of karma, affliction, and māra's works,
And though as migrators of the world, have conduct
Which is like the way a lotus is unaffected by water,
And like the sun and moon are unhindered in the sky.

For as much as the area of a field and directions
I'll utterly pacify the suffering of the bad migrations
Then set all migrators in the best of happinesses;
I will perform conduct that benefits all migrators.

I will work at completing enlightenment conduct,
Enter in harmony with sentient beings' conduct,
And utterly teach the excellent conducts;
May I do this throughout all future aeons.

May I always be accompanied by those
Whose conduct matches my own!
Moreover, through body, speech, and mind
I will perform the same conducts and prayer.

Companions who wish to benefit me,
The ones who utterly teach excellent conduct—
May I always be with them!
I will never displease them!

I will always view the conquerors in direct perception,
The guardians, buddhas surrounded by their sons.
I will also make vast offerings to them
In all future aeons without wearying.

Holding the holy dharma of the conquerors
And fully illuminating enlightenment conduct,
I will completely purify the excellent conduct
And moreover will do that in all future aeons.

May I in re-entering all becomings
Acquire unending merits and wisdoms.
May I become an unending store of method, prajñā,
Samādhis, complete emancipations, and all good qualities.

On one atom are fields as many as the atoms
And in those fields inconceivable buddhas
Seated at the centre of their buddha sons;
Doing enlightenment conduct, I will view them.

Like that so too in all directions without exception
On the breadth of merely a hair there's an ocean of buddhas
Many as their measure in the three times and an ocean of fields
And for an ocean of aeons doing the conduct, I'll utterly enter
    them.

Through the ocean of branches of sound in one speech,
The complete purity of the branches of voice of all conquerors,
Coming as voices exactly in accord with all migrators' thoughts,
The buddha speech, is what I will perpetually enter.

All the conquerors gone in the three times'
Utter turning of the modes of the wheel
And also their unending voices of speech
I too will, by the force of rational mind, utterly enter.

The entering into all future aeons is something
That I too will do but in merely an instant.
Whatever the extent of aeons in the three times
I will act to have entered them in a fraction of an instant.

I will view in a single instant
The lions of men gone in the three times.
I will perpetually enter their domains by
The force of the illusory complete emancipation.

Whatever the field arrangements of the three times,
I will make them manifest on a single atom.
Like that in all the directions without exception,
I will enter the ornamentation of conquerors' fields.

Whichever lamps of the world have not descended
Will become buddhas at the stage, turn the wheel,
And show nirvana, the final, utter peace.
I will go before all those guardians.

Forces of miracles which have all speed,
Forces of vehicle which is in all ways a door,
Forces of conduct whose quality is always good,
Force of loving kindnesses which are all pervasive,

Forces of merit which is all virtuous,
Forces of wisdom become without defilement,
Forces of prajñā, method, and samādhi—by them
I'll be truly accomplishing the forces of enlightenment.

Wholly purifying the forces of karma,
Totally destroying the forces of affliction, and
Utterly rendering powerless the forces of māra,
The forces of excellent conduct will be completed.

I will be completely purifying an ocean of fields,
Completely liberating the ocean of sentient beings,
Utterly seeing an ocean of dharmas,
Utterly realizing an ocean of wisdom,

Completely purifying an ocean of conduct,
Wholly completing an ocean of prayers,
Utterly offering to an ocean of buddhas,
And doing so tirelessly for an ocean of aeons.

The conquerors gone in the three times had their
Particular prayers of enlightenment conduct;
Becoming an enlightened buddha by excellent conduct,
I will complete all their prayers without exception.

The chief of the sons of all the conquerors is
The one whose name is "Samantabhadra"—
I utterly dedicate all these virtues here in order
To conduct myself with expertise equalling his.

The way he is expert at excellent dedications for
Completely pure body, speech, and mind, and
Completely pure conduct, and wholly pure fields,
May I too be equal to him in the same way.

For thoroughly virtuous excellent conduct
I will act as in the prayer of Mañjuśrī.
Without wearying in all future aeons
I will complete their works without exception.

May my conducts not be measurable.
May my good qualities also be immeasurable.
Due to remaining in conduct without measure
I will know all of their transformations.

As far as it would be to the final end of space
And to the end of every sentient being likewise,
And as much as to the end of karma and affliction,
It will also be that much to the end of my prayer.

Compared to one who adorns the infinite fields wherever in the
    ten directions
With jewels and offers that to the conquerors,
And offers the most enjoyable things of gods and men
For aeons as many as the atoms of the fields,

The one who hears this king of dedications
Then is utterly inspired towards and even just one time
Gives rise to faith in supreme enlightenment
Is the one who has the better superior merits.

Someone who has made this excellent conduct prayer
Will have abandoned all bad migrations,
He will have abandoned bad companions,
And he will also see Amitābha soon.

They acquire the best, are sustained in goodness,
And even in this human life can turn out well.
Moreover, whatever Samantabhadra is like,
Before long they will become like that too.

The evil deeds of the five immediates done by
Someone under the control of not knowing will,
If he recites this excellent conduct prayer,
Be quickly and without exception wholly cleansed.

He will possess wisdom, form,
Marks, family, and colour.
Many māras and Tīrthikas will be unable to affect him;
In all three worlds even offerings will be made to him.

He'll quickly go to the foot of the leading bodhi tree
And, having done so, in order to benefit sentient beings,
Will sit there, become an enlightened buddha, utterly turn the
    wheel,
And tame all the māras together with their regiments.

For whoever holds, reads or teaches
This prayer of excellent conduct
Their full-ripenings will be known by buddha.
Do not be sceptical of supreme enlightenment!

Mañjushrī knows how it is and is heroic
And Samantabhadra is like that too;
Following them in every way, I train and
Will utterly dedicate all of these virtues.

Using the dedication which all the conquerors
Gone in the three times commend as supreme,
I utterly dedicate all these roots of virtue of mine
For the purpose of excellent conduct.

When the time has come for me to die,
May all obscurations clear away;
Seeing Amitābha in direct perception,
I will utterly go to the field of Sukhāvatī.

Having gone there, may all these prayers
Without exception become manifest.
Having completely fulfilled them without exception,
I will benefit sentient beings as long as the world.

In that good and pleasing maṇḍala of the conqueror
May I be born from an exceptionally beautiful fine lotus.
Seeing conqueror Amitābha directly,
May I also obtain the prophecy there.

Having completely obtained the prophecy there,
I will with many thousands of millions of emanations
By force of rational mind, throughout the ten directions
Do many things to benefit sentient beings.

May the trifle of virtue accumulated by the one
Who has recited this excellent conduct prayer
Cause the virtues of migrators' prayers
To be obtained by them all in an instant.

May whatever infinite superior merit has been gained
In wholly dedicating this excellent conduct prayer
Cause migrators drowning in the river of unsatisfactoriness
To utterly gain the place of Amitābha.

From the great enumeration of dharmas called *Gaṇḍavyūha*, a part of the bodhisatva section of the extremely large sutra known as the *Avataṃsaka*, one part of Subhuti's respectful conduct when attending to spiritual friends is, in total, complete.

The above was translated into Tibetan language from Sanskrit then corrected and finalized by the Indian preceptors Jinamitra and Surendrabodhi, the chief editor Lotsāwa Bande Yeshe De, and others.

*Samantabhadra's Prayer
Extracted and Arranged for use
by Tibetans*

Noble One, A King of Prayers of Excellent Conduct

In Indian language: āryabhadracaryāpraṇidhānarājā.
In Tibetan language: 'phags pa bzang po spyod pa'i smon lam gyi rgyal po.

I prostrate to noble Mañjuśrī who has become youthful.

[The prayer extracted from its original place in the Gaṇḍavyūha Sutra is inserted here.]

The chief of these supreme prayers in this king of prayers
Brings benefit to all the infinite migrators;
May this scripture adorned with Samantabhadra be accomplished
And all the places of bad migrations be emptied.

Noble One, A King of Prayers of Excellent Conduct is complete.

Translated, corrected, and finalized by the Indian preceptors Jinamitra and Surendrabodhi, the chief editor Lotsāwa Bande Yeshe De, and others.

*Samantabhadra's Prayer
Extracted and Arranged for use
by non-Tibetans*

Samantabhadra's Prayer
A King of Prayers of Excellent Conduct

The following is extracted from the fifty-third chapter of the Gaṇḍavyūha Sutra in which Subhuti goes before the bodhisatva Samantabhadra to gain further insight into the meaning of the Great Vehicle.

Then, the bodhisatva mahāsatva Samantabhadra who had trod those aeons and infinite aeons and world realms one after another numbering the extremely subtle atoms of the inexpressible buddha-fields made, in order to express clearly what he had shown, this prayer in melodious verse:

[The prayer is presented in full here.]

From the great enumeration of dharmas called *Gaṇḍavyūha*, a part of the bodhisatva section of the extremely large sutra known as the *Avataṃsaka*, one part of Subhuti's respectful conduct when attending to spiritual friends is, in total, complete.

The above was translated into Tibetan language from Sanskrit then corrected and finalized by the Indian preceptors Jinamitra and Surendrabodhi, the chief editor Lotsāwa Bande Yeshe De, and others.

This arrangement for the practice of Samantabhadra's Prayer for Westerners was made by the Australian translator Tony Duff at the buddhas' place of Swayambunath, Nepal, in the spring of 2013 after consulting many Indian and Tibetan commentaries to the prayer. To remove the errors which have crept into Tibetan arrangements of the prayer, the prayer itself was translated from the sutra as found in the Derge edition of the Kangyur.

A Thorough Explanation Of Samantabhadra's Prayer
by Tony Duff

Plate 1. Lama Tony Duff teaching Mahāmudrā in retreat with a statue of Karmapa behind.

Contents

1. THE ORIGIN OF SAMANTABHADRA'S PRAYER 45
2. THE PRAYER IS AN EXTRACT 49
   1. What are the Extracts like? 49
   2. Problems with the Extracts 49
   3. Specific Problems with the Tibetan Arrangement now
      in use 50
      1. The title given is a Tibetan invention, not the
         actual name 51
      2. The prostration is a Tibetan invention 53
      3. The preamble 53
      4. A stanza added to the prayer by Tibetans 54
      5. The ending matter 55
   4. Fixing the Problems with the Tibetan framework 56
3. THE PRAYER EXPLAINED 57
   1. Topics One to Seven, the Seven Limbs that Create a
      Basis for the Prayer 58
      Topic 1: Prostrations 58
         1. Prostration through body, speech, and mind .. 58
         2. Prostration through body 62
         3. Prostration through mind 69
         4. Prostration through speech 71
      Topic 2: Offerings 75
         1. The surpassed offering 75

    2. The unsurpassed offering 77
  Topic 3: Laying Aside 80
  Topic 4: Rejoicing 84
  Topic 5: Urging 86
  Topic 6: Supplicating 91
  Topic 7: Dedication 93
2. Topics Eight to Ten, the Actual Prayer 95
  Topic 8: The Divisions of the Prayer 95
    Division 1: Thought 96
    Division 2: Not forgetting enlightenment mind   101
    Division 3: Connecting with being uncloaked . . 108
    Division 4: Benefiting sentient beings 110
    Division 5: Armour 112
    Division 6: Connecting with bodhisatvas of the
      same lot 114
    Division 7: Acting to please virtuous friends . . . 115
    Division 8: Having made the tathāgata's visible 116
    Division 9: Wholly holding the holy dharma . . 118
    Division 10: Gaining an unending store 119
    Division 11: Entering 121
      1. Entering into viewing the buddha-fields—
        two types 121
      2. Entering into the buddha speech 127
      3. Entering into turning the tathāgatas' wheel
        of dharma 129
      4. Entering into all future aeons 132
      5. Entering into viewing the tathāgatas 133
      6. Entering into their domains 133
      7. Entering into manifesting a buddha-field 134
      8. Entering into going before the tathāgatas 135
    Division 12: Forces 137
    Division 13: Accomplishing 139
    Division 14: Activities 140
    Division 15: Delineation of training following . 142
    Division 16: Conclusion 146

Topic 9: Its ending 147
Topic 10: Its benefits 148
   1. Benefits seen in this life 148
      1. Wholly holding merits that are special ... 149
      2. Seeing the tathāgatas 150
      3. Gaining the same lot with bodhisatvas ... 152
      4. Wholly ending karmic obscuration 153
   2. Benefits seen in a later life 154
      1. Benefits belonging to cause 155
      2. Benefits belonging to fruition 156
3. Dedication verses
   1. Dedication in connection with the great
     bodhisatvas Mañjuśhrī and Samantabhadra 160
   2. Dedication in connection with the tathāgatas 162
   3. Dedication for the vanishing of obscuration at the
     time of death 162
   4. Dedication for going on after death in accord with
     other shore activity 162
   5. Dedication for completing the possibilities of
     having gone to Amitābha's pure realm 163
   6. Dedication for actually being born in Sukhāvatī
     then gaining the prophesy for one's own
     buddhahood from Amitabha 163
   7. Dedication for completion of activity in Sukhavati 164
   8. General dedication of merit 166
   9. Dedication for others to gain the place of Amitabha
     166

A Thorough Explanation of Samantabhadra's Prayer by Tony Duff

1. The Origin of Samantabhadra's Prayer

It is often thought that Samantabhadra's Prayer is a standalone prayer spoken by Samantabhadra for general use, but that is not so. It is the conclusion, composed in verse, to a teaching on the conduct of a bodhisatva that was given to a young bodhisatva named Sudhana when he encountered the tenth-level bodhisatva Samantabhadra.

According to the Great Vehicle sutras Sudhana was a young man, the son of a merchant, who regularly appeared in the bodhisatva assembly congregated around Śhākyamuni Buddha. At some point Sudhana made a spiritual journey in which he undertook to meet as many of the great bodhisatvas of his time as possible in order to deepen his knowledge of the conduct or ways of a bodhisatva. By the end of his journey he had met with and received an enormous amount of teaching from each of one hundred and ten great bodhisatvas. The story of Sudhana's journey together with all of the teachings he received on the conduct of a bodhisatva became very famous. The entire story was written down in detail in fifty-three chapters that were assembled into a large sutra of the Great Vehicle named the *Gaṇḍavyūha Sutra*, which in turn is the last sutra of an extremely large collection of Great Vehicle sutras called the *Avataṃsaka Sutra*.

As Sudhana progressed on his journey, he gained increasing knowledge of the excellent conduct of a bodhisatva and increasing levels of spiritual development. His journey and his development culminated in a meeting with Samantabhadra, the greatest of bodhisatvas of his time. Samantabhadra had not only reached and also mastered the tenth bodhisatva level as had Maitreya, Mañjushrī, and some others of the time, but was known to have the greatest level of experience with the conduct of a bodhisatva and to be the one most capable of expressing it to others. Thus, there is the key point that Sudhana's journey did not merely end in receiving teachings from yet another great bodhisatva, but culminated in meeting with a bodhisatva who had mastered the highest possible level of bodhisatva training and was the most capable of teaching it to others.

The last chapter of the *Gaṇḍavyūha Sutra* recounts the story of Sudhana's meeting with Samantabhadra. The story opens with a listing of the extraordinary bodhisatva qualities that Sudhana had developed to that point on his journey. This has a meaning. It shows that Sudhana has prepared himself to the point that he could actually meet with the tenth-level bodhisatva Samantabhadra in the highest possible way, that is, in a way that was consistent with the extraordinary level of being that Samantabhadra had attained.

The chapter then paints a picture of Samantabhadra and how he was conducting himself. This part of the story shows the inconceivable mode of being of a bodhisatva who has not only reached but also accomplished the tenth and final level of a bodhisatva's training. It serves to open the reader up to the capacities and style of being of a bodhisatva at that level.

The chapter then describes the actual meeting of Sudhana with Samantabhadra. This makes the point that Sudhana did not merely meet with Samantabhadra in the way that ordinary beings would have to do but was able to enter the extraordinary, inconceivable, pervading-all-cosmoses-and-times level of being of Samantabhadra.

Sudhana's earlier meetings with bodhisatvas had often brought him into contact with the miraculous events and revelations of highly developed bodhisatvas, but his meeting with Samantabhadra brought him into contact with a direct experience of bodhisatvahood far beyond any he had experienced up to that point in his journey.

At this point the chapter gives a long description of what Sudhana entered, which starts out with his being greeted by Samantabhadra who is seated in front of the buddha Vairochana who himself is surrounded by his inconceivable retinue of bodhisatvas. Samantabhadra also is surrounded by his retinue of bodhisatvas. And as well as that there is a pure field of Samantabhadra some distance off in which there is another emanation of Samantabhadra also surrounded by his inconceivable retinue of bodhisatvas. The hair-pores of all of these Samantabhadras are filled with Samantabhadras as many as the atoms in all of the places of all of the cosmoses and each of those is surrounded by an inconceivable retinue of bodhisatvas. The description of this situation—which is actually beyond the reach of conceptual mind—in which Samantabhadra was abiding and into which Sudhana was entering goes on for many pages, painting a picture of literally mind-blowing proportions.

Once Sudhana had been drawn into Samantabhadra's cosmic vastness of being—in itself a most extraordinary experiential demonstration of the conduct of a bodhisatva—Samantabhadra gave Sudhana a formal teaching, in prose, on the conduct of a bodhisatva. At the end of the teaching, Samantabhadra composed a set of verses for Sudhana to sum up all that he had been taught—both what had been demonstrated in direct experience and what had been expressed in verbal teaching. It is those verses that, extracted out from the rest of the sutra, became known as "Samantabhadra's Prayer". Immediately at the end of the verses comes a short colophon that marks the end of the chapter and the sutra:

> From the great enumeration of dharmas called *Gaṇḍavyūha*, a part of the bodhisatva section of the extremely large sutra known as the *Avataṃsaka*, one part of

Subhuti's respectful conduct when attending to spiritual friends is, in total, complete.

Several things should be obvious from this explanation of the final chapter of the *Gaṇḍavyūha Sutra*. The most obvious is that Samantabhadra's Prayer is not, as many people think, a standalone prayer that was somewhere along the line given by Samantabhadra as a separate, nice little prayer concerning the bodhisatva's conduct. Rather, it is a set of verses that sum up a most amazing teaching given in the experiential state of the most advanced bodhisatva of the Buddha's time. Moreover, the verses have an extraordinary context that permeates their every word, so it is imperative, if the prayer is to be fully appreciated and used, to have as much knowledge of that context as possible. Unfortunately, that information is not included with the verses when they are extracted from the sutra and written out alone for use as a prayer, with the result that most people think of Samantabhadra's Prayer as merely a standalone prayer with little or no connection to anything else.

Then, there is the point that Samantabhadra's prayer is not really a prayer. Some lines do have the wording "May I ..." and the like, but most lines have the form of the statement "I shall ..." Despite the very clear wording and grammar involved, all existing translations into English from Tibetan sources reject the "I shall ..." wordings and change them to "May I" and the like. This leads those using these corrupt English translations to get a feeling for the prayer which is not there in the original. All in all, if the verses are to be recited, they should be recited in the same sense that they were given to Sudhana by Samantabhadra, that is, starting with an appreciation of the cosmic vastness of bodhisatvahood and then with an on-going sense of "I shall follow this conduct of a bodhisatva, I will perfect that conduct of a bodhisatva", and so on, exactly as the words of the verses say.

2. The Prayer is an Extract

The whole record of Sudhana's meeting with Samantabhadra is too long for convenient use for recitation. However, the concluding verses are very suited to the purpose. Therefore, at some point in ancient India the verses alone were extracted from the sutra and written down separately for use as a prayer for recitation. The same thing was done later on in Tibet.

2.1. What are the Extracts Like?

Indian Buddhists extracted the verses from the sutra and wrote them down in a very simple format—they wrote the name "Samantabhadra's Prayer" followed by the verses. Later, when the Tibetans first translated the sutra, they did the same, using the same simple arrangement as the Indians. However, the Tibetans later shifted to a complicated arrangement that packed the verses into a framework that had been royally decreed as the framework for holding all such translations. That arrangement of the verses within that framework has been in use for over one thousand years. It has sometimes been corrupted during that time, but the basic and most commonly seen form of it can be seen, translated into English, on page 33.

2.2. Problems with the Extracts

The extracts might be convenient for personal use, but there is nothing about them that tells the reader that they are an integral and important part of something larger. Instead, they give the impression that the verses are a standalone prayer with no relation to anything else. The result is that many people using the prayer never know of the its all-important context and so lose its full import. All of the arrangements, Indian and Tibetan, and now English translations of the Tibetan arrangement have that problem.

In addition, the Tibetan arrangement in normal use—the complicated one mentioned just above—has several other problems. All existing English translations of the prayer use this arrangement, so if you are a Westerner who is trying to come to a correct understanding of the prayer, it is important to know about these problems and to realize that this Tibetan arrangement is very unsuitable for use with English translations of the prayer.

2.3. Specific Problems with the Tibetan Arrangement now in use

At the time of the early translations of Buddhist works into the Tibetan language, it was set down by royal decree that translations must be placed into a framework having these features:

1. a title
2. a prostration done to indicate the validity of the translation and where appropriate to show to which section of the Buddha Word the translated material belongs
3. other prefatory material as needed to indicate the source of the work being translated
4. the translation itself
5. a colophon to indicate the end of the translation if the translated text does not include such an indication
6. a colophon showing who was responsible for the work of translation.

Tibetan commentaries to the prayer not only comment on the verses of the prayer but also comment, usually in detail, on all the parts of this framework, which makes it seem as though all of the framework is part of the original prayer. A clear example of this can be seen in the Tibetan commentary by Tenpa'i Wangchuk in volume two of this series.

2.3.1. The title given is a Tibetan invention, not the actual name

The normal Tibetan arrangement gives a title and then follows that with the title written out in both Sanskrit and Tibetan. The title as given in Tibetan is " 'phags pa bzang po spyod pa'i smon lam gyi gyal po", which translates into English as "Noble One, A King of Prayers of Excellent Conduct". This official-looking statement sends a strong message that this is a prayer that has this title that was given to it when it was composed. However, as we know from the sutra, the verses making up the prayer have no title or official name.

The Indian commentaries make it clear that the verses extracted for use as a prayer were known in India by the descriptive name Samantabhadra's Prayer. The Indian commentaries also make it clear that there were two other descriptive names for the verses used as a prayer. Firstly, they were referred to as "a prayer of excellent conduct". The words "excellent conduct" in Sanskrit are used in the same way as in English, to refer to any kind of excellent conduct. The pure conduct of bodhisatvas is one kind of excellent conduct, so excellent conduct is one of several ways of referring to a bodhisatva's conduct. Thus the verses used as a prayer were called "a prayer of excellent conduct" meaning the excellent conduct of a bodhisatva. Secondly, the verses were referred to as a "king amongst prayers" because of being regarded as the best of all prayers available at the time concerning a bodhisatva's excellent conduct. Then, it is clear from reading the commentary of Shākyamitra—one of the heart disciples of Nāgārjuna—that the last two descriptive names were also joined into one in ancient India, to give "A King of Prayers of Excellent Conduct". Finally, we know from Yeshe De's commentary that the name Samantabhadra's Prayer and the two descriptive names just mentioned were conveyed to Yeshe De by the Indian experts who were assisting him with the translation of the verses.

The title that appears on most Tibetan arrangements of the extracted verses used as a prayer, "Noble One, A King of Prayers of Excellent Conduct", is written in Tibetan in such a way as to make it look as though there was a standalone prayer that had been given that title. Moreover, all the commentaries written by Tibetans over the last several centuries proudly dissect this invented title, giving an even stronger impression that there really is a prayer with this title. Westerners have then believed that this is the actual title of a prayer! However, this Tibetan name is an artifice made up by the Tibetans.

The Indian commentaries primarily refer to the prayer simply and quite sensibly as Samantabhadra's Prayer. Why then should we not do the same? After that, if someone asks what kind of prayer it is, we could say that it is a prayer concerning the excellent conduct of bodhisatvas, those on the path to truly complete enlightenment. And then if someone asks whether it is a good prayer or not, we could say that it is regarded as supreme or a king amongst all prayers of that kind. You will see that I have named the new arrangement that I have made for the verses used as a prayer accordingly.

It has to be noted here that there are several major mistakes of translation that have followed on from misunderstanding the official title of the Tibetan arrangement. For example, the phrase "excellent conduct" is not only used in the name of the prayer but also used in several places in the prayer itself. To date, translators have seen these words in the official title and mistakenly assumed that "excellent conduct" must be the name of the prayer. However, the phrase "excellent conduct" is not a proper name for the prayer as such. It is a general phrase that has to be understood on context as referring to excellent conduct in general or to this prayer about excellent conduct of a bodhisatva. For example, one line of the prayer says "in this prayer of excellent conduct" meaning simply "in this prayer that deals with the excellent conduct of a bodhisatva", but this has been universally mis-translated into English as "in this *Prayer of Excellent Conduct*" meaning "in this prayer named the Prayer of Excellent Conduct". There are several other errors like this that derive from a mis-understanding of the name of the prayer.

2.3.2. The prostration is a Tibetan invention

The Tibetan framework for translations requires that there be a line of prostration immediately following the title. It was mandated by King Ralpachen as being a necessary part of every translation of a Buddhist text from another language into the Tibetan language. It has to be there to show both the validity of the translation and the section of the Buddha's teaching to which the translated material belongs.

The prostration used in this case says, *I prostrate to the noble one Mañjuśhrī who has become youthful.* That is explained by Tibetans to mean that the content of this prayer relates to the prajñā of the Great Vehicle, which in turn is categorized as Abhidharma. Of course, the original verses do not have this line of prostration or anything remotely connected with it. It is purely a Tibetan invention and as such should not be slavishly carried over into other languages. What *is* needed in translations into other languages is a clear preamble to the prayer that indicates the context of the prayer and the importance of that context to a proper understanding of the prayer. You will see that I have provided such a preamble in the new arrangement that I have made for the verses used as a prayer.

By they way, some Western translators will translate the word prostrate here as "homage". However, stemming from Indian cultural customs, there is a distinction made in Buddhist texts between a prostration and a homage. Here, a prostration is what is intended.

2.3.3. The Preamble

The Tibetan arrangement of the prayer usually presents the prayer next (though a few editions that I have seen have a very short preamble that mentions that the prayer is from the *Gaṇḍavyūha Sutra*). This means that the uninformed reader is not being given needed information. Having read the sutra, I found that there was one sentence prior to the actual expression of the verses which neatly summed up the context of and reason for the verses. It says:

> Then, the bodhisatva mahāsatva Samantabhadra who had trod those aeons and infinite aeons and world realms one after another numbering the extremely subtle atoms of the inexpressible buddha-fields made, in order to give clear expression to that, this prayer in melodious verse.

The first part "Then ... subtle atoms in buddha-fields" summarizes the cosmic, inconceivable experience that Sudhana met when he was drawn into Samantabhadra's space of realization. It was the context for the teaching that he was then given by Samantabhadra. The second part "in order to fully express that" says that the prayer was then given by Samantabhadra to summarize the teaching that had been given in that amazing space of realization. That excerpt from the sutra is exactly what is needed as a preamble to the presentation of the prayer itself, so it has been added to the new arrangement of the prayer.

2.3.4. A stanza added to the prayer by Tibetans

The next problem is that the Tibetan arrangement of the extracted verses adds a stanza to the end of the verses which is not part of the verses and therefore of the prayer.

The original verses were composed in a particular type of Sanskrit verse called "gāthā", which corresponds roughly to English stanzas each with four lines of verse. The official translation of the prayer into Tibetan done by Yeshe De has sixty-two stanzas in it. However, the Tibetan arrangement of the verses for use as a prayer has sixty-three stanzas in it. Whence the discrepancy? The great translator Vairochana, on the completion of Yeshe De's work of officially translating the sutra into Tibetan, wrote a stanza of dedication in appreciation of Samantabhadra's teaching having been translated into Tibetan. At some point after that, Tibetans added Vairochana's dedication to the end of the verses of the prayer and have carried on since then as though that stanza was part of the prayer.

It seems to me that the Tibetans should have marked off the end of the verses of the prayer and marked the additional verse as Vairochana's. However, that was not done, and I would note that I have many times been told by Tibetans with certainty that Vairochana's verse is part of the prayer! I have even seen a later Tibetan commentary by a so-called Tibetan expert which says the same! This mistake has continued on into English translations where Vairochana's dedication has been included with the belief that it is part of the prayer. I know of many Westerners who, because of that, have come to believe that this verse is the last verse of the original verses of the prayer.

I see no reason why Vairochana's dedication should be included in non-Tibetan versions of the verses for use as a prayer. Therefore, I have removed the stanza completely from the new arrangement for the verses used as a prayer.

Note that it is very likely that the sixty-first and sixty-second stanzas also are not part of the original verses but were additions made in ancient India, before the sutra came into Tibet. This is discussed later in this commentary.

2.3.5. The Ending Matter

There has to be something in the arrangement to indicate the end of the translated material. In most versions of the Tibetan arrangement, this is a line which simply says, "A King of Prayers of Excellent Conduct is complete". However, that makes no sense given that the last chapter of the *Gaṇḍavyūha Sutra*—the one ending with the prayer—has an ending immediately after the prayer that shows that the prayer is complete and is, therefore, ideal for the purpose. It has been used for the new arrangement for non-Tibetans:

> From the great enumeration of dharmas called *Gaṇḍavyūha*, a part of the bodhisatva section of the extremely large sutra known as the *Avataṃsaka*, one part of Subhuti's

respectful conduct when attending to spiritual friends is, in total, complete.

Following that, there has to be a colophon to indicate the translators responsible for the work. Most Tibetan arrangements use the colophon found in the official Tibetan translation of the sutra:

> Translated, corrected, and finalized by the Indian preceptors Jinamitra and Surendrabodhi, the chief editor Lotsāwa Bande Yeshe De, and others.

However, some misquote it and I have seen some texts in which it has been replaced with a line saying "Translated by Vairochana", which is total fiction! The actual colophon has been correctly added to the new arrangement of the prayer. Translations of the prayer from Tibetan into another language should have the appropriate wording added in order to indicate the translator(s) of the verses into another language.

2.4. Fixing the Problems with the Tibetan Framework

Packaging the verses of the prayer into the Tibetan framework for translations leads to the various problems just described, but this is easy to fix. All that is needed is a new framework that correctly informs the reader of the original context of the prayer and correctly provides the reader with the other, needed information. I have made such a framework for English, but it could and I hope will be used for other languages. It can be seen on page 35.

3. The Prayer Explained

All Indian commentaries agree that the prayer itself consists of ten major parts or topics. The ten topics are:

1. prostration to the tathāgatas
2. offering to the tathāgatas
3. laying aside evil
4. rejoicing in merit
5. urging to turn the wheel of dharma
6. requesting the tathāgatas to remain
7. whole dedication of the roots of merit
8. its divisions
9. its ending
10. its benefits

An easier way to understand the structure of the prayer shows that there are two main parts to the prayer, with those ten topics distributed amongst them like this:

1. Topics one to seven are the seven limbs of accumulation as they are called, which provide a preliminary to the prayer.
2. Topics eight to ten are the topics of the actual prayer. Of them, the eighth is the main part of the prayer with its many divisions. The ninth is a single verse where "ending" does not mean that the prayer is finishing but means the final reach of the prayer. The tenth is several verses on the benefits associated with the recitation of the prayer, followed by verses of dedication.

Some Tibetan commentaries present other structures for the prayer, but all of them fall within the structure just shown, which is the easiest way to understand the structure of the prayer.

3.1. Topics One to Seven
The Seven Limbs That Create a Basis for the Prayer

Topic 1: Prostrations

The first four verses are verses of prostration. The first verse is a general prostration made through body, speech, and mind. The remaining three verses are specific prostrations made though body, mind, and speech in that order.

Note that the verses of the prayer were written in a type of Sanskrit verse called gāthā. This type of verse is made of two couplets each of the same length, with each couplet made up of two equal parts. This roughly translates into four lined English verse. Observing these divisions is in some place important to understanding the prayer.

1. Prostration Through Body, Speech, and Mind

1 However many they are, all the lions of men gone
   In the three times in the worlds of the ten directions,
   I prostrate to all of them without exception,
   With admiring body, speech, and mind.

It is very clear from the grammar involved and the syntax used in this type of Sanskrit verse that the "how many they are" on the first line of the verse does not go with the "in the worlds of the ten directions" but goes with the "lions of men", as shown above. As would be expected from the grammar and syntax involved, it is explained that way in all Indian commentaries and in the earliest Tibetan commentary to the prayer, written by the chief translator of the prayer into Tibetan, Yeshe De. However, starting several centuries, Tibetan commentators lost sight of both the Sanskrit grammar and syntax involved and must have stopped looking at those early commentaries because they mistakenly claimed that the "however many they are" goes with "the worlds of the ten directions, like this:

> All the lions of men gone in the three times
> In the worlds however many they are of the ten directions

Their explanation has gradually become the accepted understanding within Tibetan Buddhist culture and, in recent times, Western translators have relied on their mistaken explanation, with the result that the verse has been incorrectly translated in all existing translations from Tibetan into English and other languages.

Here is an explanation of the grammar and syntax involved. According to the syntax, the first two couplets are composed using a particular poetic device that joins the "how many" with the lions of men. According to the grammar, the first phrase of the first couplet is, in Tibetan, "ji snyed su dag". The "ji snyed" means literally "how many" or "as many as". The "su" is equivalent to "who" and like "who" in English is only used to refer to living beings, never to inanimate things. "Su" is singular. The "dag" has been added to make it plural, as in "those who". Thus, the grammar not only supports what the syntax tells us but makes it is impossible for the "how many" to refer to the worlds of the ten directions—it can only refer to all the lions of men. Thus the first couplet reads as shown in the verse at the beginning of this section and not the way it has been mistakenly explained by Tibetans, a mistake that has now passed into translations from the Tibetan into English and other languages. There are a number of verses in the prayer, including this one, where it is crucial to understand the Sanskrit grammar and or syntax behind the Tibetan translation. It will often mean that the words and even lines of any given verse as it appears in the Tibetan translation will have to be re-ordered for the translation to match the original intent of the Sanskrit.

Next in the first couplet, we have to understand "lions of men", "gone in the three times", and "in the worlds of the ten directions". This is how they go together. This couplet is talking about the most capable of beings, lions of men, who trod and reached the end of the long path to buddhahood. They are said to be tathāgatas, that is, ones who have gone *gata* to suchness *tathā*. From our perspective, some of them have gone to suchness in the past, some have gone in our present time, and some will have gone in the future. Thus, one way to refer to all the buddhas that there ever will be is to speak of those who have "gone in the three times". Each of all of these buddhas goes to suchness somewhere in the worlds of the ten directions. In ancient India, they said "in the ten directions" to mean "throughout space in all directions" because ten directions includes the four cardinal and intermediate directions plus the directions vertically above and below. Thus the overall meaning of the first couplet is:

> However many they are, all the lions of men who have or will have gone to suchness, to buddhahood, in the three times wherever they did that in the worlds spread throughout space in every direction.

There are still more details to explain for the first couplet. Why are the ones who have gone to suchness, to buddhahood, referred to as "lions of men"? They are like lions in the sense that buddhas have no fear whatsoever of anything and therefore rule over all other beings. Well then, why not call them "lions among sentient beings"? They are specifically referred to as lions among men because, although they show themselves to all sentient beings in all of the migrations possible in samsara in order to assist them, they primarily show themselves in the form of a man to certain of the desire realm gods and to humans as a whole. As it says in the *Sutra of the Recollection of the Noble Three Jewels* "they are the teachers of gods and men". For those two reasons, they were known to the desire gods and humans whom they taught as "lions of men". Note that the correct translation here is "men" and not a re-wording of that to suit modern feminist ideas. The sutras explain clearly that they appear, in most cases, as men to humans and gods, not that they appear in diverse gender forms to humans and gods. Therefore, "men" is not only the literal but also the correct translation.

Now we have reached the second couplet:

> I prostrate to all of them without exception,
> With admiring body, speech, and mind.

One point that arises here is that the term "all" appears twice in the verse. Some think that this is either a mistake or redundancy, but it is not. The first couplet has the term because of needing to indicate "however many they are, the lions of men who have gone in all the three times". The second couplet then has "I prostrate to all of them without exception" which joins with "the however many they are" of the first couplet, to ensure every one of them is included. (This is part of why one understands from the Sanskrit syntax that "however many" joins with "lions of men".) In other words, the "all" in the first couplet includes the buddhas gone in the three times and the "all without exception" in the second couplet ensures that all of them, "however many they are", are included for the prostration.

The prostration is done to all of them with admiring body, speech, and mind. "Admiring" here is an event of mind in which one sees very clearly and therefore appreciates the good qualities of something or someone else. It is one of the three types of faith—admiring[17], longing, and trusting. It is commonly called "lucid faith" in English but that is not quite right. This is admiring faith in that one first sees something and then, because of clearly or *lucidly* seeing its good qualities, admires it. The emphasis is on the admiration of clearly-seen good qualities. Yeshe De explains that you are not merely prostrating because of being infected with someone else's enthusiasm for the buddhas, but that, through your own clear knowledge of their good qualities, you are, with admiration, prostrating to them.

The prostration is done with body, speech, and mind. If the person reciting the prayer has informed admiration for the good qualities of the buddhas, that person's mind will be prostrating to the

---

[17] Tib. dang ba'i dad pa.

buddhas as this verse is being recited. Then, because the actions of body and speech are motivated by mind, the recitation itself will be prostration through speech. Then, some people will put their palms together while reciting the verse, which is a form of prostration through body. Thus the person's body is making the sign of a prostration, the speech is prostrating through the verbal recitation, and the mind, which is driving it all, is making a prostration because of its admiration for the buddhas.

All of those words were required to give a precise explanation of the words and meaning of a single verse. From that, you can begin to understand that a very large amount of meaning is contained in this prayer, much more than might be thought from simply reading the words of the prayer. You can also see that a great deal of attention has to be paid to the grammar and syntax involved in order to correctly understand the prayer, let alone translate it correctly into other languages.

2. Prostration Through Body

Having prostrated to all the buddhas by way of admiring body, speech, and mind, those same buddhas are now prostrated to specifically by way of body:

> 2   Through the forces of excellent conduct prayer
> All conquerors are seen in direct perception by mind;
> Through utterly bowing with bodies many as the field
>   atoms,
> I utterly prostrate to all the conquerors.

All commentaries agree that the verse is structured as follows: the first and second lines set up the object to which prostration will be done, the buddhas; the third line sets up the bodies by which the prostration will be done and shows how they do the prostration; and the fourth line is the actual prostration.

Thus, the first line shows that the primary agent that makes it possible for all the buddhas in their buddha-fields to become visible directly before yourself is the forces generated by prayers for excellent conduct. The second line shows that the instrument (the complement in grammar) by which they are actually brought into direct perception before you is your ordinary, mental mind thinking of them. All commentaries agree that, having recited the two lines, each of the conquerors is now present directly ahead of you in his buddha-field and visible to your mind. On reciting the third and fourth lines, you manifest bodies as many in number as the field atoms, where field atoms in this case is considered to mean the atoms constituting all of the buddha-fields, then simultaneously bow down with all them to all of the conquerors who have become visible before you with the recitation of the first couplet. Moreover, you do not merely bow down but bow down to the utmost and therefore you do not merely prostrate to all the conquerors but prostrate to them to the utmost. That is sufficient to understand the verse and use it for recitation. Nevertheless, there are more details to be explained.

Not all commentators agree on the meaning of the first couplet. They all agree that the first line "Through the forces of excellent conduct prayer" presents the main force or, grammatically speaking, the agent, that makes it possible for the object of prostration to appear to the practitioner. However, neither "forces" nor "excellent conduct prayer" are further identified, leaving room for differing explanations. It is noteworthy that Nāgārjuna explains this line according to the literal meaning of the words of the verse, as was done in the previous paragraph, without further speculation. His explanation is most useful because it tells us that it is sufficient to stay with the general meaning and not try to pin these terms down further than has already been done. Nevertheless, all commentators following him, both Indian and Tibetan, have tried to pin down these two terms and in the process have arrived at different explanations of their meaning. In sum, they come up with two explanations of the phrase "excellent conduct prayer" and with various explanations of "forces". These will now be dealt with in that order.

First, some commentators explain that "excellent conduct prayer" means prayers for a bodhisatva's excellent conduct in general and others that it means Samantabhadra's verses about excellent conduct in particular. Whatever the case, it would *not* be correct to point to a text of Samantabhadra's Prayer packed into the Tibetan arrangement described earlier and say, "The title of the prayer here is 'Excellent Conduct Prayer' so that has to be what these words are referencing". As explained earlier, there was no formal title for Samantabhadra's prayer when it was being composed. Thus, the words here have to be understood as simply meaning "prayer of excellent conduct". That then begs the question of whether it is prayers of excellent conduct in general or Samantabhadra's prayer in particular?

Second, we can look at the word "forces" and try to identify to what it refers. Before doing so, note that it is forces in the plural not force in the singular; some translations into English have changed it to the singular and lost meaning in doing so. Now, if we take "excellent conduct prayer" to mean prayers for the excellent conduct of a bodhisatva in general, then forces means the forces of virtue that have been accumulated in the past by making prayers for the excellent conduct of a bodhisatva. On the other hand, if we take "excellent conduct prayer" to mean this excellent conduct prayer of Samantabhadra, then forces is explained by Indian commentators such as Śhākyamitra to mean the forces of each one of the many prayers contained in that prayer. Either way, it is very important to understand that the Indian commentators and Yeshe De all explain that "forces of excellent conduct prayer" refers to the forces of virtue created through making such prayers in times *prior* to the present and are unanimous in stating that it does *not* mean the forces of virtue connected with doing the current session of recitation.

A further important point is that all the Indian commentators and Yeshe De agree that forces of excellent conduct prayer are forces of virtue created through excellent conduct prayers that *you*, the person reciting the prayer, have made previously, not someone else. This last point has to be noted because some later Tibetan commentators explain that forces of excellent conduct prayer refers to the forces of prayers for excellent conduct made by buddhas previously when they were bodhisatvas. That explanation, which can be seen in Tenpa'i Wangchuk's commentary in volume II, is one of many given by Tibetans over the last several centuries that run counter to the original explanations of the Indian commentators and Yeshe De; having researched it, this seems to be purely a Tibetan invention and should not be accepted.

Also in relation to that last point, the English translation from Marpa Translation Committee changes forces to the singular and adds a "my" to the first line so that it reads "the force of my prayer for excellent conduct". This creates the completely mistaken impression that it is the force that comes from one's current recitation of Samantabhadra's Prayer that makes it possible for the buddhas to appear before the practitioner. Amazingly, I have had people tell me that the incorrect translation sounds nicer than what the prayer actually says, so they will stick with that, thank you very much! This is an example of how a badly mistaken translation can have a nice ring to it but can send the person using the prayer in a completely mistaken direction. It also illustrates how difficult it can be to overcome the prejudices of Westerners once they have started using a mistaken translation. For these and other reasons I have done the research needed and am presenting all of it here in a very detailed way.

Well then, what is the function of these forces? First and foremost, they are what makes it possible, now that you are reciting Samantabhadra's Prayer, to have all the buddhas and bodhisatvas appear to your mind directly. Besides that, some of these forces have the capacity to remove states of mind that would make the buddhas unclear, for example, they have the power to remove the distractions that would prevent the one-pointedness of mind needed to mentally make all the conquerors clearly visible before you.

Here is a summary of all those explanations of the first line. It is not necessary to identify which excellent conduct prayer is being referenced—the words literally mean any excellent conduct prayer that you have previously recited or made, including of course Samantabhadra's Prayer. By those prayers, you have created forces of virtue that have many functions. One of their functions is that they make it possible to see all of the buddhas, who were just mentioned in the previous verse, in direct perception by mind. Other functions include having the ability to overcome obstacles that would degrade your ability to see them, such as distraction, dullness, and so on.

Now we move onto the second line. It literally says, "all of the conquerors are, by mental mind, in direct perception".[18] Here, "by

---

[18] All Indian commentaries, Yeshe De's commentary, and the Derge edition of the prayer have the Tibetan phrase "yid kyis mngon sum du" "in direct perception by mental mind". The "kyis" here is a case marker that makes the "yid" or mental mind into the agent that makes the conquerors seen "mngon sum du" in direct perception.

I have seen a number of corrupt Tibetan editions of the prayer having the genitive case marker "kyi" instead of "kyis". That then means that the translation changes to "in direct perception of mind". Unfortunately, this mistake is seen in a number of the English translations of the prayer that have appeared to date. It is true that the direct perception being mentioned here is direct perception of mind, so the change in wording does not introduce a mistake of understanding. However, the change in wording makes it less explicit that the verse is not talking about wisdom direct perception. On top of that, the change in wording loses one of two agentive case markers working as a pair in the first two lines. The first marker is at the end of the first line and shows "the forces of excellent conduct prayer" to be the primary agent in causing all the conquerors to become visible. The second marker is the "kyis" here, which shows "yid" to be the complement or instrument used by the primary agent to accomplish their becoming visible.

These points of grammar might be boring to some, but they are crucial when determining what is actually being said and how to
(continued ...)

mental mind, in direct perception" is clearly explained in Indian commentaries and Yeshe De's commentary to mean that the conquerors are seen in direct perception by the ordinary mental or samsaric mind in the same way as they would be seen by the eyes in direct perception if one positioned oneself so that they were directly ahead in one's immediate line of sight. Note that in some places in Samantabhadra's Prayer seeing all the buddhas is mentioned, but is explained as something that can only be done by advanced practitioners who have reached the bodhisatva levels and see the buddhas with wisdom, not with mental mind. This second line specifically uses the word for an ordinary person's mind to indicate that this viewing of the buddhas can be done by anyone, even an ordinary person. As explained, what makes this possible is the forces of the previously made prayers of excellent conduct. Again, some later Tibetan commentaries explain that direct perception here is actually referring to direct perception by wisdom and explain that the content of this verse can only be done by someone who is on the bodhisatva levels, but such explanations are definitely mistaken for the reasons explained above.

Nāgārjuna's commentary is particularly helpful for understanding the phrase "in direct perception", which in Tibetan is "mngon sum du". "In direct perception" is a technical phrase meaning "in direct sight of one of the senses". Nāgārjuna neatly explains the meaning here using a related term, which in Tibetan is "mngon phyogs su" and means "facing directly what lies ahead". Thus, he shows that the meaning here is not that mind is merely taking whichever buddha is immediately visible in front of it and manifesting bodies as many as the atoms in that one buddha's field in order to prostrate to that buddha. The meaning here is that mind has been made to face, simultaneously, all of the buddhas gone in the three times wherever that happened in the ten directions, with the result that

---

[18](... continued)
translate and understand it correctly.

every single one of them is in direct view of the ordinary person's mental mind.

Altogether, the first two lines of this verse mean that the accumulated forces of one's various prayers for the excellent conduct of a bodhisatva done previously have provided what is needed so that all the conquerors mentioned in the first verse can be and are now being seen in direct perception by one's ordinary mentality, as though they were present directly before one. With that, the stage has been set for the prostration to be made.

Now we move onto the third line, which literally says, "by having utterly bowed down bodies many as the field atoms". It shows the cause or means by which the fourth line "I utterly prostrate to all the conquerors" is made to happen. With all of the conquerors before you in their buddha-fields, you manifest bodies of your own as many as the atoms constituting all the buddha-fields. Those bodies are facing all of those buddhas collectively—it is not that you have bodies totalling the atoms in all buddha-fields manifested before every single one of those buddhas. By simultaneously bowing down with all of those bodies to all of the buddhas in their fields before you, you utterly prostrate to all the conquerors.

Note that "fields"[19] is a general term used to indicate any discrete region in which beings exist. Thus it can mean the fields of buddhas or the fields of sentient beings or both. Here it is explained to mean buddha fields. In other places in Samantabhadra's Prayer it will have one of those three meanings and should not be automatically assumed to mean buddha fields.

The word "utterly" appears on the third and fourth lines but has been left out in all English translations to date. However, it is there, does have meaning, and must be included. Two explanations of utterly have been give. In the first, because you have created so

---

[19] Skt. kṣhetra, Tib. zhing. See field in the glossary for more.

many bodies then bowed to them you have not merely prostrated but have utterly prostrated or prostrated to the maximum extent possible. In the second, Śhākyamitra explains that because you have bowed down with the greatest respect possible, you have utterly prostrated or prostrated in the best way possible.

3. Prostration Through Mind

Prostration through mind means that buddhas are imagined to be everywhere throughout all possible places. It says:

> 3 On a single atom buddhas many as atoms
> Are seated at the centre of buddha sons;
> I imagine in that way that all the dharmadhātus
> Without exception are filled with conquerors.

The first couplet presents the idea of buddhas as many as there are atoms seated on the top surface of a single atom, with each one of them being seated at the centre of and surrounded by his retinue of buddha sons. The second couplet builds on that by saying that all possible places where phenomena exist—the dharmadhātus—are then imagined to have that same arrangement present on every single atom of those places. Keeping them in mind that way is a prostration done with mind.

One Western translation says "at the centre of buddha sons and daughters". In fact, the text says only "buddha sons". There is a very important point here. The Buddha himself specifically explained that bodhisatvas were to be called "buddha sons" because of their particular role of upholding the tathāgata family line and carrying it forward. This is a major facet of the Great Vehicle system of teaching; if you try to undo this, you undermine many aspects of the bodhisatva teaching established by the Buddha. When his system is well understood, you understand that this is not about whether one is a man or woman, but about what it means to be carrying the lineage of a Great Vehicle buddha forward. The ones who do that are the sons, which in fact is a very uplifting way of talking about the matter, and that is how it should be understood.

Of course, these sons include both men and women. There is also the point that it is not our job to modify the words of a prayer because they do not fit with our modern ideas.

Some translations into English use the wording "in a single atom". All of the commentaries both Indian and Tibetan make it clear that the wording here is "on", not "in". Nāgārjuna goes to some trouble to say that it means on the upper surface of each atom or in the area at the top of each atom. Remember that an atom in the time when Samantabhadra spoke the prayer was the tiniest individual particle possible, like the understanding of the atom in Western culture prior to the late nineteenth century discoveries which showed there was space and further structure within what had been assumed as a sold entity up to that time. This idea of something being on top of a single atom is used in a number of places in the prayer and always means on the top surface or on top of a single atom.

A dhātu is a place where something can occur or a place from which something can arise. A dharmadhātu is a place where dharmas, that is, phenomena, can occur or arise. In Buddhist texts, it is common to see dharmadhātu in the singular because it refers to the single, unending region in which all phenomena arise. The meaning is similar here, but dharmadhātu is plural in the original verse because of emphasizing all possible places in which phenomena could arise.

Thus, you imagine that in all possible vast, unending expanses of reality—the places wherein all phenomena arise, remain, and cease—every atom that there is has on it buddhas as many as there are atoms with each one seated at the centre of and surrounded by his retinue of bodhisatva sons.

For some people, this verse will raise the questions, "How can there be buddhas as many as atoms on each single atom? I cannot see this now, so how could anyone see such a thing?" The commentaries explain that this is possible because reality is non-conceptual and that the ability to see it comes with the direct sight of emptiness gained when the bodhisatva levels are gained. Until someone has that attainment, he will not be able to see such things in direct perception. Those who do not have that attainment have to have faith in the fact that people with that level of realization—the noble ones as they are called—have seen such things and have declared, from their own personal and direct knowledge, that such things are possible. Once you do have such attainment, these and many other apparently miraculous possibilities will be the norm rather than a seeming impossibility. There are extensive explanations of this point in both Indian and Tibetan commentaries, for example in the commentaries of Nāgārjuna in this volume and Tenpa'i Wangchuk in volume II.

In sum, this verse cannot actually be done until you have reached the first of the bodhisatva levels. Practitioners on the levels before that should at least try to imagine it as they do the recitation.

4. Prostration Through Speech

The next verse says:

4 Those oceans of unending commendation
   Have using all sounds of the ocean of aspects of the voice
   The good qualities of all the conquerors utterly expressed
   And I praise all of the ones gone to bliss.

"Those" in the first line refers to those buddhas visualized in the previous verse as filling all the dharmadhātus. Altogether, the line means "All of those buddhas have something about them which is worthy of commendation, which is that each one of them is an ocean of the unending good qualities of a buddha". Here, "commendation" means the things about those buddhas which are commendable and is a metaphor for the good qualities of buddhahood. Their good qualities are so vast that they cannot be enumerated; they are unending like the drops of water in an ocean seem to be unending. Thus, the buddhas are collectively referred to as oceans of unending good qualities.

Note that each buddha is an ocean of commendable qualities, not that each one is oceans of commendable qualities. There is an important point regarding the word "ocean", which is used many times in Samantabhadra's Prayer. It is used in Sanskrit poetry as metaphor for unending or inexhaustible. When used that way, it is nearly always in the singular because it is something—singular—which is unending. Western translators of Samantabhadra's Prayer, not understanding this point and also not observing the grammar of the prayer have made "ocean" into the plural "oceans", which destroys the intended meaning.

The second line begins with "have", which exactly follows the original wording of the prayer. It means "those oceans of commendable qualities have their good qualities expressed by me". You, the one reciting the prayer, commend or praise those buddhas by expressing their good qualities.

It mentions conquerors rather than buddhas or some other word on the third line because it shows they have conquered all samsaric traits and in so doing fully exposed all of the good qualities of a buddha.

And the third line says that you utterly express their good qualities, but that does not mean that you could have a list of their good qualities and read them out and be finished with it. Even if you were to extol their good qualities for as long as space lasted, you would not be able to complete the job of verbally listing them because, as mentioned on the first line, the good qualities of a buddha are unending. Here and in other places "utterly" means that you will do something to the utmost, to the very best of your ability, or in the best way possible. Here it means that you do the best possible job of extolling all those good qualities.

The best possible job in this case would include using the best voice possible, so the second line explains the sort of voice you use for the purpose. It says that you use a voice endowed with all the sounds of an enlightened voice, the voice of a buddha. There are elaborate explanations of the voice of a buddha in the sutras. One, which is seen in other verses of this prayer too, likens it to the amazing speech of the god Brahmā with its many unusual qualities. Others usually explain it to have a certain number of aspects or branches of intonation, all of which are duly explained. In the Great Vehicle sutras, sixty aspects of intonation are explained. These sixty aspects of intonation have often been translated as "the sixty melodies of buddha speech" because of a misunderstanding of the word "melody". In fact, "sixty melodies" means that the voice of a buddha has sixty different aspects to its intonation, including certain features of tone, rhythm, and so on. The voice of a buddha actually has infinite aspects to its intonation, so it is described in the second line as having an "ocean of aspects" where ocean again has the meaning unending.

The "and" at the beginning of the fourth line[20]—and with it the whole verse—can be explained in two different ways. The first is that the "and" distinguishes two separate acts of praise, one for the good qualities themselves and the other for the buddhas themselves, like this: "They have their commendable qualities utterly expressed by me and, following that, I praise all of the ones gone to bliss". The second is that it joins two parts of one act of praise, like this: "They have their commendable qualities utterly expressed by me and so, or in that way, I give praise to all the ones gone to bliss". Both understandings are equally supported by the grammar of the verse and both are explained in Indian commentaries, for instance in Nāgārjuna's commentary, as possible understandings.

The second understanding can be clearly seen in the explanation of this verse according to Adzom Gyalsay's commentary which is the basis for Tenpa'i Wangchuk's commentary in volume II:

---

[20] Tib. ching, at the end of the third line in the Tibetan.

Those conquerors with their sons stated just above, the ones who have what is worthy of ***commendation*** is the object of praise. The phrase ***"oceans of unending"*** is a metaphor for them, the object of praise, meaning "the ones, each of whom is like an ocean of unending good qualities". The mode of praise is its expression ***using all*** the various ***sounds of the*** infinite—like the drops of an ***ocean*** or grains of sand are infinite—***aspects of the voice***. Using that mode, that the objects of praise ***have the good qualities of*** the inconceivable secrets of ***all*** without exception of ***the conquerors*** is ***utterly expressed and***, in that way, ***I give praise to all the sugatas, the ones gone to bliss*** together with their sons.

The Indian commentaries explain that when the verse is understood in the second way, the fourth line of the verse is connected to the first line because the oceans of unending commendable qualities are none other than the ones gone to bliss. Note that "ones gone to bliss" is a translation of the Sanskrit "sugata"[21]. In other words, the verse in that case becomes "Those buddhas present before me are oceans of commendable good qualities so I express all those good qualities in the best way possible and in doing so have praised all those buddhas, otherwise known as the sugatas, the ones gone to bliss".

There are numerous other places in the prayer where the lines of a verse can be understood in more than one way, based on their grammar and syntax. In every case I have made the English translation as close as possible to the original, so that the various possible understandings can be seen in the English wording. In this case, you

---

[21] Sugata is fully explained in *Unending Auspiciousness, the Sutra of the Recollection of the Noble Three Jewels* by Tony Duff. The book contains many of the definitions needed to understand the terminology of the sutras, so is very useful as background reading for this book.

can understand both meanings in the English then practise it either or both ways without fault.

Topic 2: Offerings

There are two types of offering: surpassed and unsurpassed. The next two verses make surpassed offerings and a verse following them makes unsurpassed offerings.

Genereally speaking, surpassed offerings are those made by beings within samsaric existence, which mainly means the offerings of gods and men. Why of gods and men? Because of all the migrators, they are the primary disciples of a buddha and therefore the ones who engage in worship by making offerings to the buddhas. Of gods and men, gods can make offerings that are superior to those that can be made by men. In the case of mental offerings the gods are more capable of creating such offerings and in the case of physical offerings their offering substances are less coarse and superior in quality to anything that could be found in the relatively coarse human realm. Tenpa'i Wangchuk's commentary in volume II has very detailed explanations of these offerings.

1. The surpassed offering

5   I will make offerings to those conquerors
    With the finest flowers, finest garlands,
    Small cymbals, ointments, supreme parasols,
    Supreme oil lamps, and finest incense.

6   I will make offerings to those conquerors
    With the finest clothes, supreme scents,
    And mixed powders equal to Mt. Meru,
    And all with the best of excellent displays.

The two verses show, in order, what you would do in classical Indian culture for an honoured guest. You can get a sense of this by visiting India and watching the Hindus doing their worship or watching older Hindi movies in which these offerings are often shown. You invite your guest in to a room that, beforehand, has been specially decorated with flowers and flower garlands and has had the dust settled with scented water. Then you offer your guest excellent food, music, massage with fragrant oils, parasols to keep your guest shaded from the intense heat of the sun, oil lamps to brighten the place—there was no electricity when the prayer was composed, and burning incense to please his sense of smell—which is like spraying air freshener into a room nowadays. After that, you would offer clean clothing then perfume to wear. You would also have urns or bowls heaped with incense powders arranged around the room in order to mask unpleasant odours with pleasant ones. Those offerings have been listed in the verse, but there is the further point that they would not be made carelessly, but made by putting them on display, that is, arranging them, in the very best way possible.

"Finest" throughout these verses and also in other places in the prayer means "superior to all others" or "the very best". In these two verses it has exactly that sense, though to remind us that there also are special versions of any given offering that we might not think of, Tenpa'i Wangchuk says that finest can indicate another, even better level of the offering being referred to, for example, there are the flowers of the human realm and then there are the finest of all flowers which are found in the god realm.

"Garlands" refers to garlands of flowers made by stringing individual flowers on a thread then either offering them as a necklace to the person or draping them around the walls of the room. Long garlands of flowers, sometimes with jewels and other ornaments added, are hung in lattice-works around the upper walls of a room in India as a decoration. "Small cymbals" that make a pleasing "ting" sound were used in India as musical instruments. "Ointments" or unguents in ancient India were oils with fragrant substances added that were used mainly for massage. Parasols were popular as a means of keeping off the intense heat and light of the Indian sun, and the highest quality ones had gold, ivory, and so on inlaid on the handle. The text mentions "oil lamps" which in ancient India referred to a bowl-like container filled with grain or vegetable oil and supplied with a wick which hangs over the edge of the container and is lit. Given that there was no electricity, these oil lamps were also the source of light for a room. "Incense" here means any kind of burnt stick incense. "Scents" means scented waters: ancient India was a dusty place so water, or in this case scented water, was sprinkled over an entire area to bring the dust down, which was then swept away. It could also mean scented water used to set out many water offerings.

"Mixed powders equal to Mt. Meru" needs some explanation. In India, aromatic substances are powdered, combined, then mixed with glue in order to make stick incense. However, these same substances can also be powdered and mixed and then poured into bowls or urns which are placed around a room to mask unpleasant odours and create an ongoing fragrance for the room. Later, in Tibet, there was a habit of sewing these combined aromatic powders into silk or brocade packages then deploying them around a room for the same purpose, but that is a Tibetan cultural form and not what is intended in the prayer. If you were to think of a Western equivalent, the idea of potpourri or lavender bags is similar, and these days it is common to hang packages of chemical deodorants for the purpose or to use spray-can air-fresheners. Mt. Meru is the biggest mountain in Indian cosmology so it is used as an example of the magnitude of the offering of these aromatic powders.

2. The unsurpassed offering

7   The offerings which are unsurpassed, vaster,
    Those are also imagined for all the conquerors.
    Through the forces of faith in excellent conduct
    I will prostrate and offer to all the conquerors.

This verse has layers of meaning which are not obvious from the literal meaning and it has wording in the second and third lines that requires considerable explanation.

The best offerings of the last two verses go only as far as the best offerings that can be made by the gods within samsaric existence. Those offerings are surpassed by the offerings created by the power of mind of buddhas and also of bodhisatvas on the first level and above. Thus the first line actually says: "**The offerings which are** created by such buddhas and bodhisatvas are **unsurpassed** because the articles of offering that they can manifest with their powers of mind are much better than the articles of offering that can be made by ordinary beings. Such offerings also are **vaster** in extent than those made by ordinary beings because the buddhas and also the bodhisatvas on the first level and above have the power of mind needed to make offerings that pervade the entirety of the dharmadhātu—the entire region where phenomena can occur—something that ordinary beings cannot do".

The second line has the word "imagined". It translates the Tibetan term "mos pa", which has several connotations. One is "to imagine" or "to think of"; another is "to be devoted" to something or someone; another is "to be inclined" to someone or something; and there are others, too. Because of the variety of connotations for the word and the lack of context in the prayer that would pin down which connotation is intended, the exact meaning of the verse is a little difficult to understand even for the Indian masters, who then explain it in various ways.

Nāgārjuna gives the simplest explanation of all, saying that the second line means: "Those—the unsurpassed, vaster offerings—*are thought of* for all the conquerors". He omits the word "also", which is there in the original, from his explanation in order to emphasize that the wording just given is the main meaning. I have used the word "imagined" following his explanation.

The explanation given by Śhākymitra is that the word should be understood to mean "devotion". He also says that the word "also" is important in relation to that, with the first and second line meaning: "As with as the various prostrations and offerings which have been made so far out of trust in the conquerors, these unsurpassed vaster offerings will be made *also* out of *devotion* to all the conquerors". In his explanation, the also in the second line is precisely placed to emphasize that these unsurpassed offerings are once again being made, as has been done so far, out of devotion to the limitless good qualities of all the conquerors.

Another explanation says that these unsurpassed offerings can only be made by a buddha or by bodhisatvas on the first bodhisatva level and above, because of which this line is not saying that these unsurpassed offerings are being "imagined" as offerings for all the conquerors but is saying that the mind has taken interest in making this offering out of trust.

One Indian commentary explains that, as with other cases earlier in the prayer where the actual prostration or offering is beyond the capacity of an ordinary being, in this case *also* the mind is turned towards the actual activity and at least *thinks of* making such an offering, even if the person involved does not have the realization needed directly to make such an offering.

Yeshe De explains it this way:

> With *those* matchless and unbettered offerings, I will, *again* with a mind of faith and prajñā, *think* to make offering *to all* those *conquerors* who have been mentioned earlier.

This fits with Nāgārjuna's explanation and also with the use of "imagined".

Altogether, the first two lines mean: "As for the offerings which are unsurpassed and vaster in nature compared to even the best offerings that could be made by samsaric beings, an offering of those is imagined or thought of for all of the conquerors, with this being done yet again—meaning in the same way has been done in all the verses down to this point in the prayer—out of the devotion and faith and respect for the buddhas that comes from remembering their limitless good qualities".

The third line is explained in all commentaries by informing us that "excellent conduct" generally means "any kind of conduct seen as good", but also, as has been explained in many places in the sutras, is used specifically to refer to the making of unsurpassed offerings. "Unsurpassed offering" is then further explained to mean not only unsurpassed offering as explained above, but the various types of very excellent offerings that a bodhisatva makes on the path, such as the offering of arousing the enlightenment mind. "The forces of faith in" is referring to the forces of admiration, faith, and trust. Through such forces of faith in excellent conduct—and especially for excellent conduct understood as unsurpassed offering in all of the ways it was explained by the Buddha—an offering is made of both prostration and offering. Thus an offering is made on the fourth line by combining everything of the two limbs of prostration and offering that has been mentioned so far in the prayer then saying, "I will make an offering of prostrations and offerings to all the conquerors." It comes down to meaning "I will worship all the conquerors by making both prostrations and offerings to them".

Topic 3: Laying Aside

The next verse says:

8   Under the influence of desire, anger, and delusion
    And through body, speech, and likewise mind,
    The evils I have done whichever they might be,
    I lay all of them aside, each one individually.

The term "evil" is used frequently in this text. The original Sanskrit word, "papaṃ", was not a religious term but was used colloquially to mean a rotten thing to do. *Monier Williams Sanskrit-English Dictionary* gives: "a bad, vicious, wicked, evil, wretched, vile, low action". In Buddhism, it is all of that plus being an action that produces bad karma and therefore drags you down, degrades you. The word "evil" in English is not really fitting, but it is hard to find a word that fits exactly with this term. "Sins" has too many Christian overtones.

The verse has three lines to identify the evil which has been done followed by a fourth line in which it is laid aside: the first line identifies the motivating force for the evil; the second line identifies the place where the evil was done; and the third line indicates which evil was done. The verse is saying, "There are the specifics of motivation, that is, which of the three primary afflictions was involved. Then, there are the specifics of where it was done, that is, which of the three doors of body, speech, and mind was involved. Then, there are the specific bad actions I have done based on those and I lay all of them aside, each one individually".

Note that the "whichever" in the third line is a restrictive pronoun, accurately reflecting the use of a restrictive pronoun in the original. Nāgārjuna points out that the third line functions to specify which evils are the ones to be laid aside. This is done by the use of the phrase "whichever they are". In other words, the verse as a whole does not merely say "I lay aside the evils in general whatever I might have done" but says, "I identify the particular evils I have done then individually lay them aside". This construction of the verse follows the important point that the most effective way to lay aside bad actions is to remember the specifics of what one has done—the type of action, type of motivation, and so on—then to deal with the individual cases of those specific bad actions. This makes laying aside an intensive process, but if you really want to deal with bad actions, clubbing them to death with a blunt instrument is much less effective than surgically removing them with the precise knife of knowledge. That is why the traditional way of talking about laying aside is to say that it is done one by one, each evil deed individually.

Now, what does it mean to "lay them aside"? Laying aside translates the Tibetan term "bshags pa", an important term with a very specific meaning. The term has mostly been translated as "confession" but that is a major error that has long been perpetuated in English

Buddhist translations. Generally speaking, confession is the act of declaring to someone else that one has done something wrong. It functions only to make it known that one has done something wrong. Laying aside is a step further than that.

Laying aside is the name given to the process of distancing yourself from bad actions that you have done and ridding yourself of the bad karmic seeds that you have thereby accrued. It is not a process driven by guilt. It is a process driven by the clear knowledge that the bad actions that you have done have planted bad karmic seeds that will cause trouble for you in the future when they come into effect. With that clear knowledge of what you have done and how it will affect you, there is a straightforward regret about what you have done and a wish to part ways with that wrongdoing and its future, karmic effects. Based on that, you make a decision to part ways with that wrongdoing and just that is what is called "laying aside". It will be helpful at this point to know that the Tibetan term for laying aside literally means "cleaving off" or "shedding and severing all connection with".

Laying aside can be understood through the example of an addict. First an addict has to admit to himself that he has a problem and that step could be equated with confession. However, the addict still has to take the actual step of quitting or stopping or ending his addiction. Similarly, we have to admit to ourselves that we as samsaric beings have been engaged in types of behaviour that will have a later, undesirable effect. Having done that, we do the real work of severing all connection with that wrongdoing and that is given the name "laying aside".

How is laying aside done? Well, it can be done in the more general way just described in which you make the effort to understand what you have done then sever your connection with that behaviour from that point on. Or, it can be done in a very specific way by making the effort to understand exactly what you have done and then not only generally severing your connection with that behaviour, but specifically applying the four types of antidote taught by the Buddha for the purpose of mitigating and eventually ending the bad karmic seeds that were have been planted. Those four antidotes are described in detail elsewhere, but in essence they are not different from the general human understanding of how to deal with wrong types of behaviour. Generally speaking, while depending on others who are seen as models of good behaviour, you develop regret and then aversion, and finally do something to clear the whole baggage of undesirable effects that have come with the wrong behaviour.

It should be obvious from the above that laying aside is not confession! Confession is simply the act of declaring to someone else that one has done something wrong. It functions only to make it known that one has done something wrong. The specific meaning of confession as used in the Roman Catholic Christian Church of a step which automatically leads to absolution of wrongdoings—the church calls them sins—simply does not exist in Buddhism. Christianity is a theistic religion in which god has the power to absolve you of your sins if you first take the step of doing what that religion calls "confession". However, Buddhism is a non-theistic religion in which there can be no absolution of bad actions by Buddha or any other power but in which, if an individual personally lays aside bad action, the effects of the bad action can be mitigated and even eliminated by that individual for himself. It is important to understand that in Buddhism one does not confess bad actions in order to obtain absolution of wrongdoing. As the Buddha himself said, he has no ability to purify the karmic stains of sentient beings, he can only teach them how to do so for themselves. Laying aside is the method he taught.

If you are paying close attention, you will realize that laying aside itself is not confession but the psychological process of laying aside does first need an admission of wrongdoing. It is standard Buddhist teaching that laying aside is the last step of a two part process called "admitting and laying aside"[22]. To lay any wrongdoing aside in an effective way, you first have to admit to what you have done. This has the psychological effect of not hiding from what you have done and thereby accrued for yourself. That is a step of opening up to yourself so that you can proceed with clear knowledge. With that in place, it is possible to perform in a meaningful way the actual step of laying aside the wrongdoing. Therefore, it is explained that, generally speaking, laying aside has to be understood as part of the process of admitting and laying aside and that is true in this verse here where laying aside actually means "admitting and laying aside". In other words, Buddhist teaching does say admission is important, but makes a clear distinction between the first step of admission that could be seen as similar to confession and the main step of laying aside.

Topic 4: Rejoicing

9   I rejoice in all merits whoever has them,
    Those of all the conquerors of the ten directions and
    The buddha sons, of the pratyekabuddhas, of those
    In training and not in training, and of all migrators.

The Buddha made a point of teaching rejoicing as an easy but very effective practice for developing merit. Therefore, it is picked out as a separate limb of accumulation. Rejoicing is the act of wholeheartedly rejoicing in the merit that has been or is being accumulated by someone else. It has the requirement that there is no jealousy or annoyance over the good acts done or being done by the other person. Because of that, rejoicing is also taught as an antidote to jealousy or annoyance over another person's good acts. This kind of rejoicing is such that, if it can be truly done without the slightest holding back, jealousy, or other negativity at the good another person has done or is doing, it is possible for the person doing the

---

[22] Tib. mthol zhing bshags pa.

rejoicing to create an amount of merit which is equal to the other person's merit.

There is a story from the sutras which is often used to illustrate what rejoicing is and how effective it can be. It is the story of an old village woman who came into the back of the assembly hall of a king who had invited the Buddha to come and teach. The Buddha had arrived and the king was in the process of making vast offerings, praises, and so on in order to create the environment for an excellent teaching. The old lady rejoiced from the depths of her heart at the good activities of the king, whereas many of the members of the king's retinue were filled with their own petty jealousies and dislikes. The Buddha, at the end of his teaching, pointed out that the old woman had accumulated more merit than anyone else in the room because of her pure rejoicing in the good acts done by the king and, following that, by the Buddha when he taught dharma to the gathering.

In the verse, the beings who have merit are listed, starting with those who have the greatest and best merits and proceeding down through the levels of those who have lesser merits. It proceeds like this. The buddhas with their incalculable and perfect collections of merit are listed first, together with their buddha sons who have a similar type of merit. The pratyekabuddhas are listed next; their Lesser Vehicle merit is less than that of the beings—the buddhas and bodhisatvas—who have entered the Great Vehicle. The shravakas' types are listed next; their Lesser Vehicle merit is even less than that of the pratyekabuddhas. The Buddha classified the shravakas into what are called "the eight beings" and they can be summed up, as is done here, into seven types of shravakas who are still on the path, referred to in the verse as "the ones in training", and the shravaka arhats who have completed the path and are referred to as "the ones of no more training". Finally, there are all the migrators or sentient beings; their merit is purely worldly merit and lesser than that of the beings already listed. They have two types of worldly merit: the better type of merit that comes from treading a spiritual path—which in

Buddhist teaching is referred to as "superior merit" and which is mentioned in a later verse—and the plain merit of doing good for reasons other than spiritual ones, some of which could be very selfish.

The grammar of the verse in Sanskrit and Tibetan following it is said to be easy to misunderstand. It is possible to think that the term "migrators" in the verse refers to all beings, both all the ones mentioned before the term and then on top of that to all other sentient beings as well. However, that is not the case. The grammar of the verse properly understood shows that the term "migrators" indicates a specific category of beings other than the ones mentioned before it—it refers to the ordinary beings of samsara. This point is clearly stated in the Indian commentaries and the commentary by Yeshe De. Some later Tibetan commentaries explain it correctly and some do not. The existing English translations of this verse that I have seen have this and other mistakes.

The last line of the original verse has to be the last line in Sanskrit and Tibetan, but has to be moved to being the first line in English. Thus the verse starts in English by saying: "I rejoice in all merits, whoever has them", where "whoever has them" specifically refers to the listing of beings who have merit that then follows. It does not mean the more general statement "I rejoice in everyone's merits", a mistake which is seen in at least one English translation.

Topic 5: Urging

The next verse urges all of those who have become buddhas to turn the wheel of dharma:

10   Ones who are lamps of the worlds of the ten directions
     Have become buddhas at the enlightenment stage and
         gained the undefiled state;
     I urge all of those guardians
     To turn the unsurpassed wheel.

This is a supplication that conveys a sense of urging. It is not a prayer. The supplication urges buddhas who have arrived at buddhahood but who are remaining silent, not teaching, to turn the wheel of dharma. The principal reason for making this supplication is that it creates a cause for all buddhas who have not engaged in teaching the holy dharma to do so. A second reason is sometimes explained, which is that it creates a connection in general with the turning of the wheel of dharma, which will lead to one day being in the presence of a buddha's teaching.

The verse is made of two couplets with the phrase in the first line, "ones who are" connecting with the phrase "those guardians" in the third line. The first phrase has mostly been left out of English translations but is important, as will be explained below.

"Lamps of the worlds of the ten directions" is an epithet of the buddhas. They receive the name because, like lamps, they illuminate all the samsaric worlds throughout the ten directions, eliminating the darkness of ignorance with their light of wisdom. This epithet is used in this verse because the verse is primarily concerned with having the buddhas teach, in other words, with having them illuminate the worlds with their wisdom.

The second line shows what those lamps of the worlds have done that makes them into lamps of the worlds: "They have become buddhas at the highest stage or level of enlightenment, the level of enlightenment gained through following the bodhisatva's path and called unsurpassed, truly complete enlightenment[23]. Having become buddhas at that level, they have attained wisdom which cannot be affected by the defiled samsaric states of mind. Having gained that wisdom which cannot be affected by samsaric types of defilement,

---

[23] Complete explanations of "truly complete enlightenment" and the cognate phrase "truly complete buddhahood" can be found in the book *Unending Auspiciousness, the Sutra of the Recollection of the Noble Three Jewels*.

their wisdom knows everything without any possibility of the all-knowing quality being adversely affected and so reduced in its capacity. Because of that, they are the very best guardians that sentient beings can have. Because of their undefiled wisdom, they are the best possible teachers of the path to enlightenment".

However, not all of these guardian buddhas will teach the dharma. For example, Śhākyamuni Buddha on attaining his enlightenment said:

> No-one else will be able to understand this
> Nectar-like dharma that I have discovered,
> Therefore, I will remain at the edge of the forest, not teaching.

After he had been silent for seven weeks, the leaders of the gods named Brahmā and Kauśhika[24] came before the Buddha and made offerings to him and urged him to turn the wheel of dharma. As a result, Buddha Śhākyamuni relented and taught dharma widely for the benefit of others. He pointed out during his teaching that there were buddhas who appeared but who did not teach. Therefore, this supplication is done specifically to create the causes for those silent guardians to begin teaching. Secondarily, as mentioned above, doing so creates the cause for oneself to hear a buddha turning the wheel of dharma.

Therefore, the third and fourth lines are a supplication to all the guardian buddhas urging them to turn the unsurpassed wheel. Nāgārjuna explains that this specifically is the wheel of unsurpassed dharma, namely the wheel in which the Great Vehicle teachings—which include the Vajra Vehicle teachings—are given.

---

[24] Kauśhika is the personal name of the god Indra. Indra means the one having control over the others, a name given to him because of his being the chief god amongst the thirty-two other gods in the desire-realm heaven called "The Thirty-Three".

Now someone might say, "Does this verse supplicate all of the buddhas?" It does not because the past buddhas are already past, so, if they did not teach, there is no point to urging them to do so now. Thus, this verse is specifically directed at the buddhas of the present and future who might not teach unless they are urged to do so. In regard to this, Yeshe De clearly explains that the opening phrase "ones who are" implies "they who could be lamps of the worlds, if they were to teach", which can only relate to present and future buddhas. Thus, this phrase, "ones who are" is there in the original for good reason and must be included in English translations.

Finally, here are some notes on terms. The Tibetan phrase behind "undefiled state" is "ma chags pa". The phrase is derived from the word "chags pa" which has three principal meanings: to happen, to be broken, and attachment. It has been a common mistake of Tibetan scholars during many centuries to assume that "ma chags pa" used in relation to the mind of enlightenment must mean "attachment" and now Western translators read their explanation of this point and translate accordingly. However, that is a mistake. In this context, "chags pa" is on the side of "to happen" and "to be broken" and its negative form, "ma chags pa" is glossed by those Tibetan masters who correctly understand this matter to mean "mi thub pa" or "not able to be affected". That they are correct is proved by the fact that all the Indian commentaries, for example that of Nāgārjuna, definitively state that it has to be understood as "not able to be affected". Thus the use of "ma chags pa" in this verse does not mean that a buddha's mind is "unattached", but that it cannot be "adversely affected", meaning that it cannot be defiled by any type of samsaric mind and so have its all-knowing quality reduced. I have explained this clearly here because the mistaken use of "attachment" has appeared in Tibetan commentaries and in English translations following them and because the same term is used twice more in subsequent verses where its use also has been misunderstood.

"Guardians"[25] is an epithet for the buddhas. Like a child who has lost its parents needs to find a guardian who will both protect and nurture it, we sentient beings lost and helpless in samsara need to find the buddhas who will do nothing other than protect and nurture us. Note that, although this term has been translated as "protector", it means more than that—"guardian" is correct and besides, there is another term which exactly matches "protector"[26].

"Have become buddhas at the enlightenment stage" in the second line is the correct translation of a phrase which has been misunderstood starting several or more centuries ago by Tibetan experts who have explained it incorrectly and then misunderstood and mistranslated by Western translators who have followed their mistaken explanations. This is a major issue, because this same phrase appears in three verses in this prayer and has been mistakenly explained and translated in each case. The phrase is, in Tibetan, "rim par 'tshang rgya". All the Indian commentators and Yeshe De explain it according to Sanskrit. All of them agree that it is a verb phrase meaning "to become buddha at the (highest) stage (of buddhahood)". This is an unusual way of talking so they further explain that "rim par" is equivalent in this case to "rnam par", in which case the phrase means "to become buddha completely". They then explain that "to become a buddha completely" means "*to become a manifest buddha at the* highest *level* possible *of* unsurpassed truly complete enlightenment". The consistency and force of their explanations makes it impossible to consider that the phrasing means anything else. You can see Nāgārjuna's explanation of it in this book. The later Tibetan commentators because of failing to understand this as Sanskrit terminology represented in Tibetan, thought that it must mean, in Tibetan, "rim gyis", that is, "gradually" or "in stages", even though they were ignoring the grammar in doing so. They then used this same incorrect explanation in each of the three verses in which it

---

[25] Skt. nātha, Tib. mgon po. See the glossary for more.

[26] Skt. pāla, Tib. skyong.

appears. You can view an example of this type of mistake by looking at the commentary of Tenpa'i Wangchuk in volume II. The verses to look at in are verses 10, 13, and 35. You would do well to look at those verses in this commentary before proceeding to the next topic.

Topic 6: Supplicating

This next verse is a further supplication to the buddhas who were supplicated in the last verse:

11   I also will supplicate with palms joined together those
Who have asserted they will show passage into nirvana
To stay for aeons as many as the field atoms
In order to bring benefit and ease to all migrators.

"Those" on the first line connects to the buddhas who were being supplicated in the last verse. As with the last verse, it specifically means the buddhas of the present and future, given that the supplication being made here would not apply to the buddhas who have already passed. The next word "who" connects with "have asserted they will show passage into nirvana". Buddhas do not have to enter the final nirvana if they choose not to do so, so the phrase "who have asserted …" indicates that this is a supplication specifically to those who have asserted that they will enter the final nirvāṇa, which is called parinirvāṇa in Sanskrit. That is how these two words are explained in all the Indian commentaries.

In the Great Vehicle story of enlightenment, a person who manifests buddhahood as a world-leading buddha does twelve deeds as part of a complete demonstration of becoming enlightened. The deed of showing enlightenment under the bodhi tree is a demonstration of the attainment of the peace of enlightenment. However, this is not a demonstration of the final peace because the buddha concerned still has a body. The twelfth and final deed is to show the act of entering the final peace of nirvana in which there is no body remaining. Thus, it is asserted in general that world-leading buddhas will pass away into the final peace of nirvana[27] as part of their demonstration of the twelve deeds of buddhahood. This passage into the final peace of nirvana is, from the disciples' side, a great loss—they lose their teacher and the world loses a buddha in person. However, a truly complete buddha has the ability to die or not to die at will, so this verse is a supplication made from the side of us disciples to the world-leading buddhas who are present now or who will come in the future and who have asserted or will assert that they will show this final nirvana not to do so but to remain for a very long time.

How is the supplication made? It is made with palms joined together in the position called añjali. This is one of the two types of prostration done in ancient India. The other entailed fully bending down to touch the feet of the other person, which in Tibetan Buddhism became either a full- or half-length prostration.

How long do we ask them to stay? We ask them to "stay for aeons as many as the field atoms". As explained earlier, "atoms of the fields" could mean all the atoms as many as there are within all of the buddha-fields or within in all of the sentient beings' fields or within both. Nāgārjuna says that here it means the atoms of the fields of those buddhas whom we are supplicating. It has been said that we are essentially asking them to stay for so long that there is no end to their stay.

---

[27] Skt. parinirvāṇa, Tib. yongs su mya ngan las 'das pa. This refers to the final nirvana that happens for a Buddha when he shows the act of death. A Buddha can stay in his body for as long as desired, to benefit beings. By showing the act of death, he shows the final nirvana to the beings present. In the Lesser Vehicle teachings this is claimed to be the final end of that buddha. However, in the Great Vehicle teachings and above, this is only one of an unending stream of manifestations that a truly complete buddha shows for the sake of sentient beings.

Why do we ask them to stay? We ask them to stay "in order to bring benefit and ease to all migrators". The phrase "benefit and ease" is commonly used in Great Vehicle literature and is seen a number of times in Samantabhadra's prayer[28]. In this phrase, "benefit" means to gain ongoing circumstances of a good existence within samsara—birth only in the higher realms, with good circumstances, and so on. And in this phrase, "ease" means to enter the paths to enlightenment and to attain the circumstances of liberation at the level either of an arhat or truly complete buddha. Thus, we are petitioning the world-leading buddhas to stay on so that they can continue to provide goodness for sentient beings both within samsara and liberation from it. Another way to explain "benefit and ease" has the same meaning but points out that benefit is a temporary type of benefit provided for sentient beings and that ease is the ultimate type of benefit provided for them. The book *Unending Auspiciousness, the Sutra of the Recollection of the Noble Three Jewels* also explains "benefit and ease" at length.

Topic 7: Dedication

The next verse is dedication:

12 I dedicate every trifle of virtue that
I have accumulated in prostrating, offering,
Laying aside, rejoicing, urging, and supplicating
For the purpose of enlightenment.

"Trifles of virtue" are the small amounts of virtue that one has accumulated in doing each of the first six limbs. The commentaries explain that the wording "every trifle" means "each of the trifles created by prostrating, offering, and so on". I have translated according to their explanation.

All these trifles of virtue are dedicated to the great enlightenment. "Dedication" as used in the Buddhist teaching means to seal any

---

[28] A complete explanation of "benefit and ease" can be found in the book *Unending Auspiciousness, the Sutra of the Noble Three Jewels*.

virtue or merit that has been created in such a way that it will go only in a desired direction and not accidentally be lost. It is said that merit which has been created but not dedicated can easily be weakened or destroyed and lost by upheavals of affliction, but that merit which has been properly dedicated cannot be weakened or lost.

The Great Vehicle tradition in particular speaks of "wholly dedicating" which emphasizes the idea of properly dedicating merit. It means paying close attention to fully, completely, and properly dedicating the merit for the purpose of truly complete enlightenment.

There are levels of enlightenment. For example, an arhat has the enlightenment of the Lesser Vehicle teaching and a truly complete buddha has the enlightenment of the Great Vehicle teaching. The latter enlightenment is also referred to as "unsurpassed" and "supreme" and "complete" or "truly complete" in order to distinguish it from the lesser enlightenment of an arhat. It is also occasionally referred, as is done in this verse, to "great enlightenment" both because it is great compared to the arhat's enlightenment and because it is the enlightenment which is done for the sake of all sentient beings, without exception. In short, this verse dedicates all the merits, no matter how small they were, accumulated in doing the first six limbs to the specific goal of attaining the enlightenment of the Great Vehicle, that of a truly complete buddha, for the sake of all sentient beings.

There are two types of dedication: fictional and superfactual[29]. The former is a dedication in which one has not entered equipoise on emptiness of the dedicator, act of dedication, and merits dedicated. The latter is the opposite. It is explained that both are needed together for the best type of whole dedication. Later in the prayer when it mentions making a dedication following the way that Mañjushrī and likewise Samantabhadra would dedicate, it is

---

[29] For these terms, see the glossary.

referring to this point that they would not merely make a samsaric type of dedication in which there was clinging to a self in the three spheres of agent, action, and acted upon, but would make a whole dedication through both fictional and superfactual types of whole dedication.

3.2. Topics Eight to Ten, The Actual Prayer

The actual prayer consists of the last three of the ten topics that all Indian and Tibetan commentaries following them explain to be the basic structure of the prayer. The last three topics are: the divisions of the prayer, the ending to the prayer, and the benefits associated with the prayer.

Topic 8: The Divisions of the Prayer

Indian commentaries and Tibetan commentaries following them state that the actual prayer has sixteen sub-divisions. Their exact names as given by Nāgārjuna are:

1. thought
2. not forgetting enlightenment mind
3. connecting with being uncloaked
4. benefiting sentient beings
5. armour
6. connecting with bodhisatvas of same lot
7. acting to please virtuous friends
8. having made the tathāgatas visible
9. wholly holding the holy dharma
10. gaining an unending store
11. entering
12. forces
13. accomplishing
14. activities
15. delineation of training following
16. conclusion

The other Indian commentaries give the same divisions though there is an occasional slight change of wording.

Division 1: Thought

This consists of three verses that set up the general atmosphere of thought within which enlightenment conduct can flourish.

▷ The first of the three contains two thoughts in three parts:

13 May I offer to the past buddhas and the ones
    Who are seated in the worlds of the ten directions.
    Those whoever have not descended, most quickly
        completing your intentions
    Descend to buddhahood at the enlightenment stage!

The first couplet is the thought in two parts to offer to those who have become buddhas—both those of the past who were and likewise those of the present who are now seated in the worlds of sentient beings existing throughout the ten directions. It is taught in the sutras that anyone who has developed faith in another person is then obliged to treat that other person with respect and honour. The most basic forms of honouring someone according to the Buddhist way are to praise and to making offerings to the other person. Therefore, it is entirely appropriate to start the main part of the prayer on excellent conduct with a prayer to be able to honour those who have become buddhas.

The second couplet takes joy in the thought of others who have not yet achieved the ultimate goal quickly achieving it. This is the third of the four limitless ones. The couplet develops the thought that those who have yet to become buddhas should complete their particular thoughts and go to buddhahood most quickly, meaning without any delay. Note that the couplet does not say "May you who have not descended …" as has mistakenly appeared in some English translations, but ends with an imperative verb and has to be understood as shown above.

The fourth line contains a phrase which has been misunderstood then incorrectly explained by later Tibetan commentators and then mistranslated by Western translators who have followed their wrong explanations. The phrase correctly translated is "buddhahood at the enlightenment stage" as shown above. A complete explanation of the phrase's actual meaning and how it has been mistranslated appears in the explanations that go with the first appearance of the phrase, at the end of the explanation of verse ten. An example of mistaken Tibetan commentary that has appeared for this verse can be seen in the explanations of this line in Tenpa'i Wangchuk's commentary in volume II.

▷ The second verse is the thought to wholly purify a buddha-field:

14 May the fields which exist in the ten directions,
However many they are, be vast and wholly pure.
May they be utterly filled with conquerors gone
Before the leading bodhi tree and with buddha sons.

The Prajñāpāramitā teachings of the second turning of the wheel make a strong point that a bodhisatva has to complete three tasks on the way to becoming a buddha: purifying or perfecting a buddha-field; completing all prayers; and ripening sentient beings who will then be one's disciples in the purified field. This verse is connected with the first of those. The verse mentions two aspects of the purification of a buddha-field: the purification of the place or, as it is called, the support; and the purification of the beings supported by it, that is, the beings living in it.

The first line of the original prayer has a Sanskrit term that is the equivalent of English "which", but the Indian commentaries make it clear that this has to be understood as "which exist". The term was translated from Sanskrit into Tibetans with the specific term "ga la", which has the sense "which could exist". The term has been translated into English as "which exist" in accordance with the explanations of the Indian commentaries.

The first line has the word "fields" which could refer either to sentient beings' impure fields or buddhas' pure fields. The Indian commentaries and Yeshe De's commentary explain it to mean "buddha-fields". The later commentaries of Tibetans explain it to mean "sentient beings' impure fields"—for example, Lochen Dharmashrī says that it means "the impure fields" and Tenpa'i Wangchuk says that it means "the container fields", which in turn means "the impure fields that are the containers of sentient beings". Yeshe De explains it in a way which shows that there is no contradiction in these two different explanations of the meaning of fields:

> This verse concerns having the thought "May all of however many distinct buddha-fields exist in the ten directions be wholly pure". Moreover, there are two aspects of being wholly pure, so it concerns having the two thoughts of being wholly pure in relation to the support and being wholly pure in relation to the supported. Having the thought of being wholly pure in relation to the support involves the understanding that buddha-fields are places in which there are not even the words for ravines, chasms, sharp objects, disarray, general impurity, and so on present, places where the ground is made of precious substances, even like the palm of a hand, pleasant to experience, and so on, and that they are vast with everything within them making an excellent womb[30] ... Having the thought of being wholly pure in relation to the supported is having the thought, "May it be so that such fields are utterly filled with buddhas who, having gone before the king of trees, the bodhi tree, have become buddhas, and with their sons the bodhisatvas".

In other words, the first couplet is to have the thought "May all sentient beings' fields become buddha-fields which are by nature vast and completely pure" and the second couplet is to have the thought "May all those pure places, which function as supports for

---

[30] ... meaning a place where beings can be nurtured to enlightenment ...

beings to live in them, be filled with pure types of beings, buddhas who have shown the act of buddhahood and their retinues of bodhisatva sons".

What is a buddha-field like? One of the most common examples given is that of Sukhāvatī, the field of buddha Amitābha, because there are long descriptions of the arrangement of that field in the sutras taught by the Buddha. There is also an extensive description of Mañjushrī's pure field in one of the third-turning sutras[31], where the Buddha states that Mañjushrī's pure field is one of the best possible. There is also an explanation of the layout of Samantabhadra's pure field, which the Buddha said had the most perfect arrangement possible.

"The conquerors" on the third line means those who have gone before the bodhi tree in order to demonstrate enlightenment, the final conquering of all obscuration. They go before "the leading bodhi tree". Buddhists refer to the bodhi tree as the king of trees and also the leader of trees. Some English translations have it as "the powerful tree", but this is a mistake that comes from misunderstanding that the original Sanskrit term here, "indriya", translated into Tibetan with "dbang po" is used in these contexts to mean the dominant one, the leader above all others.

▷ The third verse is the special intention[32]:

15 May the sentient beings of the ten directions,
    However many, always be free of sickness and have ease.
    May all migrators' objectives of dharma be with
    Harmony and their hopes also be accomplished.

---

[31] Skt. ārya mañjushrī buddha kshetra guṇa vyūha nāma mahāyāna sūtra. Noble One, The Great Vehicle Sutra called "Arrangement of the Good Qualities of the buddha-field of Mañjushrī".

[32] For special intention, see the glossary. Here, it is an aspect of the arousing of enlightenment mind, bodhichitta.

The verse begins with praying that all sentient beings have a good existence within samsara and continues with prayers that, as they go about practising the buddha dharma, they will able to do so in an atmosphere of harmony and will have all of their wishes accomplished.

The general consensus amongst the Indian and Tibetan commentaries is that this verse is wishing that things will go easily for beings while they are in samsara and that they will do well in their spiritual pursuits as well. However, many shades of meaning appear within their explanations. It would be too much to quote every commentary here to show all these shades of meaning, so here is a general picture of what the commentators say.

The first couplet is generally accepted to be referring to sentient beings having a workable time as they stay in samsara: "May the sentient beings, however many of them there are throughout all the reaches of samsaric existence, while in their samsaric existences always be free of all types of sickness both of body and mind and, on top of that, have the ease of not having the worst of samsaric sufferings". Nāgārjuna alone differs, saying that the part concerning ease means "may they be rid of the non-ease of samsara and have the ease of the attainment of nirvana". I have to presume that his explanation of ease is based on the specific understanding of the meaning of the word ease seen in the important phrase "benefit and ease" explained earlier, where benefit refers to benefit for samsaric beings in samsaric terms and ease refers to ease for them attained by their exiting samsara and entering nirvana.

The second couplet begins with "all migrators", which connects to the sentient beings of the ten directions who are the subject of the first couplet. The second couplet is in two parts: a prayer that sentient beings' spiritual journeys—their efforts to attain their dharmic goals—go well and a prayer that everything they wish for in relation to the buddhas' dharma be accomplished.

The first part of this couplet is a prayer that all the migrator sentient beings will remain in harmony with other beings as they set about accomplishing their "objectives of dharma", where objectives of dharma is mostly explained to mean the complete range of dharmic objectives that migrators could have, from aiming for a good existence within samsara all the way to aiming for complete liberation from it for the sake of all sentient beings. The second part builds on that by praying that their hopes and wishes, again in relation to buddha dharma, will all be fulfilled. However, Yeshe De alone says that, because the word dharma can also mean "things", the second couplet is saying:

> May sentient beings' efforts within samsara to fulfill their objectives or aims for things such as food, clothing, shelter, and so on, go well and without difficulty and, on top of that, may their hopes and wishes in relation to such things within samsara be fulfilled.

Although no other commentator explains it that way, his explanation can be seen as a way of explaining the verse.

For this verse, I think it best to read the lines of the prayer and read the explanations given above and in the other commentaries while trying to get the broadest sense possible of the meaning that can be read into the words of the verse. Then you can recite the prayer according to your understanding.

Division 2: Not Forgetting Enlightenment Mind

The next main division of the actual prayer, not forgetting enlightenment mind, covers the next four verses. Of them, the first three and a half verses pick out those things which are conducive to a bodhisatva's excellent conduct and which are to be adopted, while the last half of the fourth verse picks out those things which are not conducive to a bodhisatva's excellent conduct and which are to be abandoned.

⇨ The first verse says:

16 While I perform the conducts of enlightenment
May I remember my births in all migrations.
At death transfers and births in all successive lives
May I always become ordained.

The first couplet means: "While I am performing the conducts which are to be done for the purpose of attaining the unsurpassed supreme enlightenment of a truly complete buddha, may I remember my previous births in all the migrations in which I have taken birth." In general, it is important to be able to remember all of your former lives as you proceed on your spiritual journey because it brings direct and very personal knowledge of the truth of unsatisfactoriness. If you can remember even a portion of your previous lives, you can see the karmic story that you have created and its consequences that you have and will face in past and future births, and that provides a strong incentive to get on the path to enlightenment and persevere at it. Śhākyamitra makes an excellent point in relation to this in his commentary:

> It is not good to have forgotten the succession of past lives. When you have, each new existence is like waking from sleep and not knowing who you are, where you are, and what you have and have not done before you fell asleep. Because of not knowing what you have done in the past, you might think "I have no merit" or "It takes so long to complete the accumulations for enlightenment, so how could I possibly be on the way to doing so?"

In short, you have to know your overall journey. You know that now you are practising for enlightenment, of course, but you also must know what dharma practice you have done and what you have accomplished in your previous births, in all the various types of migrations you have entered so as to know where you are on your overall journey. Note that "all types of migration" means every single type of migration you have taken because of karma, not merely the human ones.

The second couplet builds on the first, saying: "And on top of that, on every one of the occasions that I die and transfer through the intermediary state[33] then take new birth throughout the whole succession of my lives as a bodhisatva performing the conducts of enlightenment, may I only ever enter births in which I do not remain as a householder but go forth specifically into the homelessness of one who has taken ordination as a monk or nun".

Note that "death transfers" is a phrase primarily meaning "death". Some Western translators have thought it means "death and transference at death" but it is clearly explained in the Indian commentaries to mean the one thing of death and the transference from one life to another than goes with it. The Indian commentaries explain that "at death transfers and births" therefore means "on each occasion of leaving one life and entering another".

The translation of the last line is exact, with the term "ordained" being a direct and correct translation of the Sanskrit term "pravrājita"[34]. The Sanskrit term literally means "to have done what is most excellent or best". It was used by spiritual traditions in general in ancient India to refer to leaving behind household life and taking up the best circumstance for spiritual development, which in that time was regarded to be monastic life in which one was ordained as a monk or nun[35]. However, most non-Tibetan Buddhists these days do not want to be monastics. Therefore, recent translations of this last line into English have avoided the actual wording "becoming ordained" and substituted a more generic wording, such as "become a renunciant". There are two problems with this, which are covered in the next two paragraphs.

---

[33] Tib. bardo.

[34] Tib. rab byung.

[35] For an extensive teaching on this subject that is very relevant to these times, see the *Sutra of the Householder Uncouth, A Teaching of the Buddha Showing All-knowing Wisdom And the Householder's Way*.

First, this raises the issue of whether the prayer should be changed to suit our present circumstances or whether it should be translated as is. I believe that it should be translated as is and then commentaries like this should be written to clarify the matter. Therefore, here and throughout the prayer, the words of the original have been translated faithfully into English and then this and other extensive explanations have been provided so that the reader can understand unequivocally everything connected with each verse. Once the reader has been fully and correctly informed, if he or she wants to change the prayer to something more suited to one's own needs, they can do so in a way that will not have unintended effects. In this case, for example, the person wanting to use the prayer might decide to change "become ordained" to "become a renunciant" or "become a yogin", and so forth. However, changing "ordained" to something else corrupts the prayer in a way that is not immediately obvious, so this has to be examined further before you blithely change the wording "ordained" to suit yourself.

The next verse follows on directly from this aspiration to be ordained with prayers for the completely pure discipline that one undertakes as an ordained monk or nun of the Buddhist tradition. Therefore, to change "become ordained" in this verse to something else severs the continuity of the prayer and leads to a significant loss of meaning with it. In short, if we are to present the prayer and its threads of meaning without disturbance, there is no choice but to say "become ordained" in this last line of this verse.

Altogether, the prayers in this verse are the first cause mentioned for the enlightenment mind not being forgotten and so degenerating.

▷ Next is the second of the four verses connected with enlightenment mind not being forgotten:

17 May I train following all the conquerors,
    Working to wholly complete the excellent conduct

> And doing the stainless, totally pure discipline conduct
> In a way that is always uncorrupted and faultless.

As mentioned just above, this verse follows on directly from the previous verse. The previous verse ended by praying to be ordained in every subsequent life and the current verse now prays to train in the ways of a bodhisatva and in particular to have the discipline in which one's vows of ordination are kept perfectly pure in every life.

This verse, like the preceding verse has two couplets. Grammatically speaking, the preceding verse has each of the couplets as a distinct sentence, whereas this verse has the couplets joined with a conjunction—the "and" beginning the third line of the English. It is a mistake to break the two couplets into individual sentences, each one starting with "may", even though this has been done in some English translations—doing so disturbs the meaning and also the connection with the previous verse.

The Indian commentaries explain the connection between the four lines of this verse as follows. The first line makes a prayer in general to undertake training that follows or is in line with the trainings of all the conquerors, and this joins to the second line and also to the last two lines. With the first line connected to the second line, there is the prayer that one will work at that training in order to complete the excellent conduct, specifically meaning the enlightenment conduct, of the conquerors. With the first line connected to the last two lines, there is a prayer to carry out the discipline type of conduct, which itself is totally pure by nature, in a way that is consistent with its inherent purity.

In Buddhism, it is explained that "discipline conduct" means following the ways of the pure discipline taught by the buddhas as part of the enlightenment conduct. That type of conduct is not a form of discipline that was invented by someone, but is a result of and in line with reality. Accordingly, the discipline conduct taught by the buddhas is by nature stainless and totally pure. Therefore, this is a prayer that, when one undertakes the discipline conduct oneself, one will always do it in a way which is "uncorrupted and faultless". The word "uncorrupted" in the verse corresponds to the stainless aspect just described and "faultless" corresponds to the totally pure aspect just described. For more information about this, see the commentary of Nāgārjuna—it gives an extensive explanation of the two types of purity of discipline conduct when commenting on this verse.

Putting all of the above together, this verse says: "May I train in all of the trainings of all of the conquerors. As I do so, may I work to wholly complete the excellent conduct of enlightenment, and in regard to that, may I pay particular attention to the discipline conduct aspect of the excellent conduct, doing it always in a way that, being uncorrupted, does not disturb its stainless quality, and being faultless does not disturb its totally pure quality".

Altogether, the prayers in this verse are the second cause mentioned for the enlightenment mind not being forgotten and so degenerating.

▷ Next is the third of the four verses connected with enlightenment mind not being forgotten:

18 I will teach dharma in all languages—
In gods, nāgas, and yakṣhas' languages,
In khumbandha and mens' languages and
In all migrators' languages many as there are.

This is written as a statement, though the Indian commentaries say that it is to be understood as an aspiration to teach the holy dharma in all of the languages of sentient beings, as many as there are. Gods' languages are the languages of the desire realm gods and on up. Nāgas are classified as animals who interact with our human world but usually are not visible to humans; they have a powerful intellect and were amongst those involved with the Buddha's teaching. Yakṣhas are a malevolent type of being that harms humans; they are considered to be part of the asuras of the desire realm. Khumbhandas are humanoids who were renowned for having a voice so beautiful that they could seduce anyone just by the sound of it.

The prayer in this verse is the third cause mentioned for the enlightenment mind not being forgotten and so degenerating.

▷ Next is the fourth of the four verses connected with enlightenment mind not being forgotten:

19 Gentled, I'll be most diligent at the pāramitās;
    May I never forget enlightenment mind.
    May the evils become obscurations
    Without exception be totally cleansed.

Each of the first two lines is a prayer. On the first line, "gentled" is the Sanskrit term "sūrataḥ", explained in the commentaries to mean "a mindstream that has been made gentle by softening and taming it". For the bodhisatva, this means having a mindstream that has been gentled with love and great compassion. With that set as the basis, one makes an aspiration to train with the greatest or utmost diligence in the excellent conduct of a bodhisatva, which consists of the ten pāramitās. Having aspired to train in the excellent conduct in that manner, the second line is a direct prayer never to forget the enlightenment mind for as long as one has not reached the heart of enlightenment. These two lines complete the fourth cause for the enlightenment mind not being forgotten and so degenerating. One could also take the view that the first line is the fourth cause and that the second line verbalizes the not forgetting of enlightenment mind in relation to the preceding four causes.

The second couplet shows the other side of not forgetting the enlightenment mind. Rather than showing what should be developed in order to prevent it from degenerating, it shows what is non-conducive to the development of the enlightenment mind and which, therefore, is to be abandoned. It is saying, "May the all of the evil deeds that I have done, every one of which creates an obscuration to enlightenment mind, be, without exception, totally cleansed by my abandoning them".

Division 3: Connecting with Being Uncloaked

20 May I be free of karma, affliction, and māra's works,
And though as migrators of the world, have conduct
Which is like the way a lotus is unaffected by water,
And like the sun and moon are unhindered in the sky.

This verse is structured like this: may I have conduct which is free of this, done there, and done like this.

The first line deals with what one's conduct must be freed from, specifying it as karma, affliction, and māra's works. There are many types of karma and, although the verse itself does not specify which one, the commentaries state that it refers specifically to non-virtuous karma. Affliction is always an obstacle to the path of enlightenment. Nāgārjuna gives the following explanation of māra's works in this context:

> "Māra" here, given that it makes obstacles for virtue and works as an obstructor to enlightenment, functions to turn you away from the holy path, where "holy" is defined as dharma. Because māra stops the life of dharma, it is a killer, which is why it is named "māra". The activities of dharma are causes that lead to beneficial circumstances, so dharma sends you in a positive direction whereas the works of māra are causes that take you in a direction away from beneficial circumstances.

The Sanskrit term māra means to kill or cause death; it is the root of the English word "murder". Most succinctly stated, the māras are literally the kiss of death, and in Buddhist terms, they are those various negative factors that cause your spiritual path literally to be killed.

Thus, this verse is a prayer not to be cloaked by these three things, meaning not to be shrouded or covered up by them.

In terms of where one's conduct must be done, it is a fundamental part of the bodhisatva teaching that a bodhisatva does not try to escape from the world but makes the conscious decision to remain within samsara, being reborn again and again as a migrator in its various worlds. It is equally part of that teaching that what he does there is free himself from the usual worldly conduct of negative karma, affliction, and works of the māras, and keep instead to the excellent conduct of enlightenment. This core bodhisatva teaching is very much like the English saying, "In the world but not of the world". Accordingly, the commentaries explain that the second line when expanded out to its full meaning says: "And even though I go around in samsara, taking rebirths as worldly beings in the various migrations, may I conduct myself in a way which is not that of an ordinary worldly being".

What would such conduct done as a migrator in the various samsaric worlds yet without those cloaks be like? The verse contains two examples.

The first example is that it would be like a lotus flower which, having grown up above and left behind the muck of the swamp in which it started, cannot be affected by the muck of the swamp. Altogether, the third line says, "The conduct of the bodhisatva remains unaffected by the filth of samsara just as a lotus grows up above and cannot be affected by the filth contained in the water of the swamp". Note that the word "unaffected" is the same word as was previously translated as "undefiled" and explained on page 89.

The second example follows on from the first example. If you were then to ask what that conduct like a lotus unaffected by the filthy water in which it came to life is like, the answer is that it is like the sun and moon move unhindered in the sky. This second example causes all sorts of discussion in Tibetan commentaries, all of them relying on things said in the ancient Indian Buddhist tradition, but in my opinion some of them are questionable in their applicability. You will see some of them in Dza Patrul's explanations as presented in the commentary by Tenpa'i Wangchuk in volume II. In comparison, the explanation given by Nāgārjuna is short, uncomplicated, and easy to understand:

> This is the example of the sun and moon that have—as with a wish-fulfilling gem—entered the world only to work for others' sakes and that therefore move through the sky day and night unaffected by the subtlest concern for their own sakes. I too will conduct myself like that.

Shākyamitra points out that this verse teaches the pāramitā of patience as found in the bodhisatva levels connected with intentional conduct[36]. In other words, even those on the bodhisatva path who have not directly perceived emptiness can and do practice this kind of conduct, a conduct belonging to the pāramitā of patience.

Division 4: Benefiting Sentient Beings

21   For as much as the area of a field and directions
    I'll utterly pacify the suffering of the bad migrations
    Then set all migrators in the best of happinesses;
    I will perform conduct that benefits all migrators.

This verse is a prayer that arouses the thought of benefiting all sentient beings in particular. Here, Nāgārjuna points out that working to benefit others is the basic point of every arousing of enlightenment mind, as found in this and in other verses.

---

[36] Intentional conduct is a name given in the Prajñāpāramitā sutras to the first two of the five paths. The two are still involved with dualistic mind and that mind is intending to see emptiness and exit from samsara. The third path and above see emptiness in direct perception and have exited samsara so are no longer have a dualistic intention to do so.

Śhākyamitra explains that this verse follows on from the previous one in the sense that, due to the previous verse, the bodhisatva is abiding in having abandoned attachment and anger, so now this verse presents there being no arising of obstacles to doing the work of benefiting sentient beings.

The second line is a statement that one will pacify the suffering of the bad migrations—meaning the three bad migrations of birth in the hells, preta, and animal realms. All commentaries point out that the three bad migrations have sufferings that cause extreme torment for the beings there, so are picked out here. Nevertheless, this line should be understood to mean that one will pacify all the sufferings of beings within samsara, whether they are in the bad migrations or the good migrations—meaning the migrations of birth in the human, asura, and god realms.

The third line is a statement following on from that, that one will set all migrators in whatever are the very best types of happiness possible within samsara. Note that the original prayer does not have the words "best of", but the commentaries explain that it is the meaning intended and, since adding the words makes the English readable where it would not otherwise be, I have taken the liberty of adding the words. Note that some commentators say that "best of happinesses" means the three good migrations of samsara, whereas others say no, it simply means that, having removed all the sufferings of samsaric beings, that I then give them the very best of happinesses within samsara, whatever they might be.

The first line answers the question "For how long in time will one persevere at performing those two types of conduct? There are two different answers in the commentaries, as follows.

- The first explanation follows Nāgārjuna's explanation of how the wording of the line should be understood as a poetic device called an ornament. There are many types of ornament, as explained in a classic Indian text which is also used by the Tibetans called *Mirror Revealing Poetry*. The particular ornament in use here shows a length or distance and by implication shows the amount of time it would take to run across it. Nāgārjuna explains that, in the case of this verse, it means the amount of time taken to cross the area of a buddha-field and also to travel through the ten directions of such a field. Given that a buddha-field is beyond conceivable measurement, this line, according to Nāgārjuna's explanation, means an inconceivable amount of time.

- The second explanation follows various other commentators, including Yeshe De. They say that for as many migrators' realms—for example the three bad migrations—as would fit into as much as is the total volume (area and all ten directions measured together) of a buddha-field, one will do these activities in as many realms. Since the volume of a buddha-field also is inconceivable, it again comes to mean that one will be doing these activities for an inconceivable length of time.

The fourth line answers the question of why one would do those two activities, saying that one will do them specifically in order to benefit all migrators, that is, all sentient beings.

There is a further level of meaning contained in the verb structure of the verse. The second line indicates where one starts and the third line indicates what one will then do following that, with both of those activities giving worldly benefits to the migrators in samsara. The fourth line says that one will do all types of conduct for the purpose of benefiting migrators—that includes and gives the rationale for the worldly activities of the previous two lines, but it goes a step further now and includes the beyond worldly activities, which can be summed up as causing migrators to attain unsurpassed wisdom.

Division 5: Armour

The next verse is a prayer to wear the armour needed when undertaking the excellent conduct of a bodhisatva. Three types of armour are mentioned, as described below. There is a structure to the verse in relation to the three armours. The first line is concerned with *completing* the qualities of buddhahood for oneself; the second line with *entering* into those good qualities as one relates to sentient beings, and the third with, *having entered* into those good qualities oneself, now teaching them to others. This structure is conveniently summed up as: completing, entering, and having entered.

22 I will work at completing enlightenment conduct,
   Enter in harmony with sentient beings' conduct,
   And utterly teach the excellent conducts;
   May I do this throughout all future aeons.

The first line means that one will take up the armour of working to complete the buddha qualities because enlightenment conduct refers to the type of behaviour undertaken for the purpose of gaining enlightenment and working at completing it is therefore the same as working to complete the qualities of a buddha. The second line means that one will take up the armour of entering those good qualities while remaining in harmony with sentient beings; while entering the enlightenment conduct, one will be consistent with the ways in which sentient beings behave, because by doing so they will be open and one will be able to assist them. The third line means that one will take up the armour of giving dharma; the excellent conducts are the enlightenment conducts, so now the emphasis is on teaching what one has understood of those to others and thereby giving them the gift of buddha dharma.

The fourth line connects with all three preceding lines. There is a particular wording in the line which means that the line can either be understood to mean "may I do this throughout all future aeons" or "may I do this fully throughout future aeons". Some commentators have it one way, others have it another way. Nāgārjuna, who would immediately know which way the Sanskrit should be taken says that it means the former, though he makes the point that the line should be understood to mean "may I do this throughout all future aeons, to their farthest limit, doing it with a mind that never wearies of doing so". You will see that Tenpa'i Wangchuk in following Dza Patrul's lineage, does it the other way. Either way, it means to have the mind which never tires of doing it in the slightest.

Division 6: Connecting with Bodhisatvas of the Same Lot

The term "same lot" in the division heading is a specific term of Buddhism originally taught in the Abhidharma teachings. It means those beings who have the same karmic lot as oneself and who therefore are either the same as or similar to oneself. It is used to indicate two beings born in the same type of migration, such as two humans. It is also used in a more specific way, to indicate two beings not only born in the same type of migration but born in the same country and having similar cultural norms, for example, it could be two humans who follow the same religion, eat the same kind of food, have similar views, and have similar ways of doing things. "Same lot" here is used in the more specific sense, in reference to other bodhisatvas whose situation and ways are sufficiently similar to one's own situation and ways that they will be compatible and good companions on the bodhisatva path.

23 May I always be accompanied by those
    Whose conduct matches my own!
    Moreover, through body, speech, and mind
    I will perform the same conducts and prayer.

The first couplet is a prayer that one will always be connected with other bodhisatvas whose conduct on the bodhisatva path is sufficiently similar to one's own ways that they will be compatible and good companions for the journey. By having them as companions, one will be kept on the journey to enlightenment and prevented from being taken away from it by the mentality of others who either are not so fully dedicated to the same journey or are worldly types.

The first couplet can also be understood as a prayer for the best of circumstances in which one does not merely have the company of other bodhisatvas having similar ways in terms of the path, but has the company of bodhisatvas whose ways are thoroughly compatible with one's own, for example bodhisatvas of the same country, language, mannerisms, dharma affiliations, and so on. This type of companionship is the very best one can have as a bodhisatva. This additional way of understanding the first couplet derives from the more specific meaning explained above of same karmic lot.

The second couplet most exactly translated says "Moreover, I will make my conducts of body, of speech, and of mind, and as well as that of my prayers such that they are one with theirs". Note that the word "conducts" in the last line is plural because it refers to the conducts of body, speech, and mind. This couplet is a statement that one will stay within all three types of conduct and also within prayer which is in every way consistent with that of those companions. One sets this intention because there will then be nothing in either one's overall behaviour or one's aspirations that could damage one's connection to those most desirable companions for the path.

Division 7: Acting to Please Virtuous Friends

The next verse follows on from the last. The last verse prays to have a group of companions who are bodhisatvas of the same lot. This verse concerns itself with specific members of that group, the ones who are your spiritual friends. Because they have the wish to benefit you, they teach you the excellent conduct of a bodhisatva as much as they possibly can.

24 Companions who wish to benefit me,
    The ones who utterly teach excellent conduct—
    May I always be with them!
    I will never displease them!

The last verse was a prayer first to have companions in general who are bodhisatvas similar to oneself followed by a statement that one would do nothing to disturb one's connection with them. Similarly, this verse is a prayer always to be together with one's spiritual friends followed by a statement that one will not ever displease them because displeasing them is the way that one disturbs one's connection with them.

The third line is a prayer. In it, "always to be with them" means to stay close-by and be in constant contact with them.

The fourth line is not a prayer but a statement of intent in which you are urging yourself on: "I must never allow myself to displease them in any way, rather, I must ensure that I remain completely in harmony with their thoughts, wishes, actions, teachings, and so on". There are many instructions on how to relate to a spiritual teacher in a way that will allow your relationship to the teacher to work in a way that will end up leading yourself along the path. Of them, this one of never displeasing the teacher is picked out here because it is one of the main instructions on how to relate to a spiritual teacher.

Division 8: Having made the Tathagatas Visible

The name of this division refers to making those who have become tathāgatas—that is, the buddhas—visible to yourself in direct perception and, having done so, doing what is appropriate now that they are present in your perception.

25 I will always view the conquerors in direct perception,
    The guardians, buddhas surrounded by their sons.
    I will also make vast offerings to them
    In all future aeons without wearying.

The verse here has two couplets. Each couplet is a sentence in its own right. Moreover, each couplet is a statement, not a prayer. Some English translations join both couplets to make one sentence, and some make a prayer out of one or both couplets, both of which are mistakes that distort the meaning.

The first line is a statement that you will continuously view the conquerors before you, seeing them directly in front of you. Knowing something directly with your senses, such as viewing something with your own eyes, is called, in the technical language of Buddhism, viewing or seeing in direct perception.

The second line explains who those conquerors are; they are the guardians of migrators, the buddhas in their buddha-fields, each of whom is surrounded by his assembly of those who carry on his tathāgata lineage and who therefore are called "buddha sons". "Sons" here includes males and females and hermaphrodites and neuters, but it would be entirely incorrect to change the wording to something else. The point here is that the term is not used as a gender term but as a term that indicates a particular function in relation to the lineage of a tathāgata's teaching.

As explained earlier, the buddhas and their great bodhisatva sons are known as "guardians", because they watch over, protect, and nurture the infinite sentient beings.

Being surrounded by buddha sons is mentioned because the buddhas are always surrounded by their buddha sons, so, when you actually view them, that is how you will see them.

The second couplet is a statement that, now they have been made visible, you will do what is then appropriate, which is to make vast offerings to them and you will do that throughout all future aeons of time, without wearying of doing so.

This verse does not mean that anyone will suddenly see, in direct perception, the buddhas in their fields now. Rather, it is stating one's determination that that will happen for oneself at some point in the future when one has completed the third of the five bodhisatva paths and will happen continuously from that point on.

A very general way to view the meaning of this verse is that in the Buddhist teaching in general it is said that one should meet the buddhas or their ambassadors—other spiritual guides—then honour them. As mentioned before, there are several ways to honour them, with making offerings being one of them. That you would make the offerings till the end of samsara and without wearying of doing so is a statement of the style of a bodhisatva, which is to have unflagging energy for all aspects of excellent conduct.

Division 9: Wholly Holding the Holy Dharma

This division has one verse. It consists of two prayers made again in the form of a statement of what you are determined to do:

> 26 Holding the holy dharma of the conquerors
> And fully illuminating enlightenment conduct,
> I will completely purify the excellent conduct
> And moreover will do that in all future aeons.

Again, this verse is written in the form of a statement of your intent, not as a prayer. The conquerors, that is, the buddhas, are the ones who truly know everything both in the profound aspect of knowing the reality of all things and in the vast aspect of knowing every one of those things. Therefore, they are the ones who have total knowledge of the dharma, meaning the teachings that can liberate sentient beings.

The first couplet says that you will be holding—meaning fully retaining in mind through the force of non-forgetfulness—all of the holy dharma of the conquerors and then "fully illuminating enlightenment conduct", meaning truly teaching the holy dharma of the conquerors to all sentient beings. The phrase "fully illuminating", meaning "illuminating something so that it is fully visible", here means teaching and explaining the holy dharma of the conquerors—with the emphasis being on teaching and explaining the excellent conduct of a bodhisatva—so that it becomes fully known to others.

The second couplet is saying that while holding and teaching the buddhas' dharma, you will work at completely purifying the excellent conduct of a bodhisatva by removing all the impurities of mind that run counter to it. Thus, another way to say "I will completely purify the excellent conduct" is to say "I will clean the mind of all factors detrimental to it so that it will become perfect". When it says, "And moreover will do that in all future aeons", it means that you will do the first three without tiring of doing so throughout all future aeons, meaning for as long as it takes to become a buddha. Once you have become a buddha, you will hold the dharma and teach it, though in the best way possible way, in the way that only a buddha can, and you will have completely purified the excellent conduct already, so will no longer engage in doing that.

Division 10: Gaining an Unending Store

This division has one verse. It concerns gaining an unending store of bodhisatva qualities through acquiring merit, wisdom, and so on.

27 May I in re-entering all becomings[37]
    Acquire unending merits and wisdoms.
    May I become an unending store of method, prajñā,
    Samādhis, complete emancipations, and all good qualities.

The first couplet means: "May I, as I deliberately, consciously, for the sake of sentient beings, re-enter samsara again and again, going into any of all of the different rebirths within it, acquire unending merits and wisdoms". As pointed out in an earlier verse, the bodhisatva re-enters samsara again and again for the sake of sentient beings but follows the excellent conduct of a bodhisatva while avoiding the cloaks of negative karma, and so on, in which ordinary beings engage. This verse points out a further way that the bodhisatva turns re-entering samsara again and again to advantage, which

---

[37] The first line of this verse has the Tibetan "yang 'khor ba". The "yang" in Tibetan grammar has a meaning that matches the English "re-". It is coupled to "khor ba", which is the Tibetan verb form of the Sanskrit "samsara", meaning "to go about here and there in a haphazard way". Thus "yang 'khor ba" here means "to be re-entering samsara again and again". The term "becomings" means the various rebirths that one takes, all of which entail becoming this or that type of being. "All becomings" in this context means "all possible rebirths in samsara without shrinking back from any of them". Thus, the final meaning of the first line is "As I go about entering all without partiality of the various rebirths in samsara again and again".

is that by doing so he can acquire[38] unending stores of merit and wisdom. In other words, the bodhisatva thinks, "Because of taking that approach rather than the approach of seeking the personal peace of an arhat, I will constantly have the environment needed for developing all of the good qualities of a buddha, therefore, I will be able to and will gather what is needed in general to become a buddha, the two accumulations of merit and wisdom".

The second couplet then makes a prayer for becoming an unending store of all good qualities that will be developed on the bodhisatva journey while gathering the two accumulations. The full meaning of the second couplet is: "As I develop unending methods and wisdoms in that way, may I develop all of the good qualities possible of a bodhisatva, such as the most commonly mentioned ones, the methods, prajñās, samādhis, and complete emancipations.

Methods are the means by which one can skilfully benefit sentient beings and also take oneself to enlightenment. Prajñās are the correctly-knowing minds which can be used to benefit sentient beings in the most informed way possible and also to gain the insight needed for oneself to arrive at enlightenment. Samādhis, meaning one-pointed concentrations, are an important part of a bodhisatva's development. Bodhisatvas on the bodhisatva levels in particular learn to place the mind one-pointedly on all sorts of things which either aids their own progress on the path or gives them abilities through which they can aid sentient beings. An enormous number of different concentrations are taught within the bodhisatva teachings.

A "complete emancipation" is a specific emancipation gained when a bodhisatva overcomes a specific obscuration through the use of prajñā. These individual emancipations are part of a bodhisatva's

---

[38] The original term in the Derge edition is Tib. rnyed pa meaning "acquire". Other editions of *The Translated Word* have Tib. thob pa meaning "to get". Nāgārjuna's text apparently had "acquire".

overall level of emancipation, his growing enlightenment, so are, of course, beneficial to him. However, any given emancipation also comes with a specific capability which can be also be used for benefiting sentient beings. The emancipations are usually presented from the perspective of the capabilities that come with them. The reason they are properly called "complete emancipations" as opposed to merely "emancipations" is that there are many emancipations in both worldly and spiritual paths, so the Buddha used the term "complete" to indicate that the emancipations he was teaching were true emancipations. There is a further explanation of complete emancipations in Tenpa'i Wangchuk's commentary to the prayer on this same verse, in volume II of this series.

Division 11: Entering

This division has eight sub-divisions, which Nāgārjuna gives as:

1. entering into viewing the buddha-fields—two types
2. entering into the buddha speech
3. entering into turning the tathāgatas' wheel of dharma
4. entering into entering aeons
5. entering into viewing the tathāgatas
6. entering into their domains
7. entering into manifesting a buddha-field
8. entering into going before the tathāgatas

Note that "entering into" in all of these is equivalent to "engaging in".

1. Entering into viewing the buddha-fields—two types

The next two verses go together, each one being an aspiration to enter into or engage in viewing the buddha-fields. The first of the two verses says:

28 On one atom are fields as many as the atoms
    And in those fields inconceivable buddhas
    Seated at the centre of their buddha sons;
    Doing enlightenment conduct, I will view them.

Again, this verse is not presented in the form "May I" but in the form "I shall", which is the expression of a determined intent to do something to which one aspires.

The first three lines are saying: "If we consider a single atom only, there are, on top of that single atom, buddha-fields equal in number to the atoms comprising all the fields of all the buddhas who will have gone to buddhahood in the three times wherever it was in all directions. In those fields are an inconceivable number of buddhas, where inconceivable means 'beyond the range of the dualistic mind of ordinary sentient beings'. Each one of those inconceivable buddhas is surrounded by his retinue of buddha sons, the bodhisatvas whom he is teaching and leading to enlightenment".

It is important to note that these three lines do not describe a visualization that is being built up, but describe how things actually are. What is described cannot be seen by ordinary beings, but, as explained earlier, can be seen by those who have sufficient spiritual development—the buddhas and also the bodhisatvas who are on the bodhisatva levels.

The first line of the Tibetan ends in the continuative phrase linker "te", which could be understood in a number of ways. Nāgārjuna clearly shows that it has to be understood as the conjunction "and" which has been moved to the beginning of the second line of English for ease of recitation.

The wording of the fourth line in the original prayer is: "Doing the enlightenment conduct, I will view them". Nāgārjuna unravels this for us, explaining that the "will view" has to be understood first and that doing the enlightenment conduct follows. I could have changed the wording around to match the explanation given in Nāgārjuna's commentary, but it seemed best to keep the original wording as something which has to be understood through receiving an explanation of it. Nāgārjuna also explains that the "viewing" mentioned here is equivalent to the "entering" theme with which this verse is connected.

Thus, the fourth line has to be understood to mean: "I will develop myself sufficiently along the bodhisatva path that I have the capacity to view what has been as described in the verse, all those buddhas surrounded by their buddha sons, not merely as a concept but in direct perception. Having developed myself in that way, I will be able to view them, present directly before me, and then I will, in all of their various presences, practise the enlightenment conduct".

At this point, all commentaries give a long explanation to clarify the meaning of this verse. Essentially, they explain that the verse is presenting a reality that exists. The reality cannot be seen in direct perception by ordinary beings because it is beyond the reach of their concept-based mind, technically known as "dualistic, rational mind". However, it can be seen in direct perception by those who have a mind based in non-concept, which is technically known as non-dualistic wisdom.

For those who recite and use the prayer, the point to understand is that you could try to do this as a concept-based visualization and get a very rough feeling for what is being said. However, that is not the point with this verse. The point here is that you are stating your aspiration and determined intent to reach the level of development of non-dual wisdom with which you could see—or, as the commentaries explain, engage in viewing—in direct perception what has been described in the first three lines. And, having reached that level of development, you are stating your commitment to then doing—meaning practising and accomplishing—all the various types of enlightenment conduct within the actual presence of all those buddhas surrounded by their bodhisatva retinues.

The second of the two verses presents the same entering into viewing the fields in direct perception and doing enlightenment conduct within them, but expands the extent of what will be viewed to an even greater magnitude:

29 Like that so too in all directions without exception
    On the breadth of merely a hair there's an ocean of buddhas
    Many as their measure in the three times and an ocean of fields
    And for an ocean of aeons doing the conduct, I'll utterly enter them.

"Like that" directly translates the first phrase of the verse, which in Tibetan is "de ltar". All of the Indian commentaries and Yeshe De's commentary have "de ltar", but the Derge edition of *The Translated Word*, which is the basis for this translation of Samantabhadra's Prayer, has "de dag" meaning "those" instead of "de ltar". It is possible, for grammatical reasons, to see how a Tibetan mind that was editing *The Translated Word* in preparation for publishing the Derge edition of it could decide that "de dag" would be better than "de ltar" and would change it to that, and I believe that this is what has happened in this case. There are several reasons why this could be so, the most obvious being that the phrase "ma lus" that immediately follows "de ltar" is valid when coming from Sanskrit but out of place in Tibetan. A Tibetan mind, seeing this might decide that the "de ltar" would have to be a noun and would decide that it should have been "de dag" because that would both fulfil the Tibetan requirement for a noun in that position with "ma lus" following it and fulfil the need for a connection in that position to the previous verse. Nevertheless, such a change would be a mistake that would arise due to not understanding Sanskrit syntax translated into Tibetan language. The Indian commentaries and Yeshe De's too, unanimously explain that the "ma lus" goes together with the words following it and not with the "de ltar" at the beginning of the line. Therefore, believing that the Derge edition has an editorial mistake at this point, I have ignored its "de dag" and used "de ltar" instead.

The above is important for several reasons. Firstly, it shows that even *The Translated Word* can be mistaken. Secondly, it shows the importance for Western translators of not simply accepting the explanations of the Tibetan commentarial tradition. Thirdly, it shows the great need for Western translators to understand that Tibetan itself is a translation and that the general rule in the world of translation and interpreting is to go back to the original source language where possible and not to make what is already a translation into the primary source. Moreover, it should give further insight into just how difficult it is to translate Samantabhadra's Prayer and the level of detail of grammar, syntax, and the meaning of words that is required for the work. Finally, it should act as encouragement to other translators to go further into their grammar studies and not be satisfied with the less-than-correct presentations of grammar that are being given to people studying to become translators.

"Like that" means "like what has just been described in which buddha fields and so on are present on a single atom". "So too in all directions without exception" means "but now taking that further and extending it so that we are not talking about the region of a single atom alone but about all directions without exception, the entirety of space". In that entirety of space, every minute region—compared here to the size of a mere strand of hair—is filled with as many buddhas as the total number of buddhas who will have descended in the past, present, and future. This ocean—where ocean throughout this verse is a metaphor for an uncountable number—of buddhas is present within an ocean of buddha-fields also within that same minute region.

The fourth line is a statement of aspiration that, although one might not be able to view that reality in direct perception now, one will in the future develop oneself sufficiently so that one can view it in direct perception. This line when fully explained means "And I will, during an ocean of aeons, utterly—meaning to the greatest degree possible—enter into viewing them in direct perception and then, actually being present there with all those buddhas and their bodhisatva retinues, I will be continuously doing the enlightenment conduct within their assemblies".

Remember that "enter" in these two verses means "view". Thus, "utterly enter" means "utterly enter into viewing them", which carries the implication that one will be present with the buddhas and their sons.

If you look carefully, you will see that the last lines of these two verses are very similar. In the original word order, they put the conduct first and the viewing after that, but this has to be understood as viewing the buddhas then, together with that, doing enlightenment conduct in their presence. The wording here reflects the expert composition of the prayer in the Sanskrit language. The main point of each verse is entering into viewing the fields, so that has been placed in each verse as the main verb at the end of the last line, in order to highlight it. Note also that the second verse finalizes the pair of verses with the words "utterly viewing", which is a poetic device used to emphasize the main point of both verses at their very end.

It is worth noting that some commentaries, for example Dza Patrul's oral tradition of explanation that appears in Tenpa'i Wangchuk's commentary, mistakenly explain that the phrase actually found in the prayer, "the breadth of merely a hair", means "the tip of a hair". That mistake has then found its way into some English translations. In fact, the meaning here is a minute region of space, for example like the breadth of a single strand of hair.

There has also been the problem with English translations that the phrase "on top of" a hair and a single atom have been used because of not understanding that the Tibetan preposition "steng" used to convey this meaning here does not literally mean "on the top side of" but means simply "on", in the sense of "within that region of space". This was explained earlier with the explanation of the seven limbs, some of whose verses use the same image.

2. Entering into the buddha speech

The next verse is entering the buddha speech:

> 30 Through the ocean of branches of sound in one speech,
> The complete purity of the branches of voice of all conquerors,
> Coming as voices exactly in accord with all migrators' thoughts,
> The buddha speech, is what I will perpetually enter.

This verse is an aspiration, given in the form of statement of intent, to enter the buddha speech. "Enter" in this case means "I will listen to it myself"; it does not mean "I will speak it myself in future when I am a buddha"—that aspiration comes in the next verse.

Buddha speech has amazing qualities that are not present in the speech even of tenth-level bodhisatvas. One of them is that it has many aspects of intonation—it is sometimes compared to Brahma's speech, which is said to have many aspects of intonation that make it irresistible to hear and the Great Vehicle sutras speak of sixty aspects of intonation for the buddha speech and explain them. Another quality is used in this verse to encapsulate buddha speech, the quality that a single sound of buddha speech will be heard in many different ways by countless numbers of sentient beings, each one hearing it in his own language and in words that contain a meaning and style of composition that fit perfectly with the needs of that being. This quality of buddha speech is discussed at length in the other commentaries included in this book and is also explained in great detail in the book *Unending Auspiciousness*, so I will not expound on it here.

The next point is that this verse does not come out euphoniously in English unless the order of the words and lines is changed. However, making those changes causes a substantial loss of syntactic meaning, so I have kept the order as it appears in the original. In this case, it is not purely an English translation problem, for even the Indian commentaries have some difficulty explaining the verse because of the word ordering in the verse.

By looking at the Indian commentaries and then Tibetan commentaries, we can see that there was an original way that this verse was explained and a different way that it was later explained by Tibetans. The difference in explanation all hinges on how the phrase linker "kyis", which appears at the end of the first line in Tibetan, is understood. The linker has been translated here as an agentive case linker in accordance with the Indian commentaries, using the word "through". Nāgārjuna, Śhākyamitra, and other Indians, and Yeshe De too all say that the "through" should be understood to mean "I will, through listening to the speech of any one buddha, enter into listening to the buddha speech of all buddhas". The verse as a whole comes to mean, "The speech of any one buddha who is teaching dharma possesses all the amazing qualities of the buddha speech in general. All buddhas when they teach, because of the complete purity of their beings as buddhas, have speech with unfathomable, amazing qualities and abilities. I will enter into or access that buddha speech of all the buddhas, with its amazing qualities, through listening to one of them".

Yeshe De raises the point that, as one progresses through the bodhisatva levels, one will be able to hear two, three, and so on buddhas at any one time but without hearing of one of them disturb the hearing of any of the others. He explains that the aspiration of this verse to access the buddha speech through one buddha is not meant to preclude the possibility of being able to hear more than one buddha. Rather, it is an aspiration to engage the buddha speech starting with one buddha, knowing that that will change as one proceeds through the higher levels of the bodhisatva path. He says:

From *Noble One, the Sutra of Akṣhyamati*:

> The wisdom connected with the extra-perception called the God's Ear hears what all the buddhas are teaching, so that, if one is listening to one tathāgata, the dharma teaching of a second tathāgata will not be obscured. Through that wisdom, what is being taught by all the buddhas will be apprehended without sequential listening being involved.

So, this is actually a prayer saying "May I gain that sort of thing!"

The explanation of later Tibetans can be seen in Lochen Dharmaśhrī's commentary and commentaries derived from that, for example, in Dza Patrul's explanations given in Tenpa'i Wangchuk's commentary. They claim that "through" should be understood as "through the particular point that a single instance of a buddha's speech contains all the possibilities of the buddha speech, I will enter into listening to the speech of all the buddhas". This is far away from the explanation of Indian masters given above. Again, I see that a mistaken way of explaining this has developed in the Tibetan system and feel that we have to follow the Indian's explanations.

3. Entering into turning the tathagatas' wheel of dharma

The previous verse was a prayer to enter into the buddha speech in the sense of undertaking listening to it. The next verse is a prayer to enter into the buddha speech in the sense of speaking it oneself through turning the wheel of dharma as a wheel-turning buddha.

31 All the conquerors gone in the three times'
    Utter turning of the modes of the wheel
    And also their unending voices of speech
    I too will, by the force of rational mind, utterly enter.

The original wording of the verse is difficult to understand because of an unusual grammatical construction that begins at the end of the second line and carries through to the first half of the third line. There is a genitive case marker at the end of the second line, followed immediately by "they" on the third line, followed immediately by a genitive case marker[39] making the "they" into "their", and that is immediately followed by what is called an "ornament of inclusion" phrase linker in Sanskrit and Tibetan grammar, and which comes out to meaning "and also". The first line reads "All the conquerors gone in the three times". The genitive case marker at the end of the second line has to be understood as belonging to the end of that first line so that it actually reads "All the conquerors gone in the three times' (note the apostrophe at the end of line—that is the genitive case marker)". It is their "utter turning of the modes of the dharma wheel" that is being referred to on the second line. The "their" on the third line refers to the conquerors mentioned on the first line and connects them with the unending voices of buddha speech used at the time of utterly turning the modes of the dharma wheel. It has "and also" with it. Thus the third line reads "and also their unending", meaning inexhaustible voices of speech that go with their utterly turning the modes of the dharma wheel. A locative case marker at the end of the third line indicates what will be entered into, which is the two things mentioned on the second and third lines respectively, the two things of turning the dharma wheel and the unending voices of buddha speech that appear at that time. The last line says "I too will", suddenly "by the force of rational mind, utterly enter".

A point to be explained is that "modes of the wheel" refers to the fact that buddhas, for the sake of skilfully teaching sentient beings generally do not turn the wheel of dharma once, but turn it on

---

[39] The second line ends in the genitive case marker "yi" in the Derge edition and "kyi" in most other editions, without change of meaning. It is immediately followed by "de dag" or "they" which in turn is immediately followed by "gi", making the "they" into "their". That is immediately followed by "yang", an ornament of inclusion which here comes to mean "and also".

several occasions, each time with a different principal meaning. For example, Śhākyamuni Buddha taught the dharma in three modes of turning the wheel. Thus, "modes" here refers to the ways used to tame sentient beings with their various inclinations—which methods will be used to teach which dharmas at which times, on which occasions, in which places, and so on.

Another point to be explained is that when the buddhas turn the various modes of the wheel of dharma, they do so out of precise knowledge of how sentient beings are and of what are the appropriate ways to teach them. This is connected with the words on the last line "by the force of rational mind". Normally it would be very strange to mention rational mind here because rational mind usually refers to the dualistic rational mind of sentient beings and that would not be how one would teach as a buddha. However, there is also a non-dualistic rational mind of the buddhas, which is usually known as discriminating wisdom. With discriminating wisdom, a buddha never strays from non-dual wisdom but makes rational-style estimations of this being better and this worse, and so on, which is exactly what is needed for effective teaching.

When the commentaries explain this use of rational mind, they do so by referring to it as a "special rational mind" which has the meaning just explained—a wisdom form of rational mind. Moreover, some commentators—for instance Nāgārjuna—explain the fourth line using the words "suddenly enter by special rational mind". The reason for saying "suddenly" is that we are talking about wisdom, which is very rapid or sudden in its operation. Therefore, the meaning of the verse altogether is "I too will enter into the conquerors' way of turning the wheel of dharma using all the modes needed for sentient beings and to do so will enter the use of the buddhas' speech with all of its special qualities, and will do so by having the wisdom-based intelligence needed to know which of those modes are appropriate and what wording should be used".

In short, this is an aspiration to enter the buddhas' speech from the perspective of one who explains the dharma at the level of a buddha.

4. Entering into all future aeons

The next verse concerns what is called "entering into the aeons of all future aeons":

> 32 The entering into all future aeons is something
> That I too will do but in merely an instant.
> Whatever the extent of aeons in the three times
> I will act to have entered them in a fraction of an instant.

"Entering aeons", meaning "entering all future aeons wherever they are found in all directions of sentient beings worlds", is one of the many topics of the bodhisatva teachings.

The first couplet says, "Just as other buddhas and bodhisatvas enter into 'entering aeons', I too will do that, and I will do it in no more than an instant of time". The second couplet continues that idea but expands it to include the entire extent of all the aeons found in the three times in all ten directions and says, "however many aeons that is, my way of entering them will have been to do so in a fraction of an instant".

Yeshe De explains that this verse means:

> All future aeons are to be entered, and to do so may I
> know all future aeons in an instant of wisdom. May they
> appear and be seen by me in one single instant of wisdom.
> Like with that viewing of the future, but now including
> the number of aeons in the three times, may they be con-
> tained in a fraction of an instant of wisdom, one portion of
> an instant of wisdom.

The point is again that one is aspiring not to a conceptual idea of this, but to actually doing it with the wisdom of a bodhisatva who has developed himself sufficiently that he has direct access to this sort of wisdom. The same idea can be seen in Tenpa'i Wangchuk's commentary to this verse in which he explains that the wording "I will act to have entered" can be understood to be an aspiration: "May I be capable of acting like the buddhas in which case my entry into the sum total of all aeons would have been done using wisdom at their level". Whatever the case, this verse is an aspiration to do the bodhisatva's conduct called "entering aeons" in a way that is consistent with a very high level of wisdom, if not at the buddha's level.

5. Entering into viewing the tathagatas
6. Entering into their domains

The next verse contains two of the eight sub-divisions of entering, one in the first couplet and one in the second:

> 33 I will view in a single instant
> The lions of men gone in the three times.
> I will perpetually enter their domains by
> The force of the illusory complete emancipation.

The first couplet means "I will view in a single instant of wisdom the lions of men, the ones who will have gone to buddhahood in the three times". "Lions of men" was fully explained in the commentary to the very first verse on page 58 and "in the three times" implies all of them, as also explained in that verse.

In the second couplet "domains" refers to the places of the buddhas. One aspires to enter them using the power that comes with a particular complete emancipation called "the illusory emancipation". Complete emancipations are explained in the commentary to the verse for division ten on page 119. A specific and very important complete emancipation for a bodhisatva is the capacity developed through realization to stay within the state of knowing that all phenomena are illusory because of their emptiness. It is called the "all phenomena have become illusory" or "illusory" complete emancipation. With the power provided by that complete emancipation a bodhisatva can enter the domains of enlightenment—for example as Sudhana was able to do when he met Samantabhadra—and that is why it is mentioned in this verse.

7. Entering into manifesting a buddha-field

The next verse is concerned with actually making buddha-fields manifest:

> 34　Whatever the field arrangements of the three times,
> I will make them manifest on a single atom.
> Like that in all the directions without exception,
> I will enter the ornamentation of conquerors' fields.

The first couplet is a statement of aspiration which says, "I will, through a bodhisatva's miracles, make manifest on one atom only all of the fields of the buddhas of the three times, with each manifested field having an arrangement that exactly matches that of the actual field". Buddha-fields have many similarities of arrangement but each one has its own details and so has its own arrangement or "ornamentation", as it is also called. This verse in the Derge edition of *The Translated Word* has the Tibetan term "rgyan" meaning "ornamentation" where most other versions of the prayer, such as the one used for Tenpa'i Wangchuk's commentary, have the more commonly used Tibetan term "bkod pa", meaning "arrangement". There is no real difference of meaning given that "arrangement" and "ornamentation" are synonyms in Buddhist literature for the layout and decoration of a field.

The second couplet builds on that. It says, "Like that, meaning as was done in the first line where all of the field arrangements of the buddhas of the three times were made manifest on a single atom, I will also make the same exact manifestation of field arrangements manifest on every single atom throughout all the directions and all three times. I will enter those ornamentations or arrangements of the conquerors fields, that is, I will manifest them fully, in an instant of wisdom".

Making a field manifest as mentioned in this verse is done by one's own ability to perform miracles and the power of one's own samādhi or concentration. This ability belongs only to bodhisatvas on the pure levels as they are called—the eighth level and up. Therefore, this is a statement of aspiration to be at those levels in the future. Also, though it is not mentioned in the verse, Yeshe De and others makes it clear that the verse also includes the aspiration to be able to show the manifested fields to others through the power of miracles and samādhi. An example of this is Samantabhadra having the capacity to show this amazing level of manifestation of his own and other buddha-fields to Sudhana.

The imagery of this verse is very similar to that of the first verse on entering on page 121. However, Changkya Rolpa'i Dorje says in his commentary that the two verses are very different in the sense that the earlier verse concerns being able to view the existing field arrangements of other buddhas, whereas this verse concerns being able actually to manifest them by the power of one's own miracles and samādhi, show them to others, and make one's own pure field. He says that such ability is available only to those on the pure levels—the eighth to tenth bodhisatva levels—because of which those currently on the intending concept-based levels—the first and second of the five paths and the first to seventh bodhisatva levels—can only pretend to the accomplishment of what this verse mentions through the use of concentration.

8. Entering into going before the tathagatas

The next verse is aspiring to go before the buddhas:

35 Whichever lamps of the world have not descended
Will become buddhas at the stage, turn the wheel,
And show nirvana, the final, utter peace.
I will go before all those guardians.

The verse is explained by Indian commentaries and Yeshe De to have the following meaning. The first three lines explain the situation with the buddhas who have not yet come. At this point in time there are many beings who will be guardian buddhas in the future, but who have not yet come down into the worlds. These beings will appear in the future as lamps who will illuminate the darkness of the worlds at that time, as explained with the verse on urging on page 84. They will come at one time or another all the way to the very end of time, in other words, for as long as samsara exists. When they do come, they will show the twelve deeds shown when someone becomes a fully-enlightened buddha. The twelve deeds are what is being shown here but they are summed up by mentioning the act of becoming a buddha, the act of turning the wheel of dharma, and the act of showing passage into final nirvana. The meaning of the last line is aspiring to be able to go before all of those who are showing the deeds of enlightenment—not just the three specific things—whenever it might be in the future. The verse does not say so, but the Indian commentaries make it clear that to do this one will manifest a cloud of bodies who will not only go before those buddhas but who will honour them at that time by doing the accepted types of worship of making excellent offerings, praising them, circumambulating them, and so on. That is how this verse should be understood.

The phrase "become buddhas at the stage" appears in three separate locations in the prayer where it has been misunderstood then incorrectly explained by later Tibetan commentators and then mistranslated by Western translators following their mistaken explanations. The problem was explained at length at the end of the explanations connected with verse ten on page 90, which is the verse in which this phrase first appears. To restate it, this phrase means "become buddhas at the enlightenment or highest stage of buddhahood", also called unsurpassed, truly complete enlightenment. That has been misunderstood to mean "gradually become buddhas". That mistake made in this verse then helps to give a wrong impression of the overall meaning of the verse by taking the reader away from the idea of the twelve deeds of enlightenment.

The Indian commentaries and Yeshe De's commentaries go to great lengths to make it clear that the second and third lines have to be understood to mean "will show the twelve deeds of a world-leading buddha, for example, becoming buddhas, turning the wheel of dharma, showing final nirvana, and so on". Similarly, they go to pains to establish that the last line has to be understood to mean "I will go before everyone of those buddhas and be there for each of their twelve deeds".

Division 12: Forces

The twelfth division has ten parts contained in two verses:

36 Forces of miracles which have all speed,
    Forces of vehicle which is in all ways a door,
    Forces of conduct whose quality is always good,
    Force of loving kindnesses which are all pervasive,

37 Forces of merit which is all virtuous,
    Forces of wisdom become without defilement,
    Forces of prajñā, method, and samādhi—by them
    I'll be truly accomplishing the forces of enlightenment.

The verses of the original have a structure characterized by the use of "forces of" and "all" that can be translated into English in various ways. I have translated them so as to retain all of their meaning yet preserve their poetic quality.

The two verses collectively mean "by the first nine forces mentioned, I aspire to truly accomplish the tenth one, the forces whatever they are of the unsurpassed enlightenment of a truly complete buddha".

Note that in the original prayer some lines have the plural form forces and some the singular form. Accurately translating this brings a lack of euphony and lack of ease of reading the verses in English, it is true, but does reflect the original. Unfortunately, most translations into English to date have indiscriminately made the plural into the singular or vice versa, with the result that the meaning has been distorted in places.

An explanation of each of the forces can be seen in Nāgārjuna's commentary in this volume and Tenpa'i Wangchuk's commentary in volume II. Briefly, "miracles which have all speed" refers to the miracles done by bodhisatvas, they being miracles which have the greatest speed possible. In "vehicle which is in all ways a door", "vehicle" refers specifically to the Great Vehicle which is "in all ways a door" because it provides one entrance that gives all types of beings access to the completely purity of unsurpassed enlightenment. In "forces of conduct whose quality is always good", "conduct" refers to the excellent conduct of the bodhisatvas, something whose quality is always good—good at the beginning, good at the middle, and good at the end. In "force (note the singular) of loving kindnesses (note the plural) which are all pervasive", any given bodhisatva has a force of loving kindness expressed towards many beings, because of which many kindnesses are involved and, because of enlightenment mind, they will always be kindnesses which pervade the ten directions. In "forces of merit which is all virtuous", "forces of merit" refers specifically to merit gathered on the bodhisatva's path and it "is all virtuous" or nothing but virtuous because it has been made with the thought of providing benefit and ease for sentient beings. In "forces of wisdom become without defilement", the poetic use of all has been dropped in the original. "Wisdom" is the non-dual wisdom of enlightenment and "become without defilement" means that the bodhisatva is developing wisdom which has had its samsaric defilements removed. Wisdom become without defilement is a force in the sense that, like the earlier example of the lotus which cannot be affected by the filth of the swamp below it, such wisdom cannot be affected and so defiled by the afflicted states of dualistic mind. In "forces of prajñā, method, and samādhi", three individual forces are mentioned. These three are principal forces of a bodhisatva. Through these nine forces, one will be continuously truly or genuinely accomplishing or producing the forces of enlightenment.

Division 13: Accomplishing

The next verse is concerned with applying the appropriate antidote to each of three things that are representative of what is not conducive to the completion of the enlightenment forces. The same three were mentioned and partially explained in the verse for division 3 on page 108.

38 Wholly purifying the forces of karma,
    Totally destroying the forces of affliction, and
    Utterly rendering powerless the forces of māra,
    The forces of excellent conduct will be completed.

Nāgārjuna says that, given that the first line does not specify which type of karma is to be wholly purified, it must refer to all three types of karma: virtuous, non-virtuous, and unfluctuating. He then gives an exceptionally long and interesting explanation of how all these karmas are to be purified. In sum, non-virtuous karmas are to be purified by laying aside done in conjunction with the four forces of antidote and virtuous and unfluctuating karmas are to be purified by gaining insight into the absence of self.

The forces of affliction are the capabilities of the afflicted states of body and mind in samsaric existence. They make a samsaric being even more deluded than he already is. Although they can be suppressed by worldly methods and the methods taught in the Lesser Vehicle, they are taught in the Great Vehicle as things that can be taken onto and so become assistants to the path.

The forces of māra are the capabilities of the four māras. In general, māras have the capacity to create obstacles to engaging in the conduct of enlightenment. They are rendered powerless on the bodhisatva's path because they simply cannot stand up to the power of the conduct of a bodhisatva.

There is an important point of grammar on the fourth line. Grammatically, the line contains an intransitive action and says "the forces of excellent conduct will be completed". It does not have a transitive construction and so does not say, as has appeared in some English translations, "I will complete the forces of excellent conduct". This is verified by Nāgārjuna's commentary in which he makes a point that this line has an intransitive verbal action. Moreover, the use of the identifying function of the Tibetan phrase linker "ni" following "forces of excellent conduct" means that that phrase has to come first and that the "will be completed" has to follow it in order to identify what must happen with the forces of excellent conduct.

This last line of the verse finalizes this verse and the two verses before it. The meaning overall is: "Through engagement in the forces conducive to the development of the forces of enlightenment as laid out in the two previous verses and through the application of antidotes to the three things not conducive set out in this verse, it will naturally happen that the forces of excellent conduct—which includes both excellent conducts of the world and excellent conducts of enlightenment—will be completed.

Therefore, this verse serves as a reminder to oneself and an aspiration that, by accomplishing the forces conducive to excellent conduct and applying the antidotes to the things non-conducive to it, the forces of excellent conduct will, all of them, be naturally completed.

Division 14: Activities

The next two verses together show the activities of a bodhisatva:

39 I will be completely purifying an ocean of fields,
Completely liberating the ocean of sentient beings,
Utterly seeing an ocean of dharmas,
Utterly realizing an ocean of wisdom,

40 Completely purifying an ocean of conduct,
Wholly completing an ocean of prayers,
Utterly offering to an ocean of buddhas,
And doing so tirelessly for an ocean of aeons.

Overall, the two verses say, "I will be doing this and this and this, and so on—a total of seven different activities—and I will be doing them tirelessly, without wearying of doing so, for an ocean of aeons".

The use of "ocean" is a poetic feature of the original verses. As explained earlier, ocean is used in Sanskrit poetry as a metaphor for something being unending. In accord with that, all the lines of the original correctly have ocean in the singular. Not understanding this point most English translations have the singular changed into the plural "oceans" on every line, but that is not what the original says and does distort the meaning of the original. In regard to that, someone might say that the second line has ocean in the plural because the line says "sems can rgya mtsho dag" where "dag" makes the plural. However this has to be understood to mean "sems can rgya mtsho lta bu dag"—the sentient beings (plural) who are like an ocean (singular) in amount.

The first verse says, "I will be doing the task of completely purifying an ocean of buddha-fields and, together with that, will do the activity of completely liberating the sentient beings who are oceanic in number". These first two lines complement each other because purifying buddha-fields is purifying the place or the container and liberating sentient beings is liberating the beings contained in that place so that they become pure, too. The second two lines also complement each other. The third line is doing the activity of seeing for oneself, using one's prajñā, the ocean of dharmas transmitted by the buddhas—which consist of transmission through scripture and through realization. Then, there are infinite numbers of phenomena comprising all of existence, so there will be infinite wisdoms that know them, thus I will be doing the activity of realizing or having the direct experience of an ocean of wisdom.

The second verse says, "I will be doing the task of completely purifying an ocean of conduct where conduct ends up meaning enlightenment conduct, which is by nature completely pure". The term translated as "purify" has two possible meanings: purify and train. In English, we do not speak of purifying behaviour to improve it, but speak of training it. However, the commentaries all make the point that, of the two possible meanings, the one intended here is "to purify", because the enlightenment conduct in which one is still training is not yet pure, so one is engaged in the activity of purifying it. "Wholly completing an ocean of prayers" means that one engages in developing oneself on the bodhisatva path such that all of one's prayers for the enlightenment of all sentient beings, oneself and others, come to fruition. "Utterly offering to an ocean of buddhas" means that one engages to the utmost in making offerings to the ocean of buddhas. In Tibetan, there is a phrase linker at the end of the line concerned with making offerings. Mis-reading it could result in thinking that the eighth line joins to the seventh line and is saying, "And I will act to perform that offering to the buddhas tirelessly for an ocean of aeons". Nāgārjuna's commentary says it that way, but I cannot help but think that it is the error of the person who wrote down his commentary given every other commentary, including that of his principal disciple Śhākyamitra, who clearly knew Nāgārjuna's understanding of the prayer, explains it to mean "And I will stay for the long period of time during which sentient beings have many sufferings within the gaol of samsara, continuing for their sakes to do those activities untiringly for an ocean of aeons".

Division 15: Delineation of Training Following

Here, four verses in two parts delineate what it means to wholly dedicate oneself to training oneself following the teachings and examples of the buddhas and bodhisatvas. The first part, wholly dedicating to train following the example of the tathāgatas, is expressed in the next verse:

41 The conquerors gone in the three times had their
Particular prayers of enlightenment conduct;
Becoming an enlightened buddha by excellent conduct,
I will complete all their prayers without exception.

Every one of the conquerors who has gone to enlightenment in the past or present and who will have gone in the future arrives at enlightenment by first arousing enlightenment mind then, as a bodhisatva, engaging in enlightenment conduct, meaning conduct done in order to attain enlightenment. The enlightenment conduct of all the bodhisatvas who later became the conquerors gone in the three times included making their own, particular prayers for or in connection with enlightenment, prayers that they fulfilled on becoming enlightened. The person who is reciting the prayer contemplates this and arrives at the understanding that he too is on the path to enlightenment and he too can fulfill all the prayers made on the path by those who have become conquerors. Having understood that, he determines that he will, by means of the excellent conduct of a bodhisatva, become a buddha at the highest level of enlightenment and so will fulfil or complete all without exception of the particular prayers that were made by all the conquerors.

The second part, thoroughly dedicating to training yourself following the examples of the bodhisatvas Samantabhadra and Mañjushrī in particular because they were, amongst all of Shākyamuni Buddha's great bodhisatva sons, the ones most capable at making prayers for enlightenment conduct, appears in the next three verses.

The next two verses concern thoroughly dedicating oneself to having the same capabilities as the bodhisatva Samantabhadra:

42 The chief of the sons of all the conquerors is
    The one whose name is "Samantabhadra"—
    I utterly dedicate all these virtues here in order
    To conduct myself with expertise equalling his.

The first two lines are identifying who is the chief or foremost of all of the bodhisatva sons of all the conquerors. It is the noble one Samantabhadra, the bodhisatva who was also the foremost amongst all of Shākyamuni Buddha's bodhisatva sons. These words were spoken by Samantabhadra himself, so when it comes to saying that it is he who is the foremost amongst all buddha sons, he uses a humble way of saying it, which is why the second line reads, "The one whose name is 'Samantabhadra' ".

As to why he is the chief of all the bodhisatva sons, he himself indicates in the coming verse that he is especially good at making dedications. In addition, Dza Patrul's lineage of explanation as presented in Tenpa'i Wangchuk's commentary in volume II says:

> He was senior to them in four ways: years, training, good qualities, and wisdom.

In terms of years, Samantabhadra was the eldest of Śhākyamuni Buddha's eight bodhisatva heart-sons. Nāgārjuna's commentary offers no information about being the chief but his senior disciple Śhākyamitra in his commentary says:

> All the buddhas have proclaimed about Samantabhadra's field that, because it is better in all aspects when the complete environment of the different buddha-fields is considered, it is "samantabhadra" meaning "good throughout". And when his expertise in general is considered, all the tathāgatas have said that his listening, replies, retention, explanations, and dissections of the Great Vehicle being unsurpassable, fathomless, and complete in all ways, he has to be referred to as "more expert than expert".

The last two lines of the verse say, "I utterly dedicate all of the virtues, that is, good things, that Samantabhadra has taught here in the words of this prayer to developing the same expertise as Samantabhadra has in the areas in which he is expert". The words "utterly dedicate" are another way of referring to the Great Vehicle style of dedication called "wholly dedicating". The next verse follows on directly saying:

> 43 The way he is expert at excellent dedications for
> Completely pure body, speech, and mind, and
> Completely pure conduct, and wholly pure fields,
> May I too be equal to him in the same way.

This means "Samantabhadra has expertise in making excellent or superior dedications for completely pure body, completely pure speech, and completely pure mind, and also for completely pure conduct, and completely pure buddha-fields. In whatever way and to whatever degree he is expert in those things, may I also be similar to him in having that very same expertise".

The next and final verse of this division has two parts:

44 For thoroughly virtuous excellent conduct
    I will act as in the prayer of Mañjuśhrī.
    Without wearying in all future aeons
    I will complete their works without exception.

The first couplet is a dedication for the purpose of having truly virtuous—meaning truly good—excellent conduct by training oneself in the way that Mañjuśhrī has explained how the excellent conduct of a bodhisatva is to be done in what is known as Mañjuśhrī's Prayer. That prayer is found in the Great Vehicle sutras and is, together with Samantabhadra's Prayer, one of the five most important prayers of the Great Vehicle tradition, as explained in the introduction to this book. Mañjuśhrī was regarded by the Buddha as the other bodhisatva who, like Samantabhadra, was the best at expressing the excellent conduct of a bodhisatva, for which reason Mañjuśhrī's Prayer is also regarded as very special. Remember that this is Samantabhadra speaking, so he is educating us on this point, and not merely making a dedication, as is often thought.

The second couplet is a dedication for the purpose of completing all of their works. This could be taken to mean Samantabhadra and Mañjuśhrī who have just been mentioned, which would then mean, given that they make their prayers that way, that it is also a prayer for completing all of the works that buddhas' and bodhisatvas' undertake. Those works are what? They are everything that buddhas and bodhisatvas undertake in order to complete the two sakes of oneself and others. This dedication is made with the great courage of a bodhisatva, which means that these works or activities will be done with a mind that never wearies of or turns away from doing them during all future aeons.

Division 16: Conclusion

The next verse is a conclusion to the divisions.

> 45 May my conducts not become measurable.
> May my good qualities also be immeasurable.
> Due to remaining in conduct without measure
> I will know all of their transformations.

The first line is a prayer that one's application to enlightenment conduct always be so great that it never falls into becoming measurable. The second line is the same sort of prayer using the same sort of wording but made in respect to one's own good qualities, meaning the good qualities of enlightenment. Here, the literal wording of the original is "May my good qualities also have a measure which is not assessable", in other words, be immeasurable. The last couplet means "due to remaining in that way in conduct and good qualities that cannot be measured, I will come to know all of the amazing miracles—those of transformations, and so on—of the buddhas and bodhisatvas".

The word "know" in the last line translates a specific Sanskrit verb which the early Tibetan translators translated into Tibetan with " 'tshal ba " The Sanskrit verb and the Tibetan verb following it are categorized as having five different meanings. Of them, the Indian commentaries and Yeshe De's commentary explain that the meaning intended here is "know" but in the sense of arriving at that point in time at which one knows that one has such things. Therefore, it is also possible to understand that another of the five meanings, "to gain", also applies, even if it is not the meaning to be translated.

With that, the main part of the prayer with its various sub-divisions is complete.

Topic 9: Its Ending

This topic consists of one verse. The name of the topic does not indicate a conclusion to the prayer but indicates for how long the prayer will be effective and how far its effects will reach:

> 46   As far as it would be to the final end of space
> And to the end of every sentient being likewise,
> And as much as to the end of karma and affliction,
> It will also be that much to the end of my prayer.

The original verse has many poetic devices in it. It is easy to lose them and also to distort the meaning when translating them into English. However, the translation above is literal yet crafted to reflect the poetry of the original. With the poetic devices removed, the plain meaning is "just as space has no end and sentient beings likewise have no end and, following on from that[40], just the karma and affliction of sentient beings has no end, likewise there will also be no end to the effects of my prayer".

In a more detailed explanation, this verse says, "As far as one would have to go in order to reach the final limit or the end of space *and* as far as one would have to go to reach the end of sentient beings without exception—which, given that wherever there is space there are sentient beings, is the same sort of thing as how far one would have to go to reach the end of space—*and*, following on from those two, as much as it would take to reach the end of the karma and affliction of sentient beings, each of which has no end to it, my prayer also will have no end or limit to its effects". It is important to understand that there are three interconnected ideas which are used to build up the imagery of the verse: space pervades everywhere so has no limit, and sentient beings because they pervade space also have no limit, and following on from that, those sentient beings

---

[40] The Tibetan has what is called a continuative phrase linker at the end of the third line. It comes out in the English a comma at the end of the line, where the comma conveys a sense of continuation as well as pause.

being limitless, there is no end to the amount of their karma and affliction. Therefore, he says, my prayer too will be unlimited in its reach and effects, touching every sentient being through time and space and providing the antidotes needed to overcome their karma and affliction in its entirety.

This verse was spoken originally by Samantabhadra and with the intent mentioned above. However, when someone else is reciting the prayer, the wording "my" changes to mean that person's recitation of the prayer. Note also that it is "prayer", not "prayers". This verse is referring to the reach of the entire prayer for excellent conduct that one has made, not to the many sub-prayers contained within it.

Topic 10: Its Benefits

The tenth and final topic consists of the remaining sixteen verses. Although the topic is named "benefits", there are actually two subjects covered within it: the first eight verses explain the benefits of reciting the prayer and the last eight consist of dedications of the merit from reciting the prayer. The benefits are in two main parts: benefits seen in this life and benefits seen in a later life.

1. Benefits seen in this life

"Seen in this life" is a less strict translation of the technical term "seen dharmas". Seen dharmas refers to karmas created in this life whose result also manifests in this life. According to the teachings of the Buddha, it is not easy to create karma that ripens and appears in the same life as it was created; it has to be a very strong karma for that to happen. Therefore, the commentaries, by using this term in the explanations of the prayer, are not only saying that certain benefits arise in this life but are implying that the prayer is particular powerful and effective. This has four parts:

1. Wholly holding merits that are special
2. Seeing the tathāgatas
3. Gaining same lot with bodhisatvas
4. Wholly ending karmic obscuration

Some commentaries point out that there are thirteen benefits mentioned within these four parts, an approach which can be seen for instance in Tenpa'i Wangchuk's commentary.

i. The benefit that performing this prayer can lead to being a person who wholly or truly holds merits that are special

This comes in two verses that are written as and must be understood as a single sentence:

47 Compared to one who adorns the infinite fields wherever
        in the ten directions
    With jewels and offers that to the conquerors,
    And offers the most enjoyable things of gods and men
    For aeons as many as the atoms of the fields,

48 The one who hears this king of dedications
    Then is utterly inspired towards and even just one time
    Gives rise to faith in supreme enlightenment
    Is the one who has the better superior merits.

The first verse sets up a person who accumulates a certain type of superior merit. Superior or merit is merit which is better than ordinary merit made in the world because it has been made through spiritual activities. The "compared to" at the beginning of the first verse correctly translates a comparison marker found at the end of the first verse. The second verse sets up another person who, because of hearing this king of dedications, is utterly inspired towards supreme enlightenment and therefore gives rise, even if it only happens one time, to faith in supreme enlightenment. Both persons have made a superior type of merit because of their respective spiritual activities. Nevertheless, of the two persons, it is the second one whose merit is the better of the two merits accumulated.

ii. The benefit that the tathagatas will be seen

Under this heading there are three benefits altogether. The first two benefits could be thought of as helping the third benefit to happen and Nāgārjuna phrases the name of this benefit accordingly. Other commentators simply present this prayer as having three benefits, without implying that the first two affecting the third.

49   Someone who has made this excellent conduct prayer
Will have abandoned all bad migrations,
He will have abandoned bad companions,
And he will also see Amitābha soon.

The verb tenses should be noted. The commentaries agree on and show the meaning of each line as it should be understood through these tenses and that meaning is presented in the next four paragraphs.

This verse does not mean "anyone who has made this prayer concerning excellent conduct that was composed by Samantabhadra ..." It specifically means "someone who has recited this prayer repeatedly and has done so while understanding the meaning and taking it to heart".

Such a person will in this life have purified the karmas for falls into all three bad migrations—those of the hell, preta, and animal realms—and because of that will be abandoning future births in every one of the bad migrations.

That same person will also in this life have abandoned bad companions in the sense that he will either not come into contact with them or not associate with them even if he does come into contact with them. The commentaries explain that "bad companions" includes many types of undesirable companion. Nāgārjuna says that, aside from worldly people who are engaged in bad ways, it includes those on paths below the bodhisatva's path, such as śhrāvakas and pratyekabuddhas of the Lesser Vehicle path, because they could not truly be spiritual companions at the bodhisatva level, and those who follow worldly paths, good and bad. Yeshe De says that it altogether means:

> Those following the śhrāvaka vehicle, the pratyekabuddha vehicle, mistaken spiritual paths, ways not in accord with one's own ways, and those engaged in wrong ways.

That same person, this time at the time at the end of this life of passing through the intermediary state also will soon see the buddha Amitābha. In the Tibetan text of the prayer, Amitābha is referred to here and elsewhere as "Infinite Luminence"[41] and in other places as "Unfathomable Light"[42]. Both names are regularly seen in Tibetan literature and this sometimes causes confusion as to who they are. They are the same person, known in Sanskrit as Amitābha; *The Sutra of The Arrangement of Sukhāvatī* says:

> Śhāriputra! The light of the tathāgata Unfathomable Light appears unimpeded in all buddha-fields because of which he is named "Unfathomable Light" ...

and speaks extensively about the two names for the same buddha.

Why is Amitābha mentioned here and at length in the dedications at the end of this overall topic? In general, it is said that of the various buddhas, the nirmāṇakāya buddha Amitābha who resides in the western nirmāṇakāya buddha-field called Sukhāvatī or "Place of Ease", has an especially close connection with humans in this world and, because of that, humans of this world can relatively easily connect with him and his place. For that reason, it was common in Tibet and China to do prayers and practices that focussed on Amitābha in order to see him during the intervening state following death and to escape samsara at that point by being reborn into his Sukhāvatī field. In China, whole dharma traditions appeared in which the

---

[41] Tib. snang ba mtha' yas.

[42] Tib. 'od dpag med.

followers did nothing more than pray to Amitābha to be born in his pure field following death; these were called the "pure land schools". In Tibet, there were no traditions with that exclusive focus, but it was more common to do practices connected with Amitābha and his pure realm than many Westerners might think. This verse and several of the dedicatory verses clearly demonstrate this approach of turning to Amitābha for refuge and liberation at the time of death, showing that the approach was not a later invention but was very much alive at the time of the Buddha.

iii. The benefit of gaining the same lot with bodhisatvas

"Same lot" was explained earlier on page 114. Here, it means that those who recite the prayer become of the same lot as bodhisatvas, with all the benefits entailed. Three specific benefits which relate to being on the path of a bodhisatva in general are mentioned in the first couplet and then the great benefit that one later will become exactly like Samantabhadra is mentioned in the second couplet:

50   They acquire the best, are sustained in goodness,
      And even in this human life can turn out well.
      Moreover, whatever Samantabhadra is like,
      Before long they will become like that too.

"They" on the first line connects with "someone who has made this excellent conduct prayer" in the last verse. All of those referred to in the last verse gain three specific benefits that correspond to being bodhisatva-type people. Those three are the acquiring the best of all acquisitions, being sustained in goodness, and even in this life having a life that can turn out well.

The literal wording of the original is that they "acquire the best of acquisitions" and that is explained in various ways in the different commentaries. Nāgārjuna explains that it means they have acquired the very best of prayers concerning the conduct of enlightenment. Śhākyamitra as do Yeshe De, Tenpa'i Wangchuk, and others explains that it means they acquire the most meaningful thing there is, the possibility of gaining enlightenment. All commentators agree that, because of having that best of acquisitions, they are sustained in goodness, meaning that they are kept in a good state of being during the life in which they acquired the best of acquisitions. Some commentators say that they are kept in such due to the blessings of the enlightened beings in general. Others say that they are kept in the goodness that comes with the practice of enlightenment conduct. Śhākyamitra explains it very nicely:

> Everyone who works for the sake of others even in the face of suffering that threatens their lives is indeed sustained in goodness; they are unlike the others, for whom this is equivalent to death.

Then, because of both of those, they have what is needed to work at accomplishing the meaning of being human, that is, what is needed to work at gaining enlightenment. Because of having gained the best acquisition, then being sustained in goodness, and then using what those two provide for the task of gaining enlightenment, they will, in one life or another—a life which for most people is far in the future—gain all of the excellences of the great bodhisatvas and finally of a truly complete buddha. Nevertheless, because of the truth of the reality towards which they are making efforts now, then even in this human life they can have a life that turns out very well for them, as they reap the rewards that come with genuine development on the bodhisatva's path. On top of those immediate advantages in this life, they will moreover have the future advantage of becoming just like Samantabhadra.

iv. The benefit of wholly ending karmic obscuration

The name of this benefit does not mean the total ending of karmic obscuration such that one becomes a buddha; it means wholly putting an end to the karmic obscuration of having done an act of the five immediates.

> 51 The evil deeds of the five immediates done by
> Someone under the control of not knowing will,

> If he recites this excellent conduct prayer,
> Be quickly and without exception wholly cleansed.

The previous two verses have mentioned "someone" and "they" as the ones who benefit from the prayer. This verse changes to the singular because it is speaking about a specific type of person. The verse concerns a person who has done one or more of the five immediates. The five immediates are five actions that accumulate such heavy karma that their fully-ripened type of result, which is usually a birth in hell, can occur immediately. There are stories in the sutras of the ground opening up in front of such a person who is alive and the person literally falling into hell. Even if it does not occur immediately in that way, at the time of death the person immediately goes to a hellish birth, neither going on to another rebirth first then going to hell nor going into the intermediary state between births on the way to rebirth in hell.

"Under the control of not knowing" is explained in all commentaries to mean "under the control of passion, aggression, or delusion", meaning any of the non-virtuous afflictions, because un-knowing includes all of them.

Of course, purification of the commission of any of the five immediates does not come without effort. Someone who has created such heavy bad karma will have to have faith and dedicate himself to the task of intensive, clear-minded repetition of the prayer in order for recital of the prayer to have a substantial effect on the karma involved.

2. Benefits seen in a later life

This is in two parts:

1. Benefits belonging to cause
2. Benefits belonging to fruition

i. Benefits belonging to cause

This is mentioned in the next verse:

52 He will possess wisdom, form,
    Marks, family, and colour.
    Many māras and Tīrthikas will be unable to affect him;
    In all three worlds even offerings will be made to him.

With this verse, we return to any person who diligently recites, etcetera, the prayer, as explained earlier. In this case, it does not use the general singular pronoun "someone who" but uses the singular personal pronoun "he".

The first two lines list five good qualities whose causes will have been gained by reciting the prayer, and so on. "Wisdom" is what comes in future with the full accomplishment of all the conducts of enlightenment. "Form" is a truly beautiful or handsome form, as the case may be, one that is exceptionally attractive to others; it refers both to a beautiful form whilst in samsara and to the nirmāṇakāya form of a buddha when enlightenment has been attained. "Marks" are the thirty-two major marks of a buddha and this by implication includes the eighty illustrative signs as well. "Family" in the time of the prayer was either the priestly Brahman or royal kingly castes, which were the two highest of the four castes of Hindu culture; nowadays, it is a family in high standing within the society. "Colour" is the literal meaning of the original Sanskrit term "varṇa" used in this verse; this term was used in ancient India to mean complexion, just as "colour" in English can also mean "complexion", as for example in "she had good colour".

The third line, "Many māras and Tīrthikas will be unable to affect them", means that for someone who keeps, recites, and teaches this prayer of Samantabhadra, many—meaning hordes or groups or assemblies of—māras or of Tīrthikas—who attempt to harm, bring down, or overcome him will not be able to do so. "Tīrthika" is a very considerate term coined by the Buddha for those who follow a religion other than Buddhism[43]; it refers here to those followers of other religions and philosophical schools who in the Buddha's time were adversaries of and made trouble for his followers. Today's equivalents are not hard to find.

The third and fourth lines are individual sentences but the commentaries explain that the two lines go together. This is done with a semi-colon in the translation because that correctly translates the grammar of the original, though the commentaries say "and" should be understood for it. It goes like this: "On the one hand, someone who keeps, recites, teaches, and so on this prayer of enlightenment conduct will not be affected by troublemakers *and* on the other hand because such a person is involved in the virtue of the bodhisatva's path, he will be seen as someone worthy of prostrations and offerings throughout all three worlds".

Some commentaries say that "three worlds" means the three realms of samsaric existence, for example, Yeshe De explains:

> Because the person is making prayers that will result in the purposes of sentient beings being fulfilled, wherever that person is born anywhere in all three worlds, meaning all of the world realms, he will be an object of offerings in that place and gods and men will be honouring him.

Others say that it means "the three places, above, below, and on the earth". The first seems more likely, though the second is not wrong.

ii. Benefits belonging to fruition

This is mentioned in the next two verses. The first verse points out that such a person will gain enlightenment and perform the twelve deeds of enlightenment:

---

[43] For Tīrthika, see the glossary.

53 He'll quickly go to the foot of the leading bodhi tree
    And, having done so, in order to benefit sentient beings,
    Will sit there, become an enlightened buddha, utterly
        turn the wheel,
    And tame all the māras together with their regiments.

"The leading bodhi tree" means the bodhi tree, the foremost or chief or king above all other trees, as explained earlier on page 97. As a result of reciting this prayer, and so on, a person will go to the leading bodhi tree and, for the sake of sentient beings, sit at its foot, tame the māras with their army of four regiments, then attain truly complete enlightenment, manifest complete buddhahood. Although the lines of the verse put taming the māras after becoming enlightened, a buddha first sits at the bodhi tree, then tames the māras, then gains buddhahood after that. Having attained buddhahood, he teaches the dharma by turning the wheels of dharma to his utmost capacity, and so on. However, in this case, "taming the māras" in its position after turning the wheel can also be understood to mean that he tames the māras as he turns the wheels and so comes to mean that he teaches the dharma continuously, without obstacle, after having become enlightened.

The second verse concerning fruition says that whoever holds, recites, and so on this prayer of excellent conduct composed by Samantabhadra will gain results in the future consisting of both worldly and beyond-worldly perfections and that all the details of those results are known only by the truly complete buddha with his all-knowing wisdom.

54 For whoever holds, reads or teaches
    This prayer of excellent conduct
    Their full-ripenings will be known by buddha.
    Do not be sceptical of supreme enlightenment!

There are a number of different ways of explaining this verse.

The grammatical construction of the first line can be taken to mean "holds and reads and teaches" or "holds and either reads or teaches" or "holds or reads or teaches". Various people explain it in different ways but the majority of Indian commentaries fit with "holds and either reads or teaches", so it was translated that way.

Thus, the first couplet is regarded by all the Indian commentators and by Yeshe De as meaning "for someone who holds—meaning who retains the words and meanings correctly and clearly in mind—and who also reads either for himself or to others or who teaches it to others, this prayer of excellent conduct composed by Samantabhadra ..." Unfortunately, later Tibetans changed the meaning of "holds" from that just given to "keep on the body", as you will see in Dza Patrul's tradition as expressed in Tenpa'i Wangchuk's commentary. However, this change clearly comes from the Tibetan cultural habit of draping various items connected with spiritual blessings on the body in order to gain blessings and ward off problems—there is no doubt that the correct meaning is as given by the Indian commentators.

Next, the Indians and Yeshe De all understand the words "prayer of excellent conduct" as a descriptive pointer to the prayer being composed by Samantabhadra, not as a formal name. However, later Tibetan commentaries change that, claiming that it is the formal title that the Tibetan translators created for the text of the prayer, with the result that the line is explained to read "The Excellent Conduct Prayer" or "The Noble Prayer of Excellent Conduct". The words "This prayer of excellent conduct" are correctly understood to mean "this one among the many prayers of excellent conduct".

"Their full-ripenings" at the beginning of the third line correctly reflects the wording of the original prayer. A full-ripening is the maturation of a karmic seed into its result. Thus, this phrase means "their results". "Their" in "their results" does not refer to whoever is doing the activities but refers to the results of the activities of holding and reading or teaching the prayer.

All commentaries agree that "will be known by buddha" is saying that only truly complete buddhas, such as our teacher Śhākyamuni Buddha, know all the details of karmic causes and results. Therefore, the third line means "the results in all their details can only be known by a truly complete buddha and not by anyone lesser than that, for example not by śhrāvaka or pratyekabuddha arhats, nor by bodhisatvas". Because the words are literally "known by buddha" some commentaries understand it to mean "known by any buddha or the buddhas in general" whereas others understand it to mean "known by the Buddha Śhākyamuni", but the overall meaning is the same in either case.

The last line says, "Do not be sceptical of supreme enlightenment". Note that it uses the specific term "be sceptical", it does not say "doubt". With this, you are admonished to understand that the results of holding, and so on a prayer like this can include supreme enlightenment. You might be sceptical about that, but you should not be because, even though you as an ordinary being cannot know all the details of the results of the prayer, a truly complete buddha can. Therefore you should not doubt the possibility of becoming completely enlightened let alone gaining any of the other amazing results that are possible in relation to this prayer. In regard to this, Nāgārjuna explains that this verse includes all possible results of the prayer, which will include both beyond-worldly results of development along the path to enlightenment and also the worldly results such as gaining a beautiful body, and so on. Thus he explains that the last line means "do not be sceptical of supreme enlightenment nor any of the other benefits that this prayer can bring, worldly and beyond-worldly".

That completes the verses showing the benefits of the prayer. Next are the verses of dedication.

1. Dedication in connection with the great bodhisatvas Manjushri and Samantabhadra

The next verse is referred to as an intermediate-level dedication because it is in relation to high level bodhisatvas and not ordinary people or buddhas which would be the low and high level dedications respectively.

> 55 Mañjushrī knows how it is and is heroic
> And Samantabhadra is like that too;
> Following them in every way, I train and
> Will utterly dedicate all of these virtues.

There are two versions of this verse. Both were in use in India, as can be seen from the Indian commentaries, and both are in use in Tibet, even today, with each monastery using one or the other according to what their predecessors used. The overall meaning is the same in each case, but the version of the verse seen in the Derge edition of *The Translated Word*—shown just above—makes the meaning much clearer. The other version of the prayer can be seen in both Nāgārjuna and in Tenpa'i Wangchuk's commentaries, so the other wording of it can be viewed there.

The first couplet of the verse sets up Mañjushrī and Samantabhadra as the two greatest bodhisatva sons of Shākyamuni buddha. It explains that Mañjushrī is someone who knows everything just as it is. Formal explanations of a buddha's wisdom explain that it knows both the profound aspect of any given phenomenon, that is, its reality, and knows all phenomena all at once, that is, it knows them in their extent. Mañjushrī has that kind of knowledge. Note that "how it is" does not mean that he has only the first of the two wisdoms just mentioned. Here, "how it is" means that he knows all phenomena, both in their reality and their extent, so has the full knowledge of all things, like a buddha does. The first line goes on to say that Mañjushrī is an ultimate hero or warrior, that is a bodhisatva who does not flinch from the bodhisatva journey in any way at all, which connects with Mañjushrī being, like Samantabhadra, the most knowledgeable of Śhākyamuni Buddha's heart sons when it comes to the enlightenment conduct of a bodhisatva.

The second line points out that Samantabhadra has exactly the same qualities as Mañjuśhrī. Note that this line does not add Samantabhadra as an afterthought or as someone perhaps less capable than Mañjuśhrī. Rather, the first line shows that there is Mañjuśhrī with certain qualities and then, equally, there is Samantabhadra who has those qualities too. Remember that Samantabhadra is composing this verse so will put Mañjuśhrī before himself.

The third line and fourth lines go together. Because of the extreme good qualities of those two bodhisatvas, you decide that it would be right to follow them in every way. Therefore, two things happen: first, you decide in general to train as a bodhisatva following exactly the path of enlightenment conduct that they have laid out in their instructions; second, you in particular make dedications in exactly the way that they have instructed.

Mañjuśhrī and Samantabhadra explain that a bodhisatva must make dedications not only at the level of fictional enlightenment mind, that is, at the level of praying for the future appearances needed to benefit oneself and others, but also at the level of superfactual enlightenment mind, that is, at the level of praying while in direct perception of emptiness. According to the Prajñāpāramitā sutras, the way to make prayers in emptiness is that, while they are being made, the person making the prayer should have direct sight of the emptiness of the three spheres, that is, the emptiness of the person making the prayer, the object of prayer, and the action of making the prayer. Thus, the last line of this verse is not merely saying that one dedicates in the fictional way (concerning appearances) as they do, but that one specifically dedicates according to the oral instructions concerning dedication in which superfactual dedication must be present as well.

This verse is universally considered to be the one verse in the prayer that contains the whole meaning of the prayer. It is thus used in almost every set of dedications made by Tibetan Buddhists, regardless of their tradition.

2. Dedication in connection with the tathagatas

The next verse is regarded as a high level dedication because it is connected with the buddhas:

56   Using the dedication which all the conquerors
Gone in the three times commend as supreme,
I utterly dedicate all these roots of virtue of mine
For the purpose of excellent conduct.

This verse, while not considered to be the one verse that contains the whole meaning of the prayer, is considered to be so encompassing in meaning that it too is frequently recited as part of dedications generally made by Tibetan Buddhists.

"Commend" here has the sense "what all the conquerors recommend as the supreme type of dedication". Thus the verse is saying, "I will follow their recommendation and use that sort of dedication to dedicate all of the enormous roots of merit that I have accumulated through making this prayer. I will dedicate them so that they go towards developing and completing the bodhisatva's excellent conduct".

3. Dedication for the vanishing of obscuration at the time of death
4. Dedication for going on after death in accord with other shore activity

The next verse has two dedications. The first couplet is a prayer for the vanishing of obscuration at the time of death. The second couplet is a prayer for going on after death in accord with other shore activity. Other shore activity means being born in a place that is out of this shore, samsara, and belongs to the other shore, nirvana, and, while living in such a place, being only involved with activity leading to complete enlightenment.

57 When the time has come for me to die,
May all obscurations clear away;
Seeing Amitābha in direct perception,
I will utterly go to the field of Sukhāvatī.

This is saying, "When my death begins and as it unfolds, if there are any obscurations of mind that would prevent a good journey through the death process or through the intermediary state, may they clear away completely of themselves. Then, in the intermediary state, may I see buddha Amitābha with his retinue and go directly and in the best way possible to his nirmāṇakāya buddha-field called 'Sukhāvatī'".

5. Dedication for completing the possibilities of having gone to Amitabha's pure realm

The next verse continues with a prayer for the accomplishment of what can happen in general because of having gone to Sukhāvatī:

58 Having gone there, may all these prayers
without exception become manifest.
Having completely fulfilled them without exception,
I will benefit sentient beings as long as the world.

The first couplet says, "Moreover, having gone to that field of Sukhāvatī, may I actualize all of these prayers taught in this prayer of Samantabhadra". The second couplet says, "Having completely fulfilled those prayers without exception I will then benefit all sentient beings for as long as the samsaric world exists". Yeshe De explains that "for as long as the world" means "for as long as the world of sentient beings exists".

6. Dedication for actually being born in Sukhavati then gaining the prophesy for one's own buddhahood from Amitabha

The next verse continues with a prayer for actually being born in Sukhāvatī then for gaining the prophecy for one's own buddhahood from the buddha Amitābha under whom one has been training while there:

59 In that good and pleasing maṇḍala of the conqueror
    May I be born from an exceptionally beautiful fine lotus.
    Seeing conqueror Amitābha directly,
    May I also obtain the prophecy there.

"The good and pleasing maṇḍala of the conqueror" means that good and pleasing place Sukhāvatī which is the domain of the conqueror Amitābha. Thus, the first couplet is a prayer to be born in that place. There are four modes of birth: birth from a womb, birth from moisture, birth from an egg, and miraculous birth. Birth in Sukhāvatī occurs as a miraculous birth and specifically from a lotus. Descriptions of Sukhāvatī say that the lotus is made from precious substances and radiating webs of light. It is said that, on being born there, the lotus opens and one sees Amitābha directly before one. Following that, one can obtain all instructions for the path from Amitābha and his bodhisatva retinue and can practise them easily, with the result that buddhahood can be obtained there in a very short time. As one reaches and then proceeds through the bodhisatva levels, it will at the time of the eighth level be time to receive the prophecy for one's future buddhahood. At this time, Amitābha will address you and state that, "At such and such a time, in such and such a place, in such and such circumstances, you of name such and such will become the tathāgata named such and such". The second couplet concludes with a prayer for obtaining that prophecy there in Sukhāvatī.

7. Dedication for completion of activity in Sukhavati

The next verse completes the string of prayers done in relation to dying, taking rebirth into Sukhāvatī, and gaining the prophecy for future buddhahood by dedicating one's activity after the receipt of the prophesy for the sake of sentient beings:

60 Having completely obtained the prophecy there,
    I will with many emanations, thousands of millions,
    By force of rational mind, throughout the ten directions
    Do many things to benefit sentient beings.

"By force of rational mind" was also used in verse 31 on page 129 and the lengthy explanation given for it there also applies here. Rational mind here does not mean "dualistic rational mind" but the non-dualistic wisdom type of rational mind which is a feature of bodhisatvas on the levels and of buddhas. With the use of that sort of rational mind one makes precise distinctions between this and that. Thus, one will not merely send out enormous numbers of emanations indiscriminately but will send them out discriminately so that they exactly match and fulfill the needs of the beings for whom they are emanated.

The official translation of the prayer as found in all editions of *The Translated Word* ends with two more verses. However, the Indian masters Nāgārjuna, Dignāga, and Bhadravaha, and Vasubhandu do not mention these two verses, even in passing. The Indian master Śhākyamitra alone mentions and comments on both of them. This suggests that these last two verses were known in India but that most learned individuals did not accept that they were part of the prayer. Yeshe De, who I regard as the best bridge between the Indian and Tibetan versions of the prayer, indicates that the two verses were known to the Indian masters who taught him and that they, when questioned by him about whether they should be included or not, said that they were questionable, but asked that they be included anyway. As a result, the two verses given below are included in the Derge edition of the prayer. I would add here that the content of the two verses suggests that they are later additions. Why I think so would take a lot of space to explain and make this un-necessarily complicated. Suffice it to say that they could be left off the end of the prayer, but I think it better to follow the advice of the masters who were advising Yeshe De and leave them there.

8. General dedication of merit

The first of these two verses is a straightforward general dedication of all the merit gathered during the recitation of the prayer:

> 61 May the trifle of virtue accumulated by the one
> Who has recited this excellent conduct prayer
> Cause the virtues of migrators' prayers
> To be obtained by them all in an instant.

The Derge edition has "who teaches" rather than "who has recited". Most Tibetan editions, for example the one used by Tenpa'i Wangchuk have "has recited". Yeshe De's version has "has made". Nāgārjuna does not mention this verse but the version of his disciple, Śhākyamitra, clearly shows it as "has recited". I believe the Derge edition is mistaken, and should be "recite". This can easily be the case given that the Tibetan words for "show", "recite", and "make" are very similar and can easily be mistaken one for another. Therefore, I have translated it as "recited".

Note again that "this excellent conduct prayer" means "this one among many prayers of excellent conduct" and does not mean "this *Excellent Conduct Prayer*".

The verse is saying, "May the trifle of virtue accumulated by the person who has recited this prayer of excellent conduct be the cause for the various virtuous results that have been prayed for in the prayers of any given sentient being coming to pass. May that be so for all sentient beings".

9. Dedication for others to gain the place of Amitabha

The second of the two verses is again a straightforward dedication, though this time returning to the theme of Amitābha and his buddha-field being an easy place for sentient beings to go to at the time of death and an easy place in which to obtain enlightenment while staying there.

62 May whatever infinite superior merit has been gained
In wholly dedicating this excellent conduct prayer
Cause migrators drowning in the river of
    unsatisfactoriness
To utterly gain the place of Amitābha.

"Infinite superior merit" means an infinite amount of "superior merit". Superior merit was defined in the commentary to verse 9 and in the commentary on page 149. The place of Amitābha is Sukhāvatī.

The prayer ends there. The sutra then ends with its own colophons, as can be seen in the translation of the sutra earlier in the book.

May the virtue come from this painstaking effort
To establish the words and meaning of the prayer
Exposed here for those wanting to use the sutras
With uttermost confidence in their meaning

Ensure that these explanations of Samantabhadra's Prayer
Spread across the earth reaching all those who will benefit and
Become the means for all for the recitation of the Prayer and
Become the basis for correct versions to appear in all languages.

May all others obtain the same extreme joy that I have obtained
Through reading, understanding, and reciting again and again
This most marvellous and amazing Prayer of Samantabhadra;
May they fully discover its worth as a means to enlightenment.

An Explanation of Samantabhadra's Prayer By Noble Nagarjuna

Plate 2. Nāgārjuna, wall mural in Dzogchen Monastery, Tibet, 2007. Picture by the author.

Noble One, A King of Prayers of Excellent Conduct Together with Explanation
by Noble Nagarjuna

In Indian Language: āryabhadracaryā praṇidhāṇa mahārājāni bandana

In Tibetan Language: 'phags pa bzang po spyod pa'i smon lam gyi rgyal po'i shad sbyar

I prostrate to Samantabhadra.[44]

---

[44] Note that everything here from the title down to the end of the prostration to Samantabhadra has been added by the Tibetans when they translated the original manuscript from Sanskrit. The title, language indicators, and prostration all are part of the framework hat had to be added to all Tibetan translations. That has detrimental side-effects in this case because of all that it implies. For example, it suggests that there really was a prayer called "Noble One ..." and that it really had the name in Sanskrit as shown, etcetera. In fact the title is a Tibetan invention based on names in use for the prayer in India and the Sanskrit above is actually the invented Tibetan title translated back into Sanskrit. The actual text of Nāgārjuna's commentary would have had none of what is on this page but probably started with something like "Samantabhadra's Prayer with Explanation", and would have begun with the words "The meaning of ..." as seen over the page. There is an extensive explanation of the problems with the Tibetan framework in my own Thorough Explanation commentary to the prayer.

The meaning of *A King of Prayers of Excellent Conduct* can be summed up in ten topics as follows:

1. prostration to the tathāgatas
2. offering to the tathāgatas
3. laying aside evil
4. rejoicing in merit
5. urging to turn the wheel of dharma
6. requesting the tathāgatas to remain
7. whole dedication of the roots of merit
8. its divisions
9. its ending
10. its benefits

Of them, to make a prostration in general—one not specified as a prostration of body, speech, or mind—to the buddha bhagavats who are seated in the fields, and so on, of all ten directions, he[45] says: "*however many they are ...*"[46] The term "however many" literally meaning "how many" or "how much in extent", signifies the whole amount. The general term[47] "they" is a reference to the buddha bhagavats whose number is beyond assessment. Thus the phrase as a whole refers to the buddha bhagavats whose amount is beyond measure both by the phrasing just used to identify them and by their

---

[45] "He" is used extensively throughout this text to refer to Samantabhadra.

[46] Nāgārjuna is giving an oral commentary in which he says the words of the prayer then comments on them. In this translation, the words of the prayer have been marked off in bold italics and in electronic editions have additionally been given a different colour.

[47] Tib. spyi sgra. "General terms" are a part of speech defined in Sanskrit and Tibetan grammars. They are terms that make a general reference rather than a specific one, such as the pronoun they, which is general rather than specific.

actual count"⁴⁸. "*The lions of men gone in all three times*" means "the ones who will become seated as buddhas in the entirety of the three times"⁴⁹ "*in the worlds of the ten directions*" or "migrations throughout the ten directions"⁵⁰. These "lions of men" are referred to as "lions" because they are not afraid of anything and there is nothing that makes them anxious. The buddha bhagavats exhibit that quality in the worlds of gods and men. Because they are comparable to lions in those worlds, they are called "lions" in them and in addition to that they show birth as men, in which case they are men as well as lions, so are called "lions of men". He says, "*I prostrate*", that is, I utterly bow, "*to all of them*". Because of his way of expressing the first two lines, the term "all" on this line could be seen to mean a portion of them, so he adds "*without exception*" to ensure that a vast, all-inclusive approach in which not a single one

---

[48] The first phrase of the first line of the first verse is "ji snyed su dag". It could be understood in several ways so he goes to some length to explain it. The term "ji snyed" means literally "how many", and in this case means "the whole lot, as many as they are". The "su" following it is a pronoun indicating persons only, never things, so here it will be "the one" or "who". The "dag" following that makes the "su" plural, giving "the ones who" or "they". Nāgārjuna finishes by saying that the whole phrase conveys the sense "as many as they are, a number so vast that it cannot be known by conceptual mind".

[49] The second line of the verse literally says "all the lions of men gone in the three times" but the actual meaning is "the lions of men, the ones who go to buddhahood whenever they throughout the entirety of the three times". To make this as clear as possible, Nāgārjuna changes the position of the "all" in his explanation. Thus, the "all" on this line only applies to the "ones going in the three times" and does not connect with the first line which mentions them as being "in the worlds of the ten directions".

[50] In other words, "in the worlds of samsara, the worlds of the migrator sentient beings of the ten directions".

is left out[51] is indicated. He does the prostration *with* utterly ***admiring body, speech, and mind,*** where "utterly admiring" means with the greatest admiration. Mind has the greatest admiration for them and then, because body and speech are being motivated by mind, they also are showing the greatest admiration.

Now, he makes specific prostrations of body, mind, and speech. For the body prostration, he says, "***Through utterly bowing with bodies many as the field atoms …***" which means that the prostration is done by utterly bowing down bodies equal in number to the atoms of the buddha-fields. The term "many as" is a term that shows amount according to the example supplied with it and here the example shows an indefinite amount[52]. By utterly bowing bodies whose count is equal to the atoms of all the buddha-fields of the buddhas who will arrive at buddhahood in the three times somewhere in the worlds of the ten directions, "***I utterly prostrate to all the conquerors***". The buddha bhagavats are called "conquerors" because they have conquered the enemy of the afflictions and because they have conquered the māras; it is as the Bhagavat said:

> I have conquered the dharmas of evil.
> Thus, Ugata, I am a conqueror …[53]

---

[51] The second line of the Tibetan reads "all the lions of men gone in the three times". That could be restrictive. In order to indicate all of the lions of men who go in the three times and not only that but every single one of them wherever in the worlds throughout the ten directions they have gone to enlightenment, the third line says "all of them without exception".

[52] This means that the example for the amount—the atoms of the buddha-fields—is not a definitely known amount.

[53] A Brahmin named Ugata met Buddha on the road from Bodhgaya to Varanasi and asked him who he was. These two lines of verse are part of a longer reply in which the Buddha explains that he is a conqueror and what that means.

Does utterly prostrating to all those conquerors who go in the three times mean that, because mind is facing towards one bhagavat, there is utter prostration through bodies equal to just that many field atoms, a number of bodies that would be minus the other ones not being considered by mind? No. It says that the prostrations are done *"with a mind facing towards all conquerors"*[54], meaning "by a mind facing towards each one of the conquerors". Then, in *"through the forces of prayers of excellent conduct"*, excellent conduct means virtuous conduct and that virtuous conduct also being excellent conduct, there is the particular excellent conduct being referred to here of a bodhisatva's conduct. Because of aspiring to that, there is prayer in pursuit of what is meaningful. The forces of such prayers prevent being overcome by the afflictions, and so on, and definitely conquer the non-conducive side. Therefore, it says that this is done "through or by the forces of such prayers" because no other sort of thing else could successfully perform the function of turning the mind to face all conquerors then prostrate to them.[55]

Next, he makes a prostration by mind with **"On top of a single atom ..."** "On top of a single atom" means "on the top surface of a

---

[54] There is an interesting point here. The wording used in Nāgārjuna's edition of the prayer is a little different but much clearer in meaning than the wording given in all Tibetan translations. The Tibetan translation says "mngon sum du" which literally means " in direct perception". Nāgārjuna uses a similar term, which in Tibetan is "mngon phyogs" and which literally means "facing directly what lies ahead". Thus, he is explaining that the meaning here is not that mind is merely taking whichever buddha is immediately visible in front of it and manifesting bodies according to the number of field atoms involved with that one buddha's field. Rather, mind has been made to face, simultaneously, all of the buddhas wherever they are in the ten directions and three times, with the result that every single one of them is in direct view, which can also be called direct perception, of mind.

[55] This explanation is hard to follow. See the explanation of this verse in my own commentary for a clearer presentation.

single atom"[56]. "*Buddhas as many as atoms*" again is not specific, so comes out to meaning sugatas equal to the atoms of the buddha-fields of the buddhas who have arrived in the ten directions and three times being "imagined" as will be explained below. "*Seated at the centre of buddha sons*" means that each buddha individually is seated at the centre of a fathomless assembly of bodhisatvas. Exactly how are they on top of one atom? As was just said, the entirety of them without exception are there. The "*dhātu of dharmas*" refers to the nature of all dharmas, the dharmatā—that exactly is called "dhātu"[57]. That sort of dhātu of dharmas reaches to the limits of the space element, so it is mentally *imagined* in unobstructed full detail to be *filled with* the bhagavats who are individually surrounded by a fathomless assembly of bodhisatvas, all of whom are residing on top of a single atom. The actions of body and speech are motivated by mind, therefore the avenue of mind is fully shown here.

Now, he makes a prostration by speech with "*those oceans of unending commendation ...*" "Those" refers to the conquerors who

---

[56] The actual wording in Tibetan is "steng" meaning "above" or "on top of". This needs clarification, therefore he uses the word, in Tibetan "thog", that unequivocally means "on top of". Note that it has been popular amongst Western translators to say "in a single atom" but at the time this was spoken atoms were seen as solid, so there could be no description of something being inside them. The image is of the buddhas in their buddha-fields massed on the top surface of each atom.

[57] This should be understood like this: the "dharmatā" or "situation as it actually is of phenomena" is that they partake of fundamental reality. The "dhātu" or "zone or region" that is the basis for all phenomena to arise is none other than that situation as it actually is of phenomena. By definition, the zone that is the basis for all phenomena extends through every phenomenon possible and thus spreads over every possible thing. In short, the use of dharmadhātu here is equivalent to saying "everywhere possible". The only thing that knows everywhere possible is the wisdom of a buddha, which is the special mind mentioned in the next sentence.

have been clearly imagined and mentioned on the last line of the previous verse. They have an ocean[58] of commendable features, that is, an ocean of good qualities. Because the good qualities that they have do not degrade and never come to an end, the good qualities are without end, that is, unending. Note that "oceans of unending commendation" means "the ones who have unending good qualities" where the term "commendation" is understood to be a metaphor for good qualities. In "those oceans", oceans makes the plural, but all together this line is saying "to those conquerors, each one of whom is an ocean" meaning an unending amount "of commendable features" meaning good qualities.

"Using all sounds of the ocean of aspects of the voice". The term "aspects" here also stands for good qualities. What are the good qualities like in this case? In the Shrāvaka Vehicle they are said have five branches and in the Great Vehicle they are said to have sixty, ten thousand, and also fathomless branches. Because in that way they are understood to "have five branches", and so on, the line here comes to mean "using all of the sounds contained in what is a fathomless ocean of branches of voice".

The good qualities of all the conquerors—meaning the uncommon and un-assessable[59] properties of body, speech, and mind that the conquerors have had from the time they first properly aroused the

---

[58] An important note is that "ocean", which is used many times in the prayer, is glossed in Sanskrit poetry as meaning "unending" or "inexhaustible". Ocean is nearly always in the singular in the original prayer precisely because it is nearly always referring to an ocean (in the singular) as something which is unending. Nevertheless, Western translators not understanding this point have usually made "ocean" into the plural "oceans" which destroys the intended meaning.

[59] "Un-assessable" here is similar to "unfathomable". Whereas unfathomable conveys the sense of being too great to penetrate conceptually, un-assessable means that they cannot be evaluated with a conceptual mind and is very similar to "immeasurable".

enlightenment mind—are **utterly expressed**, that is, they are presented and extolled to the greatest degree possible using verbal expressions. **And I** will, as though I have gone before and am present in front of each of the sugatas or ones gone to bliss, individually, **praise all of the ones gone to bliss**. Alternatively, the sugatas, that is, the ones gone to bliss referred to on this last line, can be understood to be the unending oceans of commendable good qualities referred to on the first line in which case the prayer in this verse is about utterly expressing the good qualities of the sugatas *through* which they are praised.

───── ◆◆◆ ─────

Now, he speaks of making the two types of offering—surpassed and unsurpassed—to those buddha bhagavats. The two verses beginning **"I will make offerings to those conquerors ..."** are the surpassed offering. The finest things mentioned in these lines are those finest flowers then finest garlands, finest small cymbals, finest unguents such as made with saffron, sandalwood, and so on, finest supreme parasols, supreme oil lamps, finest incense, finest clothes, finest scents, and heaps of aromatic substances made not of one but of various powders—Sandalwood, Saffron, Camphor, Aloe, and so on—all nicely combined and prepared and equal in size to Mt. Meru. **"And all with the best of excellent displays"** means that they are arranged in the best display possible. This term "display" refers to a group of things assembled together. Thus, this assembly of the best of all the divine substances of gods and men will be offered to all of the conquerors.

He speaks also of the unsurpassed offering with **"the offerings which are unsurpassed, vaster ..."** The offerings which are created by the power of a bodhisatva's samādhi or concentration are unsurpassed and are sent into all the buddha-fields, reaching through to the end of the dhātu of dharmas, so are vaster. I strongly think of **those for all the conquerors**.

"**By the forces of faith in excellent conduct**" is that, by the forces of strongly thinking of and greatly trusting in and having great certainty in it, one thinks to perform what of many names is here referred to as excellent conduct, but which means the various types of offerings such as a bodhisatva's love[60].

Now, he sums up the prostrations and offerings that he has already expressed by saying "***I will prostrate and offer to all the conquerors***".

———— ♦♦♦ ————

He speaks of laying aside evil in terms of three aspects—motivation, place, and specific nature—with "***Under the influence of desire, anger ...***" What is the motivating cause of evil? It happens under the influence of *desire, anger, and delusion*. Where does it take place? And it takes place in the places *body, speech, and mind*. Its specific nature is "***the evils I have done whichever they might be***" which is the evils I have done, have caused to be done, and have rejoiced in the doing of, either in this or former births. *I* will, as though actually present before the conquerors together with their sons, while having as little even as an instant of regret, ***individually lay aside*** and remove ***all of them***.

———— ♦♦♦ ————

---

[60] Apart from the general usage of "excellent conduct" meaning good conduct of some kind, the Buddha also used the term to indicate the specific aspect of excellent conduct called unsurpassed offering. With that, the Buddha explained "unsurpassed offering" in a number of places to refer not only to unsurpassed offering as defined in the first line of this verse but to various aspects of the bodhisatva's behaviour such as the offerings of the practices of arousing enlightenment mind, sending love to all sentient beings, and so on.

Now, for rejoicing in merits, he says, "*I rejoice in all merits whoever has them ...*" There are the merits of *migrators* that have come from generosity, discipline, and meditation in the three times. There are the beyond worldly merits of the three times of those of the set of seven persons *in training* and of the arhats, the ones *not in training*. There are the beyond worldly merits of the two types of *pratyekas*—the rhinoceros-like ones and the ones who practise in a group. There is the accumulation of merit of all *the bodhisatvas*, the ones who have fully embraced the bodhisatva path by having initially aroused the mind[61] properly. There are the merits of those who are understood through the term used in the verse, "*conquerors of the ten directions*", to be the buddha bhagavats who have gone in the three times. The buddha bhagavats fully embraced the path after arousing the mind of enlightenment to produce worldly and beyond worldly merit collections that, un-assessable and inconceivable, are known only to buddha wisdom. The buddha bhagavats' merit collections were produced through gaining certainty in each of the pāramitās, levels, and so on, then completed at some time in the three times. Thus I rejoice in all of the merits there are, such as the ones of those beings just mentioned.

Someone might ask, "Because the term 'migrators' is a term that covers all beings, the merits of those in training, those not in training, and so on are already included within the use of that term in the verse, so what purpose is there in separately listing the merits of each type of being?" The answer is that your reasoning is faulty given that "migrator" means a being who migrates about and so has rebirths in samsara. Someone else might counter that by saying that the term "migrator", because it does not strongly convey the meaning "migration", must be intended as an inclusive term. However, that is in turn countered by pointing out that the term "migrator"

---

[61] "Arouse the mind" is the standard term used in the sutras to mean arousing the enlightenment mind, that is, bodhicitta.

never expresses the meaning "not migrating". Therefore, "migrator" does indicate a separate item.[62]

— ♦♦♦ —

Now, for urging to turn the wheel of dharma, he says ***"Ones who are lamps of the worlds of the ten directions ..."*** *The lamps* for migrators *in the worlds of the ten directions* refers to the buddha bhagavats for they are what dispels the masses of outer and inner darkness of the worlds, so they are the lamps of the worlds. ***"Have become buddhas at the enlightenment stage"***[63] means that they have become manifest buddhas at the level or stage of unsurpassed truly complete enlightenment. ***"And gained the undefiled state"*** means that they have gained the situation of not being able to be defiled—manifest truly complete enlightenment is such that the nature of everything without exception is wholly known, therefore, manifest enlightenment is true transcendence over all defilement[64]. This is hard for the

---

[62] "All migrators" on the last line could be seen as a summary of all the other types of beings with merit listed in the verse. This is a distinct possibility in the Sanskrit and Tibetan syntax wording of the verse whereas it is not an issue with the English wording. At any rate, Nāgārjuna shows that it would be wrong to take it that way because, regardless of how the wording appears, migrators only ever refers to samsaric beings and hence could not refer to all the other beings listed in the verse, for example the buddhas.

[63] A complete explanation of "become buddhas at the enlightenment stage" appears in my own commentary on page 90.

[64] "Undefiled" translates the Tibetan phrase "chags pa med pa", which is commonly used to describe the nature of the wisdom mind of truly complete enlightenment. It most literally means "incapable of being affected by samsaric defilement that would obscure its all-knowing quality".

The word "chags pa" has two main meanings, one of which is "attachment". Because of that, it has been common for Tibetan

(continued ...)

other ones who do not find meaning in and do not diligently work at manifesting the realization of profound dharma to realize, so, having been shown dharma, these ones who went on to obtain buddhahood let go of all complications, went to the foot of a supreme bodhi tree in one of the various world realms, and stayed there. *I*, for the purpose of having all those guardians of the world turn the wheel of unsurpassed dharma in order to remove the darkness of migrators' not-knowing and to illuminate unsurpassed wisdom, put my knee to the ground and join the palms of my hands[65] and, as though in front of each one of them individually, ***urge all of those guardians to turn the unsurpassed wheel*** of dharma.

---

[64](... continued)
scholars to take "chags pa" to mean "attachment" in this case. However, that is a mistake; the other meanings of the word—"to happen" and "to break"—apply here, with the negative form "chags pa med pa" coming to mean "lacking all capacity to be adversely affected". Nāgārjuna explains this himself in his commentary to a later verse where this phrase is used again, saying that this phrase means that the all-knowing mind of enlightenment cannot be harmed, degraded, defiled, or otherwise affected by samsaric factors such as the afflictions.

The example used to explain this phrase is that of the lotus flower, which is widespread in Northern India. A lotus starts off in the mud of foul water such as in a swamp. It grows not to the surface level of the water but up above the water and, in doing so, reaches a place beyond the possibility of being affected by the foul water. That is exactly the image intended with a buddha's wisdom and the defilements of samsaric mind. So, although the literal meaning is "unaffected", it comes to mean "undefiled", "without defilement" and that is how it has been translated here.

[65] This is the standard way to make a supplication to another person in the original ways of Buddhism.

Now, there is a supplication with "*I also will supplicate with palms joined together those who have asserted they will show nirvana ...*" "Those who" is non-specific[66] but, because of the context, it obviously connects to "the lamps of the worlds of the ten directions". *I will supplicate*, that is, offer a petition to, the buddha bhagavats of the ten directions who show nirvana, that is, all of *those* ones *who have asserted they will show nirvana,*[67] in order to have them stay present for a long time. For how long? I request them *to stay for aeons as many as the field atoms*, that is, for aeons equal to the atoms of all the fields of the buddhas who become realized in the three times. For what purpose? "*In order to bring benefit and ease to all migrators*", migrators who would otherwise be without guardian. Benefit here refers to migrators gaining ongoing good circumstances[68] and ease refers to their gaining the path to nirvana. Ease refers to gaining a level of behaviour counted as divine.

◆◆◆

Now, wholly dedicating the un-assessable heap of merit which has been created through the prostrations, and so on, that have been expressed so far is done with "*I dedicate ...*" I will *dedicate every trifle of virtue that I have accumulated*, that is, accomplished, *in prostrating, offering, laying aside* evil, *rejoicing* in merits, *urging*

---

[66] This "who" can be understood in two ways. It can either mean "the guardian buddhas who in general assert that they will show passage into nirvana" or it can mean "the guardian buddhas who were just mentioned and who assert ..." Nāgārjuna explains that it means the latter.

[67] In general, all buddhas show nirvana because it is the twelfth of the twelve deeds shown by buddhas. However, not all of them do that, so he re-phrases his words to indicate only the ones who have actually asserted that they will show nirvana.

[68] ... within samsara, such as a birth in the upper realms, freedom from illness, and so on, with that.

to turn the wheel of dharma, **and supplicating** the tathāgatas *for the purpose of* unsurpassed truly complete **enlightenment**.

———— ♦♦♦ ————

That was the first seven topics, now for the eighth topic, its divisions. This topic contains the main part of Samantabhadra's excellent conduct prayer, which is divided into these sixteen branches or divisions:

1. thought[69]
2. not forgetting enlightenment mind
3. connecting with being uncloaked
4. benefiting sentient beings
5. armour
6. connecting with bodhisatvas of same lot
7. acting to please virtuous friends
8. having manifested tathāgata-hood
9. wholly holding the holy dharma
10. gaining an unending store
11. entering
12. forces
13. accomplishing
14. activities
15. delineation of training following
16. conclusion

Division 1: is from the perspective of thought. This has three parts. The thought of offering to the tathāgatas and of their fully completing their understanding is *"**May I offer to past buddhas ...**" May I offer* with unsurpassed offerings *to the buddha* bhagavats who have already shown nirvana *and* may I likewise offer to *the ones* who,

---

[69] "Thought" here means to think about something in a particular way, so can also be translated as "intention". What it really means is one's mental approach to something.

alive and presently *seated*, are undertaking the task of accomplishing benefit and ease for the entirety of migrators *in the* many *world* realms *of the ten directions*. Then, *those* ones *whoever* you are who will be buddhas but *have not* yet *descended* will do so. Therefore, you must, *most quickly*, without delay, *complete your intentions and descend as buddhas at the enlightenment stage!*[70] The earlier half of this verse shows the thought to offer to the tathāgatas and the latter half shows the thought to fully complete the understanding.[71]

The thought for wholly purifying buddha-fields is what he expresses with "*May the fields which are in the ten directions ...*" *May the fields*, meaning buddha-fields, *which are*, meaning which exist, *in the ten directions however many they are*, may all of those becomings *be wholly pure throughout their extent* like Sukhāvatī. And, *may* each one of all of the abodes of the fathomless world realms become vast in area and may *they be utterly*, that is, pervasively and with no room left, *filled with conquerors*, that is, bhagavats who have *gone before the leading bodhi tree and with buddha sons*, that is, bodhisatvas.[72]

---

[70] He has explained previously that "buddhahood at the enlightenment stage" means buddhahood at the highest stage, at the stage of unsurpassed, truly complete enlightenment. A complete explanation of "become buddhas at the enlightenment stage" appears in my own commentary on page 90.

[71] The sentence in the second half of the verse is written in the imperative tense. The way to understand it is that we are included in all the ones who will descend, therefore it is saying, "We together with all the others who have not yet done so will complete our aims and intentions and become buddhas!"

[72] There is no "and" joining the two couplets of this verse, but Nāgārjuna's commentary shows that they are not two separate sentences. In other words, the two ideas expressed here go together. Tenpa'i Wangchuk clearly explains it in his commentary in volume II.

The special intention[73] of ease for all sentient beings is what he says with *"May the sentient beings ..."* *May the sentient beings of* the six classes of migrators contained in the four birthplaces in *the ten directions however many* there are, *always*, that is, perpetually, *be free of sickness* of body and mind *and* may they *have* the *ease* which, not degenerating, is the supreme ease. *May all migrators objectives of* spiritual *dharma be with harmony*, that is, be accomplished in an atmosphere of harmony, *and* may *their hopes* in regard to spiritual development *also* always *be accomplished*, that is, be fully completed.

Division 2: Now, taking the approach of highlighting the non-conducive side to be abandoned, he speaks four verses which comprise the second division, not forgetting the enlightenment mind. These verses start at *"When*[74] *I perform the conducts of enlightenment"* and go down to *"without exception totally cleansed"*.

"Enlightenment" is unsurpassed truly complete enlightenment and conduct done for that purpose is the conduct of enlightenment. *When I am doing the conducts of enlightenment may I remember my births in all migrations*. Likewise, *in all successive lives*, having gone through *death transfer and birth, may I become ordained*. The phrase "death transfer and birth" refers to the divide between lives. This is the first cause of the enlightenment mind not degenerating.[75]

---

[73] For special intention, see the glossary.

[74] Nāgārjuna's edition of the prayer clearly has "when", which is different from the edition used for the official translation into Tibetan. However, it does help to understand the sense of the first line.

[75] Note that he explains death with its transferrence as one item and birth as a second. Tibetans later explained it as death, transference, and birth as three items as can be seen in Tenpa'i Wangchuk's commentary in volume II.

Then, *"May I train following all the conquerors ..."* is a prayer to the following effect. **May I train** by *following* the trainings of *all* without exception of *the conquerors* gone in the three times, *working to wholly complete the excellent conduct and*, in order to truly accomplish that, *doing the stainless, totally pure discipline conduct in a way that is always uncorrupted and faultless*.

The discipline conduct being stainless is like a wish-fulfilling gem not possessing surface stains and its being totally pure is like being pure by nature because of being free of wrongdoings of the body. Therefore, it is to be done in an uncorrupted and faultless[76] manner.

Moreover, when done in that manner, it becomes something that fulfils all desires, dispels suffering, frees from all illness, utterly alleviates untimely death, and engages only in the accomplishment of others' sakes. Thus, the discipline of bodhisatvas is comparable to a gem. This gem, because of not being encrusted with the adventitious stains of karma and affliction is stainless and because of being free of the body fault of arousing the mind of the vehicles of the śhrāvakas and pratyekabuddhas—and because, that not being there, there is the arousing of mind of the knowledge of all superficies[77] whose nature is that of a gem—it is totally pure in all respects.

Again, out of respect for the bodhisatva's trainings, there will no doing of downfalls, therefore, the training is "uncorrupted". And, because there will not be even the slightest unhappiness caused by the process of craving as it happens through the three times—craving arises in a past life due to the experiencing of an object, then

---

[76] "Uncorrupted" fits with its being "stainless", meaning not having surface imperfections, and "faultless" fits with its being "totally pure", meaning having a nature which is free of faulty actions.

[77] "The arousing of mind of all superficies" is the arousing of the fictional enlightenment mind (see the glossary). For superficies, see the glossary.

there is strong liking for it again in a future life, and now there is the craving of strong clinging to it in this life—it is "faultless".

Again, because it becomes the basis of, like the ground for, all the buddhas and bodhisatvas' good qualities and because it totally fulfils all the wishes of migrators, it dispels all suffering and dispels all sickness, and accomplishes fathomless lives as gods and men, and only results in engagement in the accomplishment of others' sakes.

The etymological definition of "discipline" is that it is "śhīla", meaning "cooling", because it functions to dispel all sufferings of body and mind. Thus, "discipline conduct" is to conduct oneself within the disciplines and because it involves the conduct of them, it is called conduct.[78]

This, "May I always perform that kind of stainless, totally pure, discipline conduct, uncorrupted and faultless for as long as I have not reached enlightenment" is the second cause for not forgetting enlightenment mind.

"I will teach dharma in all languages ... in all migrators' languages many as there are". The spoken languages of the gods, nāgas, yakṣhas, kumbhāṇḍas, and humans are mentioned. In short, this is saying "I will teach the holy dharma to each type of being in each one's own language until each being individually has reached enlightenment", which is the third cause of not forgetting enlightenment mind.

In *"Gentled ..."*, "gentled" specifically means a gentled mindstream. *"I'll be most diligent at the pāramitās"* means to adhere tightly to

---

[78] The Sanskrit term for this is śhīla, meaning that which cools. The official Tibetan translation of it, tshul khrims, means a code of conduct in accord with the natural order of things. The English term generally used for this, discipline, means a code within which one trains oneself with the idea that it will be beneficial.

the ten pāramitās of generosity, and so on, by all means and at all times, without becoming weary of it. ***I will*** not ever, that is, ***never, forget*** the ***enlightenment mind*** until reaching the heart of enlightenment. This is the fourth cause.

With those three and a half verses he has shown the antidote to the obscurations that become the side not conducive to enlightenment mind. Now, with a half verse he shows the not conducive side to be abandoned, saying, "***May the evils*** which have ***become obscurations*** that create obstacles for enlightenment mind all of them ***without exception, be totally cleansed***, that is abandoned, by me".

Division 3: Now, for the third one, connecting with being uncloaked, he takes a "from where, in where, and like what"[79] approach, saying, "***May I be free of karma, affliction, and māra's works ...***" The type of karma has not been specified, so it could be taken as any of the three types of karma—virtuous, non-virtuous, and unfluctuating—but it refers to non-virtuous karma. Being free of non-virtuous karma, affliction, and māra's works, you perpetually live your lives ***as*** one of the ***migrators of the worlds*** but while having conduct that is not cloaked by those things. What would that be comparable to? ***Conduct which is like the way a lotus is unaffected by water*** gives the example of the lotus which, having completed its growth is not dirtied by the water. You will act without your conduct being cloaked by the worldly dharmas of karma, affliction, the works of māra, and so on. Similarly, you will also act without being defiled by virtuous and unfluctuating karmas, that is, independent of karmic result. You will act in that way only for the sake of producing benefit for the entirety of migrators, which is a central

---

[79] The three things in this list sum up the threefold structure of this verse. Where the absence of cloaking will come from is given in the first line, where the bodhisatva will do the excellent conduct without the cloaking is given in the second line, and examples of what that conduct would be like are given in the third and fourth lines.

issue of "the bodhisatva's way"[80]. And to what could that be compared? It would be to act unhindered *"like the sun and moon are unhindered in the sky"*. This is the example of the sun and moon that have—as with a wish-fulfilling gem—entered the world only to work for others' sakes and that, therefore, move through the sky day and night unaffected by the subtlest concern for their own sakes; You too will conduct yourself like that.

"Māra" here, given that it makes obstacles for virtue and works as an obstructor of enlightenment, functions to turn you away from the holy path meaning the dharma path. Because māra stops the life of dharma, it is a killer, which is why it is named "māra"[81]. The activities of dharma are causes that lead to beneficial circumstances, so dharma sends you in a positive direction, whereas the works of māra are causes that take you in a direction away from beneficial circumstances.

Division 4: The fourth one, working to benefit others, which is the point of every arousing the mind as found in this and other verses, is what he says with *"For as much as the area of a field and directions, I'll utterly pacify the suffering of all the three types of bad migrations…"* Why does this speak of pacifying only the suffering of the bad migrations? They have been picked out above all others because they create extreme torment, but this should be understood

---

[80] He is saying that it is an essential part of the bodhisatva way that one rids oneself of the obscuring factors. However, rather than doing that as part of finding a place of personal peace, one does it while staying in the worlds as a migrator yet not being affected by the obscuring factors. This point is also clearly explained in Tenpa'i Wangchuk's commentary and my own commentary. This corresponds exactly to the English adage "In the world but not of the world".

[81] The Sanskrit term "māra" means to kill or cause death; it is the root of the English word "murder". Most succinctly stated, the māras are literally the kiss of death and, in Buddhist terms, they are those various negative factors that cause your spiritual path literally to be killed.

to mean "pacifying all the sufferings of samsara". ***Then***, he says, *"**set all migrators in the best of happinesses**"*. Why do that? *I will perform conduct* in order to *benefit all migrators* without weariness and without any other aim, for the purpose of causing them to gain unsurpassed wisdom. "Will perform conduct" means "will exert myself at". For how long in time will one do that? *For as much as the area of a field and directions* where "as much as" comes to mean "how long" and "area of a field" is an ornament[82] indicating to run as fast as possible through the area of a buddha-field however far that might be, which in this case comes down to what it would take to pass through such a field. "Directions" connects with the idea of conducting oneself in the ten directions of such a field for as long as that takes.

Division 5: The fifth one is armour, which has three aspects: working to complete the buddha qualities; undertaking doing that in harmony with sentient beings' conduct; and utterly giving the holy dharma. In the line *"**I will work at completing enlightenment conduct**"*, enlightenment conduct is conduct done for the purpose of enlightenment, so to work at completing it has the same meaning as working to accomplish the buddha dharmas. And then, having known the mentality of or mental *conduct of sentient beings* in each of their births, if I can naturally—for no ulterior reason—befriend them, they will be happy because of which *I will* be able to *enter* being with them in a way that is *in harmony with* their ways. And then, in "*and utterly teach the excellent conducts*", excellent conduct is understood as teaching the dharma. Teaching because someone has asked you to do so is one aspect of the "excellent conduct", so it is to be done. This verse concludes by saying "***May I do that***

---

[82] In Sanskrit and Tibetan languages grammatically speaking, "ornaments" has two meanings: it is the name for a particular part of speech and it is also the name for a group of poetic devices. Nāgārjuna says that the phrase used here is a case of a particular ornament used in poetry and then explains it.

throughout all future aeons" to their farthest limit, doing it with a mind that never wearies of doing so.

Division 6: The sixth one, concerns having the company of bodhisatvas of the same lot[83]. *May I always be accompanied by those* bodhisatvas *whose conduct* is equal to my own, meaning whose conduct *matches my own* in whatever I do. May I always be accompanied by them, that is, be in their company, means "may I stay together with them until reaching enlightenment, however long that takes". *Moreover, through body, speech, and mind I will,* together with them, *perform the same* bodhisatva *conducts and* the same *prayer*, that is, I will remain as one who is not one of the totally afflicted[84].

---

[83] Tib. skal mnyam. "Same lot" is a technical term defined in the Abhidharma teachings. It is explained to mean those beings who have the same or similar karmic lot. It can be used more generally and more specifically. For example, it can be used to mean beings born in the same migration in samsara and can be used to mean beings not only of the same samsaric migration but also birthplace, circumstances, views, and ways. Here it means to find the company of other bodhisatvas who are human and inhabit the same area and have the same language and other circumstances of life. In other words, it means other bodhisatvas with whom one can easily stay and do the work of treading the bodhisatva's path because of having a karmic situation very similar to theirs.

The term could also be translated as "equal fortune" which would mean equal karmic situation, not equal good fortune. If translated that way, it leads to thinking that the prayer here is saying to find other bodhisatvas whose good fortune is equal to one's own, but that is not the meaning intended.

[84] "Total affliction" refers to the samsaric side of existence and "complete purification" refers to the nirvanic side. Those who are totally afflicted are the ordinary beings in samsara doing their ordinary things under the constant influence of affliction.

Division 7: The seventh one is a prayer made from the perspective of pleasing spiritual friends by accomplishing the teachings they have provided due to their thoughts of benefiting others. The ***companions who wish to benefit me*** means those companions who, because of their role of benefiting others by teaching the dharma, are ***the ones utterly teach the excellent conduct. May I always be*** together ***with them!*** That is, may I always stay close by them. Moreover, ***I will never***—not even sometimes—***displease them!*** I must not cause them the slightest annoyance, but instead, until I have become enlightened, however long that is, must steadily remain in harmony with them.

Division 8: The eighth one is making the tathāgatas visible and making offerings for a long time without wearying of the task. *"**I will always view the conquerors in direct perception, the guardians, buddhas surrounded by their sons.**"* The conqueror buddha bhagavats in all ten directions are called "guardians" because they only act as supporting kinsmen to the migrators. They are totally surrounded by assemblies of bodhisatvas[85]. With unobstructed vision of the eye ***I will always view them in direct perception***, where "direct perception" means that they will actually be visible in front of me as viewed with the eyes. And, ***I will also*** in each individual instant ***make vast offerings to them*** of the best of all things. These offerings will be as vast meaning as extensive as space—they will pervade the entire dharmadhātu. And for how long a time would I do that? *"**In all future aeons without wearying**"*, that is, I will do it tirelessly throughout all future aeons to their farthest limit.

Division 9: The ninth one is holding the holy dharma of the conquerors, that is, the ones who totally hold the holy dharmas through the activities of holding and teaching it. *"**Holding the holy**

---

[85] His point in explaining it this way is that the prayer could be read to mean that "conqueror" refers to the buddhas and their surrounding bodhisatvas or could refer to the buddhas alone. He carefully indicates that it is the latter.

dharma of the conquerors" means that, using the force of retention[86], I will be holding—truly[87] holding—the dharma taught by all the conquerors of the three times as contained in the twelve branches of the excellent speech[88]. *And* I will by way of teaching dharma be truly explaining it, which is what *fully illuminating enlightenment conduct* for migrators means. Here "enlightenment conduct" is a noun phrase[89]. *I will completely purify the excellent conduct"*, where the excellent conduct is the bodhisatva's conduct and completely purifying it is removing all imperfections from it so that it is perfect. *And moreover I will do* or will exert myself at *that in all future aeons* without any exception, that is, for a long time.

Division 10: The tenth one is acquiring merit and wisdom, and so on and thereby gaining an unending store of them. *"May I in re-entering"* or in being reborn again and again for the sake of all sentient beings in *all* the desire realm and other *becomings acquire unending merits and wisdoms*, that is, come to possess merits and wisdoms that could not come to an end. Similarly, *May I become an unending store of method*, and *prajñā*, and *samādhis* such as the Space Store, Stainless Light, and so on, and similarly *complete emancipations* such as Great Compassion, Stainless, Illusory, and so on, *and* due to that *all* of the bodhisatva's common and uncommon *good qualities*. This is saying, "May I, for the purpose of creating benefit and ease for all migrators, become a basis of good qualities that could not come to an end.

---

[86] "Force of retention" means the ability to retain in mind without forgetting.

[87] "Truly" here means actually and correctly and with effort, all three.

[88] When Śhākyamuni Buddha's words were recorded for posterity, the sutra teachings were put into the three categories of Vinaya, Sutra, and Abhidharma, and were also divided into a set of twelve categories. The twelve categories are listed in the *Illuminator Tibetan-English Dictionary*.

[89] He has to make this observation in order to prevent someone taking this to be a verb phrase as in "doing the conduct of enlightenment".

Division 11: The eleventh one, entering, has eight parts:
- entering into viewing the buddha-fields—two types
- entering into the buddha speech
- entering into turning the wheel of dharma of the tathāgatas
- entering into entering aeons
- entering into viewing the tathāgatas
- entering into their domain
- entering into producing a manifest buddha-field
- entering into going before the tathāgatas

• **Entering into viewing the buddha-fields—two types** is what he says in two verses starting with "*On one atom fields as many as there are atoms …*"

On top of *a single atom* itself are buddha-*fields* equal in number to *the atoms* of the fields of those who reach buddhahood in the ten directions and the three times, *and* what is *in those fields* is *inconceivable*, that is, could not be conceived of, is beyond the range of concept. In those fields are *buddha* bhagavat*s* who are *seated at the centre of buddha sons*, where "buddha sons" means bodhisatvas. Those ones seated there should now be connected with "*will view them*" and with "*performing enlightenment conduct*", meaning accomplishing the conduct of enlightenment, understood to come after that. Here, "will view" means "will engage in viewing".[90]

---

[90] The fourth line is written in a way that is unexpected—it literally says "performing enlightenment conduct, I will view them". What it means is that one first engages in being able to view them actually in person as described in the first three lines and then, whilst viewing them, one gets on with engaging in enlightenment conduct. Note the point that "to view" here actually means "to enter those fields and be there in person". In other words, this is not merely about viewing a field conceptually as most of us would be limited to, but about actually entering those fields, countless numbers of them, all at once with one's wisdom mind, as
(continued …)

If that sort of thing were impossible, it would mean that the result sought by such a prayer would not exist and hence that bodhisatvas would not make such a prayer. Here is another way to say the same thing. You might say, "If it is not possible for me to see a single buddha-field together with the entirety of its individual details on top of each single atom, how could I make the prayer 'May I see on top of a single atom separate buddha-fields equal to the atoms of the fields of the buddhas who will have arrived in the three times, buddha-fields filled with buddha bhagavats—bhagavats who, compared to the first case are beyond count—seated at the centre of their retinue of bodhisatvas?'" The answer is that that is not the right reasoning for this. The reasoning to be used here is that, just as there are the various world realms manifested by inconceivable karmas in the different places above, below, and straight ahead, why could there not be inconceivable wisdom manifestations on top even of a single atom? This has been expressed with:

> It is inconceivable but
> Why do experts in the levels
> Have not the slightest amazement
> Over it, when they are amazed at
> Concepts produced by the faculties[91]?
> The guardians of the world who protect it
> Taught this as the four inconceivable things

---

[90](... continued)
Samantabhadra was able to do, and then practising enlightenment conduct in their actual presence.

[91] These are the ideas that something is there when in fact there is not, for example, the belief that the illusions of a conjurer are there when in fact they are not. The verse sarcastically points out that so-called experts in the details of the bodhisatva levels show amazement at the illusions made by a conjuror, trickery which in fact is minor, worldly ability, yet show no amazement at the truly inconceivable things being discussed in this verse.

Of the nāgas with their mode of karmic states of
    absorption[92] and
Of the greater beings, the buddhas.

Therefore, what is being spoken of here is not impossible, but those who are incapable of making such transformations with their rational minds need to have real faith, thinking "All of these things spoken of by the buddha are exactly as he has said". This has been made extremely clear in these words:

Those who develop some doubt over
Hidden things[93] spoken of by the buddha
Should have trust that this sort of thing
Really does happen within emptiness.

In the world even, there is the specific case of seeing the whole sky adorned with planets, stars, constellations, and so on, within an exceptionally small container filled with pure water. Because of that the bhagavat said:

Dharmas are analogous to reflections,
Having the character of floaters and dreams,
They are comparable to illusions and mirages,
And are like gandharva's cities.

There is another verse later in this prayer which says "whatever arrangements of fields of the three times" which serves to clarify the verse here.

---

[92] Nāgas can make things appear in the human realm by the power of their concentrated states of mental absorption produced within samsara. The buddhas have utterly perfected all types of absorption, worldly and transcendent, so what they can manifest is amazing.

[93] Hidden means those things which cannot be directly known by ordinary sense consciousnesses because they are too subtle for it—bacteria and atoms are two examples of things that cannot directly be perceived by eye consciousness. A buddha has direct knowledge of even these hidden things because a buddha's wisdom directly knows all phenomena.

"*Like that*" means "like the way mentioned in the previous verse that there are on one atom fields as many as there are atoms, and so on". *So too in all directions without exception* means "in the entirety of the directions, none left out". In "*On the breadth of merely a hair*", "breadth of a hair" means on a hair. This is what it is saying, "In the space of a mere strand of hair, *there is an ocean of buddhas* as *many as their measure in the three times*, that is, the buddhas included within the three times, and *an ocean of* their *fields*, and *for an ocean of aeons, doing the conduct* meaning 'continuously doing the conduct', *I will be utterly entering them*".

• **Entering into the buddhas' speech** is what he says with "*Through the ocean of branches of sound in one speech …*" The sounds that come from the ocean of voices comprising the speech of one tathāgata when he is teaching dharma are such that, from the perspective of the listener, a single sound only will, due to the specific orientations of the countless beings who are listening, appear differently, as one or another words and letters for one another of the migrators. In exactly the same way, for all the conquerors seated in the ten directions and three times who are teaching dharma, because of *the completely purity of* their *branches of voice*, there are for all of the fathomless migrators who are listening, *voices exactly in accord with* their *thoughts, the buddha speech* itself that has come forth in that particular way. *I will* in the same way as them enter it by hearing it with my ears; I will enter *the* *ocean of branches of sounds of the speech of a single* tathāgata[94]. That has also been said like this:

> When the manifold retinue of
> Ones having various aims
> Is taught with one instance of speech,
> It is heard in many different ways,
> With all the beings believing that
> "This was spoken for me".
> What is more wondrous than this?
> What is more amazing than this?

Similarly, it is as said in Maitreya's story in the *Noble Gaṇḍavyūha*:

> This is a topic for those who, even though they have remained in the supreme vehicle without being stupid about it and have done so for many hundreds of thousands of millions of aeons, because of having a mind which is still not satisfied, work to become consistent with the cloud of dharma of the tathāgatas of the ten directions.[95]

---

[94] In this verse, "enter" means that one will engage in listening to the buddha speech of amazing qualities; it does not mean that one will engage in becoming a speaker of it. The verse is saying that the infinite sounds that can come forth as the speech of a single buddha when he is speaking are fully representative of the infinite sounds that can come forth as the speech of the infinite conquerors. Therefore, by engaging in listening to the speech of a single buddha, one will engage in listening to the buddha speech in general. This is explained in further detail in my own commentary.

[95] In other words, the speech of the buddha is an amazingly profound topic, so much so that even those who have been intelligently learning the buddhas' teachings for cosmic lengths of time still have to work at fully comprehending it. The original sutra can be read in PKTC's publication *Maitreya's Sutras and Prayer with Commentary by Padma Karpo*, by Tony Duff.

The previous two verses were primarily about being a great type of listener and the subsequent two verses are primarily about being a great type of explainer.

Some people say that it should be:

> The ocean of branches of sound contained in one speech—
> The completely pure branches of the voices of all conquerors ...

asserting that the ending should be a sevenfold singular term which they view as a padding term "ste".[96]

• **Entering into turning the wheel of dharma** is what he says with "*The conquerors of the three times ... wheel ... of ...*" There is a genitive case marker at the end of the second line, followed immediately by "they" on the third line followed immediately by a genitive

---

[96] The first line of the couplet in all editions that I have seen have the Tibetan indicator of an agent "kyis" as the ending, which means "by way of". However, some people say that it should be what is called in Tibetan grammar the la-equivalent "la", which has seven variants and a number of possible meanings. One of the possible meanings is the same as the phrase linker "ste" in its specific function as what is called a boundary marker that is doing no more than filling in the number of words needed on the line. What that means can be understood from the English shown here.

This verse is not easy to understand, hence his comment. The point is that the first line mentions the speech of a single tathāgata as a subset of the speech of all the buddhas. Hence the second line follows, and all of them, whether a single tathāgata or all of the tathāgatas have a speech with the amazing qualities shown on the third line. That is the buddha speech, whether known through one or all tathāgatas. I will get involved with the buddha speech by listening to the speech of any given tathāgata who I happen to be with.

case marker⁹⁷ making the "they" into "their"⁹⁸. What does the first genitive case marker mean? It should be understood to add to the end of the first line to connect ***All the conquerors gone in the three times'*** to ***utter turning of the modes of the*** dharma ***wheel*** on the second line. The "their" on the third line refers to the conquerors mentioned on the first line, giving ***and also***⁹⁹ ***their unending***, beyond ending, ***voices of speech*** that come together with their acts of utterly turning the modes of the dharma wheel. Those, ***I too will*** enter suddenly ***"by the force of rational mind***"—meaning a great type of knowing¹⁰⁰— and so ***utterly enter*** them.

"Modes" here is viewed as referring to the ways used to tame sentient beings with their various inclinations—which methods will be

---

⁹⁷ This is the explanation of a the Tibetan words "de dag gi yang" on the third line of the Tibetan verse, which can be difficult to understand. The "de dag" meaning "they" or "those" refers to all the conquerors mentioned on the first line of the verse and the "gi" is a genitive case marker making the "they" or "those" into "their".

⁹⁸ The second line ends in Tibetan "yi" in the Derge edition and Tibetan "kyi" in most other editions, without change of meaning. It is immediately followed by Tibetan "de dag" at the beginning of the third line, which in turn is immediately followed by "gi".

⁹⁹ The Tibetan "de dag gi" glossed just now is then followed by Tibetan "yang" which, grammatically speaking, is an ornament of inclusion that translates here into "and also".

¹⁰⁰ Skt. mati, Tib. blo. See rational mind in the glossary. Rational mind is mainly used in reference to the rational aspect of dualistic mind, in which case it is a pejorative term. However, a buddha's wisdom does have the ability to make precise rational distinctions between this and that—it is an aspect of the fourth of the five wisdoms, the one which knows things individually. That kind of discriminative ability, but in wisdom mode, is what is needed in order to teach the dharma skilfully, for example through the three levels of the modes of turning the wheel just mentioned. Therefore, "rational mind" here refers to a greater type of knowing, that is, a wisdom type of knowing.

used to teach which dharmas at which times on which occasions in which places. The term "voices" has the meaning of a padding term[101].

- Entering into entering aeons is what he says with "*The entering into all future aeons ...*" The "entering aeons" as it is called of *entering into all aeons of the future* is that, in short, *I will* enter into all the aeons which arise one after another.

"*Whatever the extent of aeons in the three times, those*"—all of those, however many of them are in the three times—*I will act to have entered*—meaning will have entered—*them in a fraction of an instant*, that is, a part of one single instant of knowing[102].

- Entering into viewing the tathāgatas and entering their domain is what he says with "*The lions of men gone in the three times ...*" Whoever are the lions of men, the ones who will have gone in the ten directions' three times, the buddha bhagavats, *I will view them in a single instant* of knowing and *I will* also *perpetually enter their domains*, that is, their places. "*By the force of the illusory complete emancipation*" is a particular complete emancipation of a bodhisatva called "illusory" which has the nature of wisdom, and through its force, I will perpetually enter their domains.

---

[101] In this verse, Samantabhadra could simply have said "and also their unending speech". However, in order to fill the line of verse so that it has the right metre, he has had to add a padding term. The term he has added is "voices". This type of addition is, in Sanskrit and Tibetan grammar, referred to as "verse padding". Why does Nāgārjuna bother to mention this? He does so because it informs us that the emphasis here is on buddha "speech" as a whole and not on the various aspects or "voices" of that speech.

[102] Knowing here has to be understood, according to all other commentaries, to be referring to a buddha's wisdom.

- **Entering into making a buddha-field manifest** is what he says with *"Whatever the field arrangements of the three times ..." Whatever* is *the* ocean of *field arrangements of the three times, I will make* those field arrangements *manifest on a single atom* by the force of miracles. *"Like that in all the directions without exception"* means "and like that, I will make an arrangement of fields just exactly as was done on a single atom but now in all directions without exception" and then *I will*, in an instant of knowing[103], *enter the ornamentation of conqueror's fields.*[104]

Someone says, "If for me the different details of nature, extent, colour, and shape of any given buddha-field are not now present on a single atom, how could the different details of nature, and so forth, as they are of the fields of buddhas of the three times without exception existing in the ten directions be present on top of a single atom unobstructed and unmixed[105]. They could not, so, how can I trust this?" I will explain it here. Because of not being able to take it in all at once, you do not know it. To take it in all at once, you need to have meditated on all dharmas lacking essentiality yet coming out in an illusory way; on their being unborn and unceasing, primally peaceful as with falling hairs[106]; on their being by nature completely in nirvana; and on their being thoroughly dissected by

---

[103] Knowing here means wisdom type of knowing.

[104] Tib. rgyan. "Ornamentation" is an older terminology which has been supplanted by the more commonly used term for it "arrangement" (Tib. bkod pa).

[105] ... without getting in the way of each other and without getting mixed up with each other ...

[106] "Falling hairs" is one of several names for a particular fault of the eye called "floaters" in English. The medical term is *muscaris volante*. It is not cataracts. They appear as hairs falling before the eyes but in fact are not there. The point here is that phenomena are empty illusion-like appearances—as with the example of falling hairs—and when that is realized, there is peace at the primal level.

mere thought that inspects them for what they actually are, yet finding they have all sorts of differing natures. Then[107], if samādhis having different contents and specific complete emancipations are used to experience inconceivable arrangements, you will be able to have a good meditation on those arrangements.

This has to be clearly defined at this point. Even in the world where there is much harmfulness and little trust, there are makers of visual illusions that have tremendous ability, illusions that make even those of the best intelligence react with amazement. Those are nothing more than visual tricks, therefore, you should have trust in all that has been expressed here, not doubting it at all.

• **Entering into going before the tathāgatas** is what he says with "*Whichever lamps of the world have not descended ...*" There are buddha bhagavats—the lamps of the world—who have not yet descended and will not descend all the way to the farthest limit of future time. They, seated here and there throughout the farthest reaches of the world realms of the ten directions, are beyond count yet are within the domain of the buddhas' wisdom. Some, together at the same instant of time, will be becoming manifest buddhas at the level of unsurpassed truly complete enlightenment. Similarly, others together at the same time will be turning the wheel of dharma. Similarly, others will be showing nirvana. I will go before those who the verse says "*will become full buddhas, turn the wheel*", and so on. "They" at the beginning of the second line is in the agentive case[108], so some among them will be manifesting as complete buddhas, similarly some will be turning the wheel of dharma, and some will be showing nirvana. *I will go*—meaning at the same time—***before*** the feet of ***all*** of ***those*** individual ***guardians*** of the

---

[107] ... if you have meditated on and successfully seen emptiness in direct perception ...

[108] Tib. de dag gis. By saying this he clarifies the meaning of the second and third lines; it shows that *they will do* what follows.

world. By the force of rapid mind-miracles[109] I will suddenly pervade the future ten directions with a cloud of bodies, then make offerings to each one of them with uncountable, supreme, especially good clouds of offerings pervading space, and offer praises to them all, and circumambulate them one hundred times, one thousand times. And I will go before them for as long as there is samsara.

"***Become buddhas in full***"[110] means become manifest buddhas. "***The final, utter peace***", which has been used to explain "***show nirvana***" is understood to be a phrase whose purpose is padding. Because those three are most meaningful among all the deeds, the prayer speaks of them. Nevertheless, like moons in water, there are the occasions of: being seated in the immeasurable palace of Tuṣhita, showing death and transference, entering a womb, being born, going to the god realms, showing crafts and skills, going forth into homelessness, becoming a renunciant, being an ascetic, going to the heart of enlightenment, being seated on the lion seat at the foot of the bodhi king of trees, and then taming the māras. I will go before their feet at those times also, going at one and the same time before every one of them who is showing the same deed. It has also been said like this:

> It is because un-assessable sentient beings
> Are in each one of the world realms
> Instant by instant becoming buddhas that
> It is not worthwhile to shrink from the task.

---

[109] The miracles of wisdom occur very quickly.

[110] The wording of the text is literally "become buddhas at the stage". He has previously explained that "at the stage" means "completely" or "in full", so here he is explaining it that way again. "Buddha at the stage" he says means *buddha at the* highest *stage* of enlightenment, which is also called a manifest buddha. A full explanation of this phrase appears in my own commentary on page 90.

Division 12: is force and it has ten sub-divisions. It starts with *"By forces of miracles which have all speed ..."*

- *"Forces of miracles"*. A "miracle" involves production of something; a "special miracle" requires an authentic type of production and its coming out in exact accordance with another's wishes[111]. Well then, how should "special miracles are miracles" be understood? When miracles are used to win over and gratify ordinary sentient beings, they are special miracles. Their "force" is that they are meaningful. *"All speed"*[112] is, for example, like the way that bodhisatvas, rather than going by some other means, go suddenly in the ten directions by the miracle of total freedom of movement.

- *"Forces of vehicle ..."* means by the forces of the Great Vehicle. Because it functions to take someone somewhere, it is called "vehicle"[113]. It is both a vehicle and also a great one, so it is the Great Vehicle, or, alternatively, it is the vehicle of buddhas and great bodhisatvas, so it is the Great Vehicle. What is its nature? It is the

---

[111] Tib. rdzu 'phrul, cho 'phrul. The Buddha used these two words in his teaching. The common Tibetan word "rdzu 'phrul" or "ṛiddhi" in Sanskrit means something which is a marvel, marvellous, miraculous. There is a less common word in Tibetan, "cho 'phrul", which is used only to indicate the miracles done by buddhas and highly developed beings for the sake of others. Unfortunately, we do not have a clear set of different terms to cover these two in English, so I have used miracle for the first and special miracle for the second.

[112] Tib. kun tu myur ba. The words in the text literally mean "very rapid" but to maintain the poetic device used by Samantabhadra in these verses, the literal wording "all speed" has been used.

[113] This is simply re-stating the definition of a vehicle, which is "that which is able to convey something somewhere". If something does not have that capacity, then it cannot be called a vehicle. For example, the vehicle of the śhrāvakas is capable of taking a person to the arhat-hood of a śhrāvaka, so it is a vehicle for that, but is not capable of taking a person to truly complete enlightenment, so it is "not a vehicle" for that.

path which causes a person to obtain a buddha's enlightenment—the Great Vehicle is comprised of "merit and wisdom"[114]. Alternatively, it has with it the pāramitās[115], so is the Great Vehicle.

Its "force" means "that which is not impeded by anything else and which cannot be overpowered by anything on the side which is not conducive to it". *"Which is in all ways a door"* means that it is a door which provides entry in every way. How is that? It is seen as a doorway that allows access to the totally pure domain[116] for all those who have not yet given birth to enlightenment mind and who have not yet seen benefit and ease for all sentient beings as commendable, and also for those who do not even have such ideas.

• *"Forces of conduct ..."* The type of conduct is not specified, so it means the forces of both bodhisatva conduct and excellent conduct. It is conduct *"whose quality is always good"* because of its being virtuous at the beginning, middle, and end.

• *"Force of loving kindnesses"* is to have been filled with thoughts of happiness for all types of sentient beings. *"Which are all pervasive"* is that those kindnesses pervade the ten directions.

---

[114] The Great Vehicle is defined in terms of a buddhahood that is the result of completing the accumulations of merit and wisdom. The buddhahood of the arhats is not defined that way, given that their level of buddhahood has neither a complete accumulation of merit or wisdom.

[115] The pāramitās, whose name literally means "gone to the other shore", are practices which are not done in connection with any of the lesser levels of enlightenment but only in relation to the other shore, truly complete enlightenment itself. Therefore, anything which proceeds by way of them is by definition the greatest level of vehicle.

[116] ... of the tathāgata's reality ...

- ***"Forces of merit ..."*** Merit comes from behaving in a pure way and also from doing ritual activities of purity. Alternatively, merit comes from making oneself good again and again. Its force comes from doing it with the arousing of enlightenment mind. It has been said like this:

> If the merits of enlightenment mind
> Were given form,
> They would totally fill space
> And even then there would some left over.

Similarly, by holding the profound and vast dharmas possessed by the Great Vehicle, reading about them, teaching them, aspiring to them, retaining even two verses of them, and wholly dedicating merits to truly complete enlightenment, your merit will become like that, and that is how "forces of merit" is understood. It is ***"all virtuous"*** or virtuous in every way because it was made by the thought of providing benefit and ease for all sentient beings.

- ***"Forces of wisdom"*** are in relation to a knower which knows all knowables. That wisdom knower has ***"become without defilement"*** meaning that it has no defilement of it occurring ever in the three times.

- ***"Force of prajñā"*** is that it comprehends the meaning exactly.

- ***"Force of method ..."*** It is method because it works precisely in relation to the need. Its force is that it is meaningful.

- ***"Force of samādhi ..."*** It is samādhi because it truly holds, it deeply and definitely holds, it is a steadiness of thought[117]. Its force is that through it there is no impediment to producing the good

---

[117] ... Where "deeply and definitely holding" is the direct translation of the Tibetan for "samādhi" and where "firmess of thought" is the direct translation of the Tibetan for "dhyāna", the more general word for meditative concentration.

qualities of the extra-perceptions, and so on, needed to work for the sakes of the entirety of migrators. The force of samādhi is understood through that.

• "*By* all of *them I'll be truly accomplishing the forces of enlightenment*" means that by the development of all of those forces I will be truly accomplishing the power of whatever are the forces of unsurpassed truly complete enlightenment.

Division 13: is antidote. To defeat the forces of karma, affliction, and the work of māra all of which are on the side which is not conducive to the side shown above, there are three activities starting with "*wholly purifying the forces of karma ...*" This does not specify which karma, so it is the three types of karma—virtuous, non-virtuous, and unfluctuating karma.

Of the three types of karma, first there is the force of non-virtuous karma that definitely will be experienced. It has the capacity to create the three bad migrations, so it must have the forces that will wholly purify it, dispel it, completely reject it, and so on applied to it! As has been said:

> I scolded myself completely for the utterly endless
> Evils I have done, then set out to lighten them.
> It has been explained with certainty that, by utterly laying
>   them aside
> And taking vows against them, their roots are pulled out.

Going further with that, the way to completely purify non-virtuous karmas is to use the force of an antidote. This is like the beloved daughter who created non-virtuous karma by harming her mother. When that karma later matured into its full-ripening result, it caused her to enter a reality in a field different to the one she had been in. She had experienced only a little of this karmic result when, producing an exceptionally good special intention in her mind, she aroused the enlightenment mind with a prayer for the sake of sentient beings and just that caused that karma to be entirely uprooted and destroyed. What was her prayer for the sake of sentient beings that aroused the enlightenment mind like? She said, "For the sake of whoever of the sentient beings amongst all the migrators has, like myself, done harm to her mother, may the infinitely great mass of suffering that came with my beating her over the head, an action that will cause me to experience misery uninterruptedly for as long as there is samsara, mean that this never again happens to even one sentient being".

Moreover, non-virtuous karmas are completely purified using the force of reliance. This is like in the narrative of realization of the sow[118]. In it, there was a being who was a son of the gods[119] who had reached the end of his life and saw that he was about to experience the result of a karma that would cause him to take birth in the womb of a sow. However, he took refuge in the Three Jewels, which permanently uprooted that karma in its entirety. Then, he died and transferred from his place amongst the gods of the Thirty-Three to a rebirth amongst the gods of Tuṣhita.

Morever, their roots will permanently uprooted through realizing that all phenomena are without a self. As the Buddha said in the *Sutra of Completely Cleaning Obscurations of Karma*:

> For example, another bhikṣhu committed two defeats by engaging in non-chastity and by killing his mother. Later, he became sorry for it and was pained in his heart. Like a madman he went from temple to temple, town to town,

---

[118] The narratives of realization are stories of the buddha's journey to enlightenment through various births. The one here is his almost being born to a sow but purifying the karma through the fore of reliance on the Three Jewels.

[119] "Son of the gods" is a term of ancient India that means a god who rules over one of the thirty-three heavens in the desire realm. He is a bright star amongst the gods, a son to the gods even higher than him.

and path to path, and in front of all beings said, "I am defeated".

By the force of his truly declaring "I am defeated" and wailing "Alas, alas" and by the force of his laying aside the evil deeds, he began to rid himself of that karma and continued with that until it was much lessened. Another bodhisatva who had gained the extra-perceptions and knew of his torment taught him profound dharma, showing him how things are. Because of that he realized that all phenomena are selfless which altogether and totally uprooted every single bit of that evil and he gained the forbearance in regard to all phenomena being unborn[120].

It is necessary to have faith in the statement that "The strong belief in profound dharma dispels all downfalls and regrets and does the work of completely cleansing all obscurations of karma". As was said in *Noble One, Sutra of the Store of the Tathāgata*:

> Kāśhyapa! In regard to what else it is, it is also that acting to remove the life of a pratyekabuddha is, within the acts of killing, a heavy one. It is like this: stealing the goods of the Three Jewels is, within the acts of taking what has not been given, a heavy one. It is like this: having sexual relations with one who is both mother and an arhati, is, within the acts of having wrong sexual relations due to desire, a heavy one. It is like this: denigrating the tathāgata is, within the acts of lying, a heavy one. It is like this: making a schism in the saṅgha is, within the acts of divisive speech, a heavy one. It is like this: criticising the noble ones is, within the acts of rough speech, a heavy one. It is like this: distracting those wanting dharma is, within the acts of gossip, a heavy one. It is like this: having a mind to

---

[120] "Forbearance in regard to" is a standard way of saying that he was able to meet with the fact of something and stay with it fully and completely, not being afraid of and rejecting it in any way.

steal the acquisitions of those who have entered reality and those who are engaged in reality is, within the acts of covetous mind, a heavy one. It is like this: getting ready to do one of the immediates is, within the acts of a harmful mind, a heavy one. It is like this: development of a dense thicket of views is, within the acts of wrong views, a heavy one. All of these ten paths of non-virtuous action are wrongdoings[121].

Kāśhyapa! Suppose one or more sentient beings were to become possessed of these great wrongdoings, the karmas of the paths of the ten non-virtuous actions, and, moreover, were to enter into the tathāgata's dharma teaching that has with it information about causes and conditions and think, "There is not at all a self or sentient being or life-force or person[122] who has done this or will experience something because of it", and were like that to engage all phenomena as being a contrivance and not compounded and without total affliction and illusory dharmatā and by nature luminosity, and were to develop true faith in and strong belief in all phenomena being primally complete purity. If they developed this strong belief, I would not say that those sentient beings would be going to the bad migrations.

Why is that? For the afflicted things there is no existence as an assemblage—because all afflicted things are born and perish, they degrade. They are born due to the assemblage of causes and conditions and immediately they are born, they also cease. Whatever is that perishing connected with birth is also what is called the perishing of

---

[121] Tib. kha na ma tho ba. This term, literally meaning "unmentionable", covers all types of wrongdoings in general.

[122] These things were enumerated by the Tīrthikas of the Buddhas time as the various attributes that truly existed. Therefore, here the Buddha is using their wrongly stated ideas of a self to present the idea of non-self.

all afflicted things. Whenever there is belief in what I have said, for that person there is no downfall and no topic of downfall. In the absence of obscuration, what would become a topic of downfall is a non-topic, is without status.[123]

Similar to that, there is motivated non-virtue that has been created in the case of downfall from enlightenment mind and that has an extreme need to be cleared. It has been said like this in the *Sutra Petitioned by Noble One Upāli* :

> Suppose a bodhisatva were to have a downfall in the morning then at midday were to again bring forth enlightenment mind. That bodhisatva's aggregate of discipline would be known to be limitless.
>
> Similarly, if at midday he had a downfall and in the afternoon were to again bring forth enlightenment mind, that bodhisatva's aggregate of discipline would be known to be limitless.

Saying the same thing, the *Gaṇḍavyūha Sutra* also says:

> Son of the family! Enlightenment mind, because it definitely incinerates everything bad that has been done, is like the consuming fire of the aeon ...

And the *Three Hundred* also teaches it with:

> Subhuti! Those sons of the family or daughters of the family who, for this sutra section with a nature like that,

---

[123] Topics are topics for explanation that can validly be discussed and non-topics are topics which have no basis—or status as the Buddha said—for discussion. Thus, for a person who has overcome karmic obscurations by realizing non-self, the issue of downfalls which would otherwise be a topic for those who have created them, becomes a non-topic, meaning that there is nothing to be discussed, that there is no basis for a discussion.

will hold it in mind and will keep it and will read it and will work to take it in entirely, will suffer, will suffer enormously. Why is that? What those sentient beings in their past succession of lives have done of non-virtuous karmas that are consistent with the production of bad migrations, will be fully experienced as a seen reality[124]. Therefore, they will suffer because of the exhaustion of those non-virtuous karmas of the past.

In that and other ways it has been taught that the karmas of evil that are definitely to be experienced can be utterly, wholly purified.

One person asks, "It seems that small and medium karmas of evil will be utterly removed by the force of laying aside evil, and so on, yet how will the heavy karmas of the immediates, and so on, be altogether cleansed, from the root?" The answer is that, of the smaller, middling, and greater divisions of intention, the ones motivating the immediates of conqueror, birth-mother, arhat, and so on[125] and which mean having to remain in the Unremitting Torment[126] hell for an aeon or close to an aeon or half an aeon, will give rise to a mind suffering with extreme regret. Those karmas are lessened by the force of truly laying aside. The buddha said, "It is like this: in regard to that, the result of that karma will have been truly experienced during merely the time it takes for a ball to fall.[127]" The person asks, "Well, does that mean that just that much will result in

---

[124] That those karmas will be "fully experienced" means that the sentient beings who have created them will have no choice but to experience them fully. For example, if a karma results in a hell realm the sentient being y will experience it as though it were real, etcetera—it will be experienced as a "seen reality" meaning it will be the conscious experiences of some lifetime.

[125] ... meaning wounding the tathāgata with malicious thought, which is one of the five immediates, killing mother, an arhat, and so on ...

[126] Skt. Avīci.

[127] In English we would say, "in the blink of an eye".

the karma being totally pulled out from the root, or not?" The answer is that one plough will not be enough for an unploughed field! The person asks, "Well then, supposing there is no change except for just the amount of a fly's leg, how will the accumulation of definite karmas be totally ended?" The answer is that, if you exert yourself at entering into the mind of the antidote, it can only result in its being ended. The person asks, "Well then, how should we take this, which was taught by the Buddha:

> Well, even in a thousand million aeons
> Karmas will not simply waste away;
> If there is assemblage[128] and the time has come,
> Bodied beings will have the fruition brought forth ..."

The answer is that it has to be understood that this was taught in relation to any karmas that have not been rejected and lightened by the forces of complete rejection, full application, and so on[129]. Consistent with that, the Buddha said this:

> Those who are not skilled might do a small evil but it will
>   stay there, lurking below, and
> Those who are skilled might do a big one but it will be
>   totally abandoned and become meaningless.
> Iron, though small, if placed on water will sink, and
> It, though big, if made into a vessel will float.

Moreover, the karmas of evils whose experience is not certain, those of the three times, beyond count, must be wholly purified. In order to really bring benefit and ease to sentient beings born in the bad migrations, by having control over karma, all of a sudden, in the ten directions and uninterruptedly for as long as samsara persists, one takes a birth whose details of type of being, shape, colour, and extent are the same as theirs. For that, one has to be certain of the purification of all types of non-virtuous karma.

---

[128] ... of causes and appropriate conditions for the karma to ripen ...

[129] These are the four forces for completely purifying karma.

Moreover, one also has totally to purify the forces of virtuous karma that have the capacity to create a result within becoming. How is that done? One eliminates the full-ripening results[130] then develops certainty of direction by wholly dedicating with prayers for enlightenment itself.

Then the same is also done for the karmas motivated by the dhyānas and formless realms, the unfluctuating karmas that result in living in the form and formless realms. They also are removed and then, in accordance with the need for control over karma, for the sake of sentient beings one makes efforts for certainty. Applying oneself to this is what this line in the prayer is talking about.

"*Totally destroying the forces of affliction*"[131]. Due to allowing the continua of body and mind to become afflicted, there is affliction—desire, and so on. "Their force" is that, because of them, the entirety of migrators enter an even greater degree of unknowing in relation to all things—for example, as journeying and not journeying, benefiting and not benefiting, heavy and light, and so on. Destroying the afflictions by the meditations on ugliness, and so on, and overwhelming them by worldly paths can be done, but the essence of it is that, by gaining control over the afflictions, they themselves become part of the meditation of enlightenment.

---

[130] ... of the virtuous and non-virtuous karmas of the desire realm by applying the various methods laid out so far—the four powers of antidote, laying aside, and on ...

[131] The afflictions can be overcome by worldly methods and they can be destroyed by the methods of the Lesser Vehicle, such as overcoming desire by a set of meditations on ugliness. However, here, "totally destroying" means using the methods of the Great Vehicle in which they are not rejected but are controlled by using them as the path.

"And utterly rendering powerless the forces of māra". "Māra" refers to the māras of "son of the gods", and so on[132]. Their forces are capable of making obstacles for the bodhisatva's conduct, and so on, so utterly rendering them forceless is to make them what is called "pale and powerless" by the forces of the extra-perceptions, and so on.

"All forces of excellent conduct will be completed". The forces of excellent conduct are not overcome by the side not conducive to them, so they are spontaneously entered[133]. "All" means "without exception"[134]. "Will be completed" means will be completed through the ten types of forces—miracles and so on—expressed earlier and this set of three antidotes just now explained.

Division 14: The fourteenth one is showing what the bodhisatvas' activities are. The activities are of eight types—wholly purifying buddha-fields, and so on—which he speaks of in two verses starting *"I will be completely purifying an ocean of fields ..."*

In each instant *I will be completely purifying an ocean of fields* like those of Sukhāvatī, Padmāvatī, and so on. And, similarly, I will be *completely liberating the ocean of sentient beings*—with ocean meaning the whole amount of sentient beings—who are tightly

---

[132] These are the four maras of the aggregates, the afflictions, the Lord of Death, and son of the gods.

[133] The words in Tibetan are pointing out that that this is an intransitive verbal action, which is important to understanding how this verse is being phrased. This is explained further in my own commentary.

[134] Nāgārjuna's text has "all" in this line as shown. None of the Tibetan editions have it. Instead, they have a marker which shows clearly that this line is not "I will complete them" but that "they will be completed", which implies—exactly in accord with how Nāgārjuna explains it—that the foregoing three antidotes are part of the means for completing them.

bound by the steel shackles of affliction in the prison of samsara, by gratifying them with both miracles and the special miracle of total expression[135] then using the special miracle of teaching them appropriately. And, I will be **utterly seeing an ocean of dharmas** meaning that I will in each instant be seeing or viewing with the eye of prajñā the ocean of dharmas taught and the ocean of dharmas of realized. And, knowables are infinite so wisdom is infinite, thus I will be in each instant **utterly** entering and **realizing** those oceans of wisdom—here referred to as "**an ocean of wisdom**"—meaning that such wisdoms will actually be seen.

And, I will be "**completely purifying an ocean of conduct**" where "conduct" has not been specified so can be understood to mean both enlightenment conduct and excellent conduct. In regard to this, enlightenment conduct is the accumulation of wisdom done to accomplish the buddha qualities and excellent conduct is the accumulation of merit that fits with the creation of benefit and ease for the entirety of migrators. Furthermore, excellent conduct is also enlightenment conduct precisely, because both are done to attain buddhahood. Thus, it ends up being merely the difference between what are called "direct and implied" statements[136]. So, I will in each instant, by the force of the extra-perceptions be completely purifying and making stainless an ocean of conduct.

And, I will in each instant be **wholly completing an ocean of prayers** by the forces of discipline and samādhi. And, I will in each instant be **utterly offering to an ocean of buddhas** of the ten directions using offerings pervading space. **And**, I will be **doing so tirelessly for an**

---

[135] "Total expression" is the speech of a bodhisatva or buddha which is able to speak whatever needs to be spoken in any given situation.

[136] "Enlightenment conduct" directly states what it is and "excellent conduct" indirectly states what it is.

ocean of aeons meaning that "I will make offerings with a mind that does not tire of doing so"[137].

Division 15: The fifteenth division is wholly dedicating to training following the buddhas and bodhisatvas. It has two sub-divisions.

Wholly dedicating to train following the tathāgatas is what he says starting with *"The particulars of the prayers of enlightenment conduct ..."* The person reciting the prayer has contemplated and genuinely come to understand that *the particulars of the prayers of the enlightenment conduct of whoever are the conquerors gone in the three times* when they were bodhisatvas will, all of them without exception, be completed by the person's becoming *an enlightened buddha*. *Thus,* the person determines, *I will by excellent conduct*—the conduct of excellence—achieve unsurpassed truly complete enlightenment and so *become an enlightened buddha.*

Wholly dedicating to train following the bodhisatvas Noble Samantabhadra and others through body, speech, and mind conducts, fields, and prayers that are completely pure is what he says with *"The chief of the sons of all the conquerors ..."* Because for the bodhisatva mahāsatva Noble Samantabhadra all of the many conducts of excellence of the bodhisatvas, and the many complete emancipations of the bodhisatvas, and the many samādhis of the bodhisatvas—in short, all of the many good qualities of the bodhisatvas—have gone

---

[137] The grammar involved makes it seem as though this line is a continuation of the last line, which is how Nāgārjuna seems to be explaining it. However, he is not explaining it in detail. All other commentaries make it clear that this line is a conclusion to the seven preceding lines.

to the far side, have become pāramitā[138], he is the chief of the sons[139]. *The* one who has become the ***chief*** among or ***of the sons of all the conquerors is*** the great bodhisatva ***whose name is*** the noble one "***Samantabhadra***". *I* wholly ***dedicate*** in each instant ***all these virtues*** that he has taught in these words ***here in order to conduct myself*** throughout this aeon ***with expertise equalling his*** expertise in whatever he is expert.

"***The way that he is expert at excellent dedications for completely pure body, speech, and mind, and ...***" refers to his expertise at dedications for complete purity of body, speech, and mind, and ***conduct, and fields***[140]. The words "***he is expert***" refers to Noble Samantabhadra. "***Excellent dedications***" means making whole

---

[138] There is conduct, such as generosity, which looks like the bodhisatva's action of the pāramitā of generosity but which, because it has not gone to (itā) and become something of the (pāram) other shore, is not considered to be pāramitā. Anything which has gone to the other shore is regarded as pāramitā.

[139] At the beginning of this sentence, the "excellent conduct" in general is also referred to as the "totally excellent" conduct where totally excellent is the word "samantabhadra". In this case "samantabhadra" is not the name of the bodhisatva Samantabhadra but another name for the conduct of excellence of the bodhisatvas which both emphasizes the extent of the excellence of the bodhisatva's conduct and also makes a connection with Samantabhadra who was regarded as the most capable of the Buddha's heart sons at the bodhisatva's conduct.

[140] The "and" at the end of the line translates the Tibetan phrase linker "kyang" which gives the meaning "as well as". Nāgārjuna is saying that it means "complete purity of body, speech, and mind, and complete purity as well of conduct and fields". Some Tibetans say that it simply ends the list of body, speech, and mind giving the intensified sense "all of them", which corresponds to a separate use of the phrase linker. Indian commentators agree with Nāgārjuna. At any rate, there are five items in the list, starting with body.

dedications. *"May I too be equal to him in the same way"* means "may I be exactly like him in abilities".

"For thoroughly virtuous excellent conduct" refers to excellent conduct that is virtuous in the beginning, middle, and end and has the character of being fundamentally good. For that, *I will act as in the prayer of Mañjuśhrī*, meaning the prayer of noble Mañjuśhrī. What is that prayer? It was spoken by the noble Mañjuśhrī, who had become a king of space, when he said this and much more like it:

> How long to the beginning in the past
> Of beginningless samsara,
> For that long for the sake of benefiting sentient beings
> I will course in conducts past fathomable.

"Without wearying in all future aeons" means throughout all future aeons, with mind neither wearying of it nor switching to some other idea during that time, *I will complete their works*—the buddhas' and bodhisatvas' works—*without exception*.

Division 16: The sixteenth division, in which he talks about application, measureless good qualities, and remaining in the conduct, is what he says with *"May my conducts not become measurable ..."* This is effectively saying "May my conducts be measureless". *May my good qualities also be immeasurable.* Moreover, *due to remaining in* both *conduct without measure* and good qualities without measure, *I will know* the time of *all* the amazing miracles *of the transformations*, and so on, of those buddhas and bodhisatvas.[141]

---

[141] The word "know" in this line translates the Tibetan word " 'tshal". The early Tibetan translators explained that the Tibetan word has five meanings. If them, the Indian masters such as Dignāga and the ones who were advising Yeshe De say it is "know". Tenpa'i Wangchuk says that it is "gain". How can this be resolved? Nāgārjuna shows us with his commentary. "Know" in this case means "knows the time of" which in turn means knowing that one has arrived at point where those things
(continued ...)

Those were the sixteen sub-divisions of the eighth topic of the prayer.

——— ♦♦♦ ———

Now, there is the ninth topic, the end of the prayer. For *as far as it would be to the final end of space and* for as far as it would be *to the end of every* existent *sentient being, and* for *as* far as it would be *to the end of* migrators' *karma and* for as far as it would be to the end of *affliction*, may the *end of my prayer* meaning this current prayer of mine of Samantabhadra's conduct *also be* as far away as *that*. In other words, space and the other items mentioned in this verse are without a final end, without a point of completion, and may my prayer likewise be without a final end, without a point of completion.

——— ♦♦♦ ———

Now there is the tenth topic, the prayer's benefits. This has two parts: benefits connected with seen dharmas[142] and benefits connected with another life.

Benefits connected with seen dharmas are in these four parts, each one taking up one verse: wholly holding merits that are special; seeing the tathāgatas; gaining same lot with bodhisatvas; and wholly ending karmic obscuration.

---

[141](... continued)
are present. That in turn can be understood as "gained" which is another of the five meanings of the term " 'tshal". Thus, the line is "will know all of their transformations" meaning "will come to know in one's own experience that one has gained the use of their transformations".

[142] "Seen dharmas" is the technical name for karmas which are accumulated in this life and which also ripen in this life.

- First, compared to the example of the merit of having offered to special places various types of vast and numerous things which are the best of their type, the merit that one comes to hold from turning the mind towards seeking enlightenment due to this prayer is best. There is a son or daughter of the family who *adorns the* boundless, *infinite* buddha-*fields* of *the ten directions with* clothes, canopies, umbrellas, victory banners, streamers, various forms, small cymbals, *jewels*, bells, garlands, flowers, incense, rows of oil lamps, and so on, *and offers that to the conquerors and* who makes an offering of *the most enjoyable things of gods and men* such as food and comestibles possessing five hundred flavours *for aeons equal to the atoms of the buddha-fields* to the buddha bhagavats. And there is another person *who hears this king of dedications then is utterly inspired towards and even just one time*—meaning on one occasion—thinking "This is how it is"—*gives rise to faith in supreme enlightenment*. Who would that second person be? It would be a person totally involved with seeking supreme enlightenment, a person of the Great Vehicle. That one *is the one who* will gain superior merit that is *better* than the superior merit arising from the first-mentioned generosity. Two persons are involved and the final line says that, of the two, it is the merits of this latter person which are the better of the two superior merits.

- Second, by having abandoned downfalls of wrongdoing and bad companions, the tathāgatas are seen. *Someone who has made this excellent conduct prayer will have abandoned all* of the three *bad migrations* and *he also will have abandoned bad companions* such as śhrāvakas, and so on, those who are not virtuous spiritual friends[143]. *And,* at the time of death, *he also will see* the bhagavat tathāgata *Amitābha soon*. Who will see him? Someone who has taken to heart both this text about the excellent conduct and its meaning will see him.

---

[143] Anyone who follows the Lesser Vehicle, such as a śhrāvaka, is not a virtuous spiritual friend given that virtuous spiritual friends are by definition followers of the Great Vehicle.

• Third, because of gaining the most commendable acquisition and sustenance and life, such people eventually reach the same level as the bodhisatva. ***They acquire the best***, an unsurpassed jewel of a prayer. Because they have acquired this unsurpassed jewel of a prayer, they ***are sustained in goodness***. Because of those, the things they need to pursue and the supreme attainment come to them ***and*** then, if they set about actually gaining it, ***even in this human life*** their lives ***can turn out well***, meaning turn out in a virtuous way. ***Moreover, whatever*** the noble ***Samantabhadra is like, before long they will become like that too***.

• Fourth, there is the benefit of ending karmic obscuration. It says, "***The evil deeds of the five immediates***—killing mother, and the other four—that have been ***done by someone under the control of not knowing…***" Note that "under the control of not knowing" means that it could be desire or anything else because not knowing is the root of all of them. To ascertain what is being said here, understand that, ***if*** that person has now wet his mind with the water of utter purity and made it good and if ***he recites this excellent conduct prayer*** with strong inspiration and keeps it in mind and teaches it day and night to the entirety of migrators, then the immediates ***will be quickly and without exception wholly cleansed***, that is, they will be uprooted and ended.

The benefits connected with another life has two parts: benefits belonging to cause and benefits belonging to fruition. They take up the next three verses.

• Benefits belonging to cause refers to having the characteristics of good form, marks and signs, good caste, good family, being harmless, and being someone worthy of offerings. "***He will possess…***" "***Possess***" means that such a person will come into the possession of the things listed, where possession means always truly possessing and being connected with them. "***Will***" means "will have accomplished" these things through the prayer. "***Wisdom***" refers to what comes with the true accomplishment of all the conducts. "***Form***" is a very attractive form. "*Marks*" means the thirty-two marks of a great being—the mark of the uṣṇīṣha on the crown, and so on—and because the illustrative signs are included together with the marks, possessing the illustrative signs is also understood to be included. "Caste" is the caste whichever it might be of brahman and kingly castes. "*Family*" means having the extra-perceptions superior to all others. "***Many māras and Tīrthikas will be unable to affect him***" means that someone who keeps and teaches this prayer of Samantabhadra's conduct will not be able to be affected, that is, overcome, by the hordes of māras and Tīrthikas, and, *in all three worlds even offerings will be made* to him.

• Benefits belonging to fruition. The characteristics of going to the heart of enlightenment, showing being seated on the lion throne, taming the māras, manifesting enlightenment, turning the wheel of dharma, and so on, are what he says with "***He'll quickly go to the foot of the leading bodhi tree ...***" He who has this unsurpassed jewel of enlightenment conduct and has gathered the accumulations of merit and wisdom will quickly go to the foot of the leading bodhi tree *and having done so*, moreover, for the sake of being able *to* accomplish *benefit* for all *sentient beings will sit there* on the lion throne with his legs crossed up. Moreover, having sat there, he will defeat the regiments of māras following which he will *become* a manifest complete *buddha* at the level of unsurpassed truly complete *enlightenment*, and then will *turn the wheel* of unsurpassed dharma, in short, will be teaching.

Furthermore, there is the benefit of gaining worldly and beyond worldly perfections without exception. *For whoever holds, reads or teaches this prayer of excellent conduct*, what *their full-ripenings* will be is something that *will be known* in this world *by buddha*, meaning the great bhagavats, not by the others lesser than them, the śrāvakas and pratyekabuddhas. What do they know the full-ripening of this jewel of a prayer to be like? He says, "***supreme enlightenment***", which is the result, unsurpassed truly complete enlightenment. If there were no perfections of the worldly ones, that would not happen, so this here has to be viewed as an expression of the presence also of the benefit of gaining the perfections without exception of the worldly ones. Therefore, ***do not be sceptical*** about the possibilities of this prayer; do not give rise to doubts about that!

───── ♦♦♦ ─────

Now comes dedications. First he gives a dedication in relation to the middling level ones, the bodhisatvas, with **"*How the hero Mañjushrī knows and ...*"** It says, "In that same way as noble Mañjushrī knows and likewise bodhisatva Samantabhadra knows, in order for me to train following them, I utterly dedicate all of these virtues".[144]

Second, he gives the dedication of the tathāgata level. It says, "***Using the dedication which all the conquerors*** who have ***gone in the three times*** have ***commended as*** the ***supreme***, unsurpassed one, a whole dedication which expresses benefits and good qualities, ***I*** will supremely ***dedicate all of these*** verses recited possessing an oceanic accumulation of ***roots of virtue for the purpose of excellent conduct***."

Third, he gives half a verse for separating from obscuration and a further half for entirely keeping one's things consistent with the other shore. ***When the time has come for me to die***, that is, the time when life has become obstructed, ***may*** even the slightest of ***obscurations*** be ***cleared away*** by the excellent conduct, then, ***seeing*** bhagavat ***Amitābha in direct perception, I will utterly go to the buddha-field of Sukhāvatī***.

Moreover, ***having gone there*** to that buddha-field of Sukhāvatī, ***may*** I actually ***manifest*** in direct perception ***all without exception*** of ***these prayers*** that have been taught here. Moreover, having wholly,

───────────

[144] This verse is explained according to one of the two, distinct editions of it that exist. The Derge edition uses the other edition and the English translation of the prayer in this book uses that. That version of this verse is explained in my own commentary.

without exception, completed or *fulfilled them, I will benefit* all *sentient beings* for *as long as the world* meaning "for as long as there are migrators".

Following this there are verses for gaining the prophecy and accomplishing the sakes of sentient beings. What are they? It says, "*In that good and pleasing maṇḍala of the conqueror ...*" where "maṇḍala of the conqueror" means "in the maṇḍala of the retinue of the tathāgata". In "*may I be born from a beautiful fine lotus*", "born" is to have arisen, and "*fine lotus*" is a supreme lotus, and "*beautiful*" is that it has light, that it is giving off webs of light rays. Due to *seeing* the bhagavat *Amitābha directly*—in direct perception—he will make a prediction, therefore, *may I also obtain the prophecy there* directly from the conqueror, with him saying this sort of thing: "You will become in such and such world realm, such and such tathāgata, arhat, truly complete buddha".

I will obtain the prophecy from him, the bhagavat Amitābha, and *having completely obtained* it *there I will* make a cloud of *many emanations, thousands of millions* of them that will pervade *the ten directions*, and then, *by the force of* wisdom without defilement, without impediment—which is the greater type of *rational mind*—I will, in every instant and for as long as there are migrators, *do many*—a number which is beyond count—*things to benefit sentient beings* throughout the ten directions.

◆◆◆

The stainless merit, the virtue, that has been obtained
From making this explanation in combined with the text of this king
   of prayers

Is sent and wholly dedicated consistent with the cause[145].
In order to accomplish the sakes of migrators may this be used again and again.

This explanation combined with the noble Samantabhadra's *King of Prayers, the Excellent Conduct Prayer* given verbally by Master Nāgārjuna is complete.

The Kashmir Preceptor Thigle Bumpa and the great translator of written texts, the Śhākya bhikṣhu Lodan Sherab, translated it into Tibetan, corrected, and finalized it.

---

[145] This line means "Is sent and wholly dedicated to a result which is consistent with the cause" where the cause was an elucidation of a prayer concerning enlightened conduct done for the sake of others and the result, buddhahood, result will follow accordingly.

GLOSSARY

Affliction, Skt. kleśha, Tib. nyon mongs: This term is usually translated as emotion or disturbing emotion, etcetera, but the Buddha was very specific about the meaning of this word. When the Buddha referred to the emotions, meaning a movement of mind, he did not refer to them as such but called them "kleśha" in Sanskrit, meaning exactly "affliction". It is a basic part of the Buddhist teaching that emotions afflict beings, giving them problems at the time and causing more problems in the future.

Arousing the mind, Tib. sems bskyed: This is general term used to mean the deliberate rousing of a particular mind. It is frequently used in the Great Vehicle to mean "arousing the enlightenment mind". The Great Vehicle path can be summed up as: arousing the mind of enlightenment, engaging in the conduct of enlightenment, and making prayers for enlightenment. This summary is readily apparent in the commentary in this book to Samantabhadra's Prayer. Note that there are two types of arousing the mind—fictional and superfactual; see under fictional enlightenment mind and superfactual enlightenment mind.

Authoritative statement, Skt.agama, Tib lung. Although often translated as "scripture", authentic statement means statement made by someone who has the true knowledge needed to make fully reliable statements about a subject. It is often used to indicate dharma taught by the Buddha or his disciples which is authoritative because of its source. It is also used in the pair "authoritative statement and realization" which, the Buddha explained, summed up the ways of transmitting his realization.

Bardo, Tib. bar do: Literally, "interval" or "in-between place". The general teachings of Buddhism explain this as the intermediary state between one life and the next.

Becoming, Skt. bhāvanā, Tib. srid pa: This is another name for samsaric existence. Beings in samsara have a samsaric existence but, more than that, they are constantly in a state of becoming—becoming this type of being or that type of being in this abode or that, as they are driven along without choice by the karmic process that drives samsaric existence. It is sometimes used to mean any kind of existence, whether on the side of nirvana or samsara, for example in the phrase "appearance and becoming" explained earlier in the glossary and used in the commentary to Samantabhadra's Prayer.

Bliss, Skt. sukha, Tib. bde: The Sanskrit term and its Tibetan translation are usually translated as "bliss" but refer to the whole range of possibilities of everything on the side of good as opposed to bad. Thus, the term will mean pleasant, happy, good, nice, easy, comfortable, blissful, and so on, depending on context.

Bodhicitta, Tib. byang chub sems: See under enlightenment mind.

Bodhisatva, Tib. byang chub sems dpa': A bodhisatva is a person who has engendered the bodhichitta, enlightenment mind, and, with that as a basis, has undertaken the path to the enlightenment of a truly complete buddha specifically for the welfare of other beings. Note that, despite the common appearance of "bodhisattva" in Western books on Buddhism, the Tibetan tradition has steadfastly maintained since the time of the earliest translations that the correct spelling is bodhisatva; see under satva and sattva.

Clinging, Tib. zhen pa: In Buddhism, this term refers specifically to the twofold process of dualistic mind mis-taking things that are not true, not pure, as true, pure, etcetera and then, because of seeing them as highly desirable even though they are not, attaching itself to or clinging to those things. This type of clinging acts as a kind of glue that keeps a person joined to the unsatisfactory things of cyclic existence because of mistakenly seeing them as desirable.

Complete purity, rnam dag: This term refers to a buddha's situation given that a buddha is completely free of the impurity of samsara.

Cyclic existence: See under samsara.

Dharmadhatu, Skt. dharmadhātu, Tib. chos kyi dbyings: This is the name for the *dhātu* meaning range or basic space in which all *dharma*s, meaning all phenomena, come into being. If a flower bed is the place where flowers grow and are found, the dharmadhātu is the dharma or phenomena bed in which all phenomena come into being and are found.

Dharmata, Skt. dharmatā, Tib. chos nyid: This is a general term meaning the way that something is, and can be applied to anything at all; it is similar in meaning to "actuality" *q.v.* For example, the dharmatā of water is wetness and the dharmatā of the becoming bardo is a place where beings are in a samsaric, or becoming mode, prior to entering a nature bardo. It is used frequently in Tibetan Buddhism to mean "the dharmatā of reality" but that is a specific case of the much larger meaning of the term. To read texts which use this term successfully, one has to understand that the term has a general meaning and then see how that applies in context.

Dhyana, Skt. dhyāna, Tib. bsam gtan: A Sanskrit term technically meaning all types of mental absorption. Mental absorptions cultivated in the human realm generally result in births in the form realms which are deep forms of concentration in themselves. The practices of mental absorption done in the human realm and the godly existences of the form realm that result from them both are named "dhyāna". The term also means meditation in general where one is concentrating on something as a way of developing oneself spiritually.

Endurance World, Tib. mi mjed 'jig rten: The Buddha named our planet and its cosmic zone "Endurance World" because the humans inhabiting the planet endure suffering. He also called it Endurance Field meaning the entire cosmic field within which our planet exists.

Enlightenment mind, Skt. bodhicitta, Tib. byang chub sems: This is a key term of the Great Vehicle. It is the type of mind that is connected not with the lesser enlightenment of an arhat but the enlightenment of a truly complete buddha. As such, it is a mind which is connected with the aim of bringing all sentient beings to that same level of buddhahood. A person who has this mind has entered the Great Vehicle and is either a bodhisatva or a buddha.

It is important to understand that "enlightenment mind" is used to refer equally to the minds of all levels of bodhisatva on the path to buddhahood and to the mind of a buddha who has completed the path. Therefore, it is not "mind striving for enlightenment" as is so often translated, but "enlightenment mind", meaning that kind of mind which is connected with the full enlightenment of a truly complete buddha and which is present in all those who belong to the Great Vehicle.

Evil, evil deed, Skt. papaṃ, Tib. sdig pa: The original Sanskrit means something which someone has done which is truly bad, rotten. Anyone who has done such a thing is looked down upon. The Tibetan for it relates to the idea of a scorpion, a nasty creature that will sting you and injure you. In Buddhism, the term does not have the Christian sense of evil but simply means action done that, being done under the influence of an affliction, degrades you now in other's eyes, degrades you now because of the bad karmic seeds that you have planted by doing it, and degrades you in the future because of the ripening of the bad karmas into unpleasant results.

Excellent conduct, Skt. bhadracharya, Tib. bzang po spyod pa: This is a general term for all ways of behaviour which are seen as good, commendable, excellent. Each group of beings has their own idea of what constitutes excellent conduct. Therefore, this one term includes all types of conduct which are seen as good, both worldly and spiritual. Although that is understood in Buddhism, it is often used to indicate the excellent conduct of a bodhisatva in particular. In that latter case, it is excellent because it is the conduct by which one gains the goodness of enlightenment and in that case it is equivalent to the more specific term "enlightenment conduct" which refers only to the conduct of a bodhisatva done for the purpose of attaining enlightenment.

Fathom, fathomless, unfathomable, Tib. dpag pa, dpag tu med pa: "To fathom" means "to penetrate something fully by a probing or calculating type of dualistic mind. Fathomless and unfathomable mean that the thing being referred to is to large to be fully penetrated by that sort of mind.

Fictional, Skt. saṃvṛtti, Tib. kun rdzob: This term is paired with the term "superfactual" *q.v.* In the past, these terms have been translated as "relative" and "absolute" respectively, but those translations are nothing like the original terms. These terms are extremely important in the Buddhist teaching so it is very important that they be corrected, but more than that, if the actual meaning of these terms is not presented, then the teaching connected with them cannot be understood.

The Sanskrit term saṃvṛtti means a deliberate invention, a fiction, a hoax. It refers to the mind of ignorance which, because of being obscured and so not seeing suchness, is not true but a fiction. The things that appear to that ignorance are therefore fictional. Nonetheless, the beings who live in this ignorance believe that the things that appear to them through the filter of ignorance are true, are real. Therefore, these beings live in fictional truth.

Fictional and superfactual: Fictional and superfactual are our greatly improved translations for "relative" and "absolute" respectively. Briefly, the original Sanskrit word for fiction means a deliberately produced *fiction* and refers to the world projected by a mind controlled by ignorance. The original word for superfact means "that *super*ior *fact* that appears on the surface of the mind of a noble one who has transcended samsara" and refers to reality seen as it actually is. Relative and absolute do not convey this meaning at all and, when they are used, the meaning being presented is simply lost.

Fictional truth, Skt. saṃvṛtisatya, Tib. kun rdzob bden pa: See under fictional.

Fictional truth enlightenment mind, Tib. kun rdzob bden pa'i byang chub sems: One of a pair of terms explained in the Great Vehicle; the other is Superfactual Truth Enlightenment Mind. See under fictional truth and superfactual truth for information about those terms. Enlightenment mind is defined as two types. The fictional type is the conventional type: it is explained as consisting of love and great compassion within the framework of an intention to obtain truly complete enlightenment for the sake of all sentient beings. The superfactual truth type is the ultimate type: it is explained as the enlightenment mind that is directly perceiving emptiness.

Field, Field realm, Tib. zhing, zhing khams: This term is often translated "buddha-field" though there is no "buddha" in the term. There are many different types of "fields" in both samsara and nirvana. Thus there are fields that belong to enlightenment and ones that belong to ignorance. Moreover, just as there are "realms" of samsara—desire, form, and formless—so there are realms of nirvana—the fields dharmakāya, saṃbhogakāya, and nirmāṇakāya and these are therefore called "field realms".

Five paths, Tib. lam lnga: In the Prajñāpāramitā teachings of the Great Vehicle, the Buddha explained the entire Buddhist journey as a set of five paths called the paths of accumulation, connection, seeing, cultivation, and no more training. The first four paths are part of journeying to enlightenment; the fifth path is that one has actually arrived and has no more training to undergo. There are a set of five paths that describe the journey of the Lesser Vehicle and a set of five paths that describe the journey of the Greater Vehicle. The names are the same in each case but the details of what is accomplished at each stage are different.

Floaters, Tib. rab rib: This term has usually been mistakenly translated as "cataracts". It is the medical term for eyes with a disease known as *Muscaria volante* in Western ophthalmology. The disease is common to a large portion of the world's population and has the common term "floaters" given to it by the medical profession. Almost anyone who looks out at a clear source of light will see grey threads, sometimes twisted, sometimes straight, floating in the field of vision. When an eye is moved, because the gel of the eye shifts, the floaters can seem to be like hairs falling through the field of vision and so are sometimes called "falling hairs". They seem to be "out there" when in fact they are shadows being cast on the retina by fissures in the gel inside the eye. The point is that they seem real when in fact they are an aberration produced by an illness of the eye.

Foremost instruction, Skt. upadeśha, Tib. man ngag: There are several types of instruction mentioned in Buddhist literature: there is the general level of instruction which is the meaning contained in the words of the texts of the tradition; on a more personal and direct level there is oral instruction which has been passed down from teacher to student from the time of the buddha; and on the most profound level there are foremost instructions which are not only oral instructions provided by one's guru but are special, core instructions that come out of personal experience and which convey the teaching concisely and with the full weight of personal experience. Foremost instructions or upadeśha are crucial to the Vajra Vehicle because these are the special way of passing on the profound instructions needed for the student's realization.

Great Vehicle, Skt. mahāyāna, Tib. theg pa chen po: The Buddha's teachings as a whole can be summed up into three vehicles where a vehicle is defined as that which can carry a person to a certain destination. The first vehicle, called the Lesser Vehicle, contains the teachings designed to get an individual moving on the spiritual path through showing the unsatisfactory state of cyclic existence and an emancipation from that. However, that path is only concerned with personal emancipation and fails to take account of all of the beings that there are in existence. There used to be eighteen schools of Lesser Vehicle in India but the only one surviving nowadays is the Theravāda of south-east Asia. The Greater Vehicle is a step up from that. The Buddha explained that it was great in comparison to the Lesser Vehicle for seven reasons. The first of those is that it is concerned with attaining the truly complete enlightenment of a truly complete buddha for the sake of every sentient being where the Lesser Vehicle is concerned only with a personal liberation that is not truly complete enlightenment and which is achieved only for the sake of that practitioner. The Great Vehicle has two divisions: a conventional form in which the path is taught in a logical, conventional way, and an unconventional form in which the path is taught in a very direct way. This latter vehicle is called the Vajra Vehicle because it takes the innermost, indestructible (vajra) fact of reality of one's own mind as the vehicle to enlightenment.

Guardian, Skt. nātha, Tib. mgon po: This name is a respectful title reserved for the buddhas. It means that they both protect and nurture sentient beings who they oversee, like a child who, having no parents has been given or has found a guardian. It is often translated as "protector" but that correctly translates another Sanskrit term to start with and on top of that is insufficient because it does not include the aspect of nurturing. It is also given to other beings such as bodhisatvas who have a similar quality, for example, Guardian Nāgārjuna and Guardian Maitreya.

Intentional conduct, Tib. mos spyod: A name in the Great Vehicle for the path activities done at levels of both accumulation and connection. At this level, one is still intending to directly realize emptiness. Note that intention is the name of one of the fifty-one mental events. Thus this name implies that it is conduct still at the level of dualistic being, though it is a good mind because it intends to reach non-dualistic being. Also, by definition there is no real accomplishment until the path of seeing is reached, so there is no real accomplishment at the level of intentional conduct. Intentional conduct as non-accomplishment followed by the three paths which are levels of accomplishment is a general presentation contained in the common vehicle.

Kaya, Skt. kāya, Tib. sku: The Sanskrit term means a functional or coherent collection of parts, similar to the French "corps", and hence also comes to mean "a body". It is used in Tibetan Buddhist texts specifically to distinguish bodies belonging to the enlightened side from ones belonging to the samsaric side.

Enlightened being in Buddhism is said to be comprised of one or more kayas. It is most commonly explained to consist of one, two, three, four, or five kāyas, though it is pointed out that there are infinite aspects to enlightened being and therefore it can also be said to consist of an infinite number of kāyas. In fact, these descriptions of enlightened being consisting of one or more kāyas are given for the sake of understanding what is beyond conceptual understanding so should not be taken as absolute statements.

The most common description of enlightened being is that it is comprised of three kāyas: dharma, saṃbhoga, and nirmāṇakāyas. Briefly stated, the dharmakāya is the body of truth, the saṃbhogakāya is the body replete with the good qualities of enlightenment, and the nirmāṇakāya is the body manifested into the worlds of samsara and nirvana to benefit beings.

Dharmakāya refers to that aspect of enlightened being in which the being sees the truth for himself and, in doing so, fulfils his own needs for enlightenment. The dharmakāya is purely mind, without form. The remaining two bodies are summed up under the heading of rūpakāyas or form bodies manifested specifically to fulfil the needs of all un-enlightened beings. "Saṃbhogakāya" has been mostly translated as "body of enjoyment" or "body of rapture" but it is clearly stated in Buddhist texts on the subject that the name refers to a situation replete with what is useful, that is, to the fact that the saṃbhogakāya contains all of the good qualities of enlightenment as needed to benefit sentient beings. The saṃbhogakāya is extremely subtle and not accessible by most sentient beings; the nirmāṇakāya is a coarser manifestation which can reach sentient beings in many ways. Nirmāṇakāya should not be thought of as a physical body but as the capability to express enlightened being in whatever way is needed throughout all the different worlds of sentient beings. Thus, as much as it appears as a supreme buddha who shows the dharma to beings, it also appears as anything needed within sentient beings worlds to give them assistance.

Lay aside, Tib. bshags pa: This term is usually translated as "confession" but that is not the meaning. The term literally means to cut something away and remove it from oneself. In Buddhism, it is used in the context of ridding oneself of the karmic seeds sown by bad karmic actions.

Lesser Vehicle, Skt. hīnayāna, Tib. theg pa dman pa: See under Great Vehicle.

Mara, Skt. māra, Tib. bdud: The Sanskrit term is closely related to the word "death". Buddha spoke of four classes of extremely negative influences that have the capacity to drag a sentient being deep into samsara. They are the "maras" or "kiss of death": of having a samsaric set of five skandhas; of having afflictions; of death itself; and of the son of gods, which means being seduced and taken in totally by sensuality.

Migrator, Tib. 'gro ba: Migrator is one of several terms that were commonly used by the Buddha to mean "sentient being". It shows sentient beings from the perspective of their constantly being forced to go here and there from one rebirth to another by the power of karma. They are like flies caught in a jar, constantly buzzing back and forth. The term is often translated using "beings" which is another general term for sentient beings but doing so loses the meaning entirely: Buddhist authors who know the tradition do not use the word loosely but use it specifically to give the sense of beings who are constantly and helplessly going from one birth to another, and that is how the term should be read.

Mind, Skt. chitta, Tib. sems: There are several terms for mind in the Buddhist tradition, each with its own, specific meaning. This term is the most general term for the samsaric type of mind. It refers to the type of mind that is produced because of fundamental ignorance of enlightened mind. Whereas the wisdom of enlightened mind lacks all complexity and knows in a non-dualistic way, this mind of un-enlightenment is a very complicated apparatus that only ever knows in a dualistic way.

Noble one, Skt. ārya, Tib. 'phags pa: In Buddhism, a noble one is a being who has become spiritually advanced to the point that he has passed beyond cyclic existence. According to the Buddha, the beings in cyclic existence were ordinary beings, spiritual commoners, and the beings who had passed beyond it were special, the nobility.

Ones Gone to Bliss: see under sugata.

Prajna, Skt. prajñā, Tib. shes rab: The Sanskrit term, literally meaning "best type of mind" is defined as that which makes correct distinctions between this and that and hence which arrives at correct understanding. It has been translated as "wisdom" but that is not correct because it is, generally speaking, a mental event belonging to dualistic mind where "wisdom" is used to refer to the non-dualistic knower of a buddha. Moreover, the main feature of prajñā is its ability to distinguish correctly between one thing and another and hence to arrive at a correct understanding.

Rational mind, Tib. blo: Rational mind is one of several terms for mind in Buddhist terminology. It specifically refers to a mind that judges this against that. With rare exception it is used to refer to samsaric mind, given that samsaric mind only works in the dualistic mode of comparing this versus that. Because of this, the term is mostly used in a pejorative sense to point out samsaric mind as opposed to an enlightened type of mind.

This term has been commonly translated simply as "mind" but that fails to identify this term properly and leaves it confused with the many other words that are also translated simply as "mind". It is not just another mind but is specifically the sort of mind that creates the situation of this and that (*ratio* in Latin) and hence, at least in the teachings of Kagyu and Nyingma, upholds the duality of samsara. In that case, it is the very opposite of the essence of mind. Thus, this is a key term which should be noted and not just glossed over as "mind".

Realization, Tib. rtogs pa: Realization has a very specific meaning: it refers to correct knowledge that has been gained in such a way that the knowledge does not abate. There are two important points here. Firstly, realization is not absolute. It refers to the removal of obscurations, one at a time. Each time that a practitioner removes an obscuration, he gains a realization because of it. Therefore, there are as many levels of realization as there are obscurations. Maitreya, in the *Ornament of Manifest Realizations*, shows how the removal of the various obscurations that go with each of the three realms of samsaric existence produces realization. Secondly, realization is stable or, as the Tibetan wording says, "unchanging". As Guru Rinpoche pointed out, "Intellectual knowledge is like a patch, it drops away; experiences on the path are temporary, they evaporate like mist; realization is unchanging".

Reference and Referencing, Tib. dmigs pa: Referencing is the name for the process in which dualistic mind references an actual object by using a conceptual token instead of the actual object. Whatever is referenced is then called a reference. Note that these terms imply the presence of dualistic mind and their opposites, non-referencing and being without reference imply the presence of non-dualistic wisdom.

Refuge, Skt. śharaṇaṃ, Tib. bskyab pa: The Sanskrit term means "shelter", "protection from harm". Everyone seeks a refuge from the unsatisfactoriness of life, even if it is a simple act like brushing the teeth to prevent the body from decaying un-necessarily. Buddhists, after having thought carefully about their situation and who could provide a refuge from it which would be thoroughly reliable, find that three things—buddha, dharma, and saṅgha—are the only things that could provide that kind of refuge. Therefore, Buddhists take refuge in those Three Jewels of Refuge as they are called. Taking refuge in the Three Jewels is clearly laid out as the one doorway to all Buddhist practice and realization.

Samsara, Skt. saṃsāra, Tib. 'khor ba: This is the most general name for the type of existence in which sentient beings live. It refers to the fact that they continue on from one existence to another, always within the enclosure of births that are produced by ignorance and experienced as unsatisfactory. The original Sanskrit means to be constantly going about, here and there. The Tibetan term literally means "cycling", because of which it is frequently translated into English with "cyclic existence" though that is not quite the meaning of the term.

Satva and sattva: According to the Tibetan tradition established at the time of the great translation work done at Samye under the watch of Padmasambhava not to mention the one hundred and sixty-three of the greatest Buddhist scholars of Sanskrit-speaking India, there is a difference of meaning between the Sanskrit terms "satva" and "sattva", with satva meaning "an heroic kind of being" and "sattva" meaning simply "a being". According to the Tibetan tradition established under the advice of the Indian scholars mentioned above, satva is correct for the words Vajrasatva and bodhisatva, whereas sattva is correct for the words samayasattva, samādhisattva, and jñānasattva, and is also used alone to refer to any or all of these three sattvas.

All Tibetan texts produced since the time of the great translations conform to this system and all Tibetan experts agree that this is correct, but Western translators of Tibetan texts have for last few hundreds of years claimed that they know better and have "satva" to "sattva" in every case, causing confusion amongst Westerners confronted by the correct spellings. Recently, publications by Western Sanskrit scholars have been appearing in which these great experts finally admit that they were wrong and that the Tibetan system is and always has been correct!

Special intention, Tib. lhag bsam: This term is used in general to refer to all specially pure intentions. In Great Vehicle literature it will more often refer specifically to bodhicitta but even then, it can be used to mean bodhicitta in general or an especially pure instance of bodhicitta.

Sugata, Tib. bde bar gshegs pa: This term is one of many names for a buddha. It has the twofold meaning of someone who has gone on a good, pleasant, easy journey and who has arrived at a place which is good, pleasant, and full of ease. The meaning in relation to buddhahood is explained at length in *Unending Auspiciousness, the Sutra of the Recollection of the Noble Three Jewels* by Tony Duff, published by Padma Karpo Translation Committee, 2010, ISBN: 978-9937-8386-1-0.

Superfactual, Skt. paramārtha, Tib. don dam: This term is paired with the term "fictional" *q.v.* In the past, the terms have been translated as "relative" and "absolute" respectively, but those translations are nothing like the original terms. These terms are extremely important in the Buddhist teaching so it is very important that their translations be corrected but, more than that, if the actual meaning of these terms is not presented, the teaching connected with them cannot be understood.

The Sanskrit term literally means "the fact for that which is above all others, special, superior" and refers to the wisdom mind possessed by those who have developed themselves spiritually to the point of having transcended samsara. That wisdom is *superior* to an ordinary, un-developed person's consciousness and the *facts* that appear on its surface are superior compared to the facts that appear on the ordinary person's consciousness. Therefore, it is superfact or the holy fact, more literally. What this wisdom knows is true for the beings who have it, therefore what the wisdom sees is superfactual truth.

Superfactual truth, Skt. paramārthasatya, Tib. don dam bden pa: See under superfactual.

Superfactual truth enlightenment mind, Tib. don dam bden pa'i byang chub sems: This is one of a pair of terms; the other is Fictional Truth Enlightenment Mind *q.v.* for explanation.

Superfice, superficies, Tib. rnam pa: In discussions of mind, a distinction is made between the entity of mind which is a mere knower and the superficial things that appear on its surface and which are known by it. In other words, the superficies are the various things which pass over the surface of mind but which are not mind. Superficies are all the specifics that constitute appearance—for example, the colour white within a moment of visual consciousness, the sound heard within an ear consciousness, and so on.

The authentic, Tib. yang dag: This is a term commonly used in the sutras as a synonym for reality. For example "view of the authentic" means "view of reality" not a correct view. The term "limit of the authentic" meaning final or utmost reality, that is, nirvana, was also frequently used in the sutras.

The Translated Treatises, Tib. bstan 'gyur or Tangyur: This is the name of the collection of the official translations into the Tibetan language of the treatises of Buddhist masters that were made to support and clarify the meaning of the Buddha-word. These treatises are mainly those of Indian Buddhist masters but also include some by masters of other countries. The commentaries on Samantabhadra's Prayer preserved in the *Translated Treatises* are ones that were composed in the Sanskrit language by Indian masters and translated into Tibetan at the time of the great translations in Tibet.

The Translated Word, Tib. bka' 'gyur: This is the name of the collection of the official translations into the Tibetan language of the Buddha-word and words of great Buddhist masters in the time of the Buddha. There are seven major editions of *The Translated Word* in Tibetan. When doing this work, I used a recently produced version of the Derge edition which has all differences between it and the remaining six major editions carefully noted.

Tīrthika, Skt. tīrthika, Tib. mu stegs pa: This is very kind name adopted by the Buddha for those who did not follow him but who, because they followed some other spiritual path, had at least started on the path back to enlightenment. The Sanskrit name means "those who have arrived at the steps at the edge of the pool". A lengthy explanation is given in the *Illuminator Tibetan-English Dictionary* by Tony Duff and published by Padma Karpo Translation Committee. In the prayer, it is used to indicated followers of religions other than the Buddhist tradition who had antipathy towards and created trouble for the Buddhists because of religious disagreement.

Unsatisfactoriness, Skt. duḥkha, Tib. sdug bngal: This term is usually translated into English with "suffering" but there are many problems with that. When the Buddha talked about the nature of samsaric existence, he said that it was unsatisfactory. He used the term "duḥkha", which includes actual suffering but means much more than that. Duḥkha is one of a pair of terms, the other being "sukha", which is usually translated as, but does not only mean, bliss. The real meaning of duḥkha is "everything on the side of bad"—not good, uncomfortable, unpleasant, not nice, and so on. Thus, it means "unsatisfactory in every possible way". The real meaning of its opposite, sukha, is "everything on the side of good"—not bad, comfortable, pleasant, nice, and so on. Therefore, that he is completely liberated from the sufferings actually means that he has completely liberated himself from the unsatisfactoriness of samsara, which includes all types of suffering and happiness, too.

Wisdom, Skt. jñāna, Tib. ye shes: This is a fruition term that refers to the kind of mind, the kind of knower possessed by a buddha. Sentient beings do have this kind of knower but it is covered over by a very complex apparatus for knowing, dualistic mind. If they practise the path to buddhahood, they will leave behind their obscuration and return to having this kind of knower.

The Sanskrit term has the sense of knowing in the most simple and immediate way. This sort of knowing is present at the core of every being's mind. Therefore, the Tibetans called it "the particular type of awareness which is there primordially". Because of the Tibetan wording it has often been called "primordial wisdom" in English translations, but that goes too far; it is just "wisdom" in the sense of the most fundamental knowing possible.

About the Author, Padma Karpo Translation Committee, And Their Supports for Study

I have been encouraged over the years by all of my teachers to pass on the knowledge I have accumulated in a lifetime dedicated to study and practice, primarily in the Tibetan tradition of Buddhism. On the one hand, they have encouraged me to teach. On the other, they are concerned that, while many general books on Buddhism have been and are being published, there are few books that present the actual texts of the tradition. Therefore they, together with a number of major figures in the Buddhist book publishing world, have also encouraged me to translate and publish high quality translations of individual texts of the tradition.

My teachers always remark with great appreciation on the extraordinary amount of teaching that I have heard in this life. It allows for highly informed, accurate translations of a sort not usually seen. Briefly, I spent the 1970's studying, practising, then teaching the Gelugpa system at Chenrezig Institute, Australia, where I was a founding member and also the first Australian to be ordained as a monk in the Tibetan Buddhist tradition. In 1980, I moved to the United States to study at the feet of the Vidyadhara Chogyam Trungpa Rinpoche. I stayed in his Vajradhatu community, now called Shambhala, where I studied and practised all the Karma Kagyu, Nyingma, and Shambhala teachings being presented there and was a senior member of the Nalanda Translation Committee. After the vidyadhara's nirvana, I moved in 1992 to Nepal, where I have been continuously involved with the study, practise, translation, and teaching of the Kagyu system and especially of the Nyingma system of Great Completion. In recent years, I have spent extended times in Tibet with the greatest living Tibetan masters of Great Completion, receiving very pure transmissions of the ultimate levels of this teaching directly in Tibetan and practising them there in retreat. In that way, I have studied and practised extensively not in one Tibetan tradition as is usually done, but in three of the four Tibetan traditions—Gelug, Kagyu, and Nyingma—and also in the Theravada tradition, too.

With that as a basis, I have taken a comprehensive and long term approach to the work of translation. For any language, one first must have the lettering needed to write the language. Therefore, as a member of the Nalanda Translation Committee, I spent some years in the 1980's making Tibetan word-processing software and high-quality Tibetan fonts. After that, reliable lexical works are needed. Therefore, during the 1990's I spent some years writing the *Illuminator Tibetan-English Dictionary* and a set of treatises on Tibetan grammar, preparing a variety of key Tibetan reference works needed for the study and translation of Tibetan Buddhist texts, and giving our Tibetan software the tools needed to translate and research Tibetan texts. During this time, I also translated full-time for various Tibetan gurus and ran the Drukpa Kagyu Heritage Project—at the time the largest project in Asia for the preservation of Tibetan Buddhist texts. With the dictionaries, grammar texts, and specialized software in place, and a wealth of knowledge, I turned my attention in the year 2000 to the translation and publication of important texts of Tibetan Buddhist literature.

Padma Karpo Translation Committee (PKTC) was set up to provide a home for the translation and publication work. The committee focusses on producing books containing the best of Tibetan literature, and, especially, books that meet the needs of practitioners. At the time of writing, PKTC has published a wide range of books that, collectively, make a complete program of study for those practising Tibetan Buddhism, and especially for those interested in the higher tantras. All in all, you will find many books both free and for sale on the PKTC web-site. Most are available both as paper editions and e-books.

It would take up too much space here to present an extensive guide to our books and how they can be used as the basis for a study program. However, a guide of that sort is available on the PKTC web-site, whose address is on the copyright page of this book and we recommend that you read it to see how this book fits into the overall scheme of PKTC publications. Other sutra publications of interest would be:

- *Unending Auspiciousness, the Sutra of the Recollection of the Noble Three Jewels* by Tony Duff, published by Padma Karpo Translation Committee, 2010, ISBN: 978-9937-838-61-0.
- *Maitreya's Sutras and Prayer, with Commentary by Padma Karpo*, by Tony Duff, published by Padma Karpo Translation Committee, February 2013, ISBN 978-9937-572-62-0. The book presents two sutras petitioned by Maitreya and his famous prayer, and a commentary to the prayer by Padma Karpo.
- *The Noble One Called "Point of Passage Wisdom", A Great Vehicle Sutra*, t by Tony Duff, published by Padma Karpo Translation Committee, 2010, ISBN: 978-9937-572-58-3. The root sutra of the ten profound essence sutras of Other Emptiness of the third turning of the wheel.
- *Sutra of the Householder Uncouth, A Teaching of the Buddha Showing All-knowing Wisdom And the Householder's Way*, by Tony Duff and Tamás Agócs, published by Padma Karpo Translation Committee, 2013, ISBN 978-9937-572-56-9.
- *Samantabhadra's Prayer Volume II, with commentary by Tenpa'i Wangchuk*.

We make a point of including, where possible, the relevant Tibetan texts in Tibetan script in our books. We also make them available in electronic editions that can be downloaded free from our web-site, as discussed below. The Tibetan texts for this book were too large to include, so they have been made available in digital format for download on the PKTC web-site.

Electronic Resources

PKTC has developed a complete range of electronic tools to facilitate the study and translation of Tibetan texts. For many years now, this software has been a prime resource for Tibetan Buddhist centres throughout the world, including in Tibet itself. It is available through the PKTC web-site.

The wordprocessor TibetDoc has the only complete set of tools for creating, correcting, and formatting Tibetan text according to the norms of the Tibetan language. It can also be used to make texts with mixed Tibetan and English or other languages. Extremely high quality Tibetan fonts, based on the forms of Tibetan calligraphy learned from old masters from pre-Communist Chinese Tibet, are also available. Because of their excellence, these typefaces have achieved a legendary status amongst Tibetans.

TibetDoc is used to prepare electronic editions of Tibetan texts in the PKTC text input office in Asia. Tibetan texts are often corrupt so the input texts are carefully corrected prior to distribution. After that, they are made available through the PKTC web-site. These electronic texts are not careless productions like so many of the Tibetan texts found on the web, but are highly reliable editions useful to non-scholars and scholars alike. Some of the larger collections of these texts are for purchase, but most are available for free download.

The electronic texts can be read, searched, and even made into an electronic library using either TibetDoc or our other software, TibetD Reader. Like TibetDoc, TibetD Reader is advanced software with many capabilities made specifically to meet the needs of reading and researching Tibetan texts. PKTC software is for purchase but we make a free version of TibetD Reader available for free download on the PKTC web-site.

A key feature of TibetDoc and Tibet Reader is that Tibetan terms in texts can be looked up on the spot using PKTC's electronic dictionaries. PKTC also has several electronic dictionaries—some Tibetan-Tibetan and some Tibetan-English—and a number of other reference works. The *Illuminator Tibetan-English Dictionary* is renowned for its completeness and accuracy.

This combination of software, texts, reference works, and dictionaries that work together seamlessly has become famous over the years. It has been the basis of many, large publishing projects within the Tibetan Buddhist community around the world for over thirty years and is popular amongst all those needing to work with Tibetan language or deepen their understanding of Buddhism through Tibetan texts.

INDEX

A King of Prayers of Excellent
   Conduct 34, 36, 55, 172
abandoned bad companions .. 30,
                           150, 223
Abhidharma ... 53, 114, 192, 194
accumulation of merit . 180, 207,
                                 218
accumulation of wisdom 218
accumulations of merit and
   wisdom 207, 225
acquiring merit and wisdom . 194
act of turning the wheel of dharma
   136
acting to please virtuous friends
   .... 42, 95, 115, 184
activities ... 42, 85, 95, 108, 112,
   140, 142, 145, 149, 158, 184, 190,
          193, 208, 209, 217, 237
activities of dharma 108, 190
admiring 23, 58, 61, 62, 174
admiring, longing, and trusting 61
admission of wrongdoing 83
admitting and laying aside ... 84
advantages
   future 153
   immediate 153
Adzom Gyalsay xxi
Adzom Gyalsay's commentary 73

affliction 26, 29, 30, 94, 108,
   109, 139, 147, 148, 187, 189, 192,
      209, 212, 218, 222, 230, 233
agentive case 66, 128, 204
all dharmas lacking essentiality
   203
all phenomena are without a self
   210
all-knowing quality 88, 89
Amitābha . xi, 30-32, 43, 99, 150-
   152, 163, 164, 166, 167, 223, 226,
                                 227
   Infinite Luminence 151
   Unfathomable Light 151
an ocean of wisdom . 29, 140, 141
antidote .. 83, 84, 139, 189, 209,
                               215, 216
antidote to the obscurations . 189
añjali 92
arhat's enlightenment 94
armour 42, 95, 112, 113, 184, 191
army of four regiments 157
arousing of enlightenment mind
   .... 99, 110, 208
arousing the mind 180, 187,
                               190, 230
assemblage of causes and
   conditions 212

INDEX

assistants to the path 139
atoms of the fields .. 30, 92, 149, 195, 196
authoritative statement 230
Avataṃsaka Sutra .... xiii, 45
bad companions 30, 150, 223
　explanation 150
bad migrations 6, 26, 30, 34, 110, 111, 150, 190, 209, 212, 214, 215, 223
bardo 103, 231, 232
beautiful fine lotus 32, 164
become buddhas at the enlightenment stage
　explanation 90
become buddhas at the stage
　.................... 28, 135
become ordained ... 26, 102, 186
becoming .. xxviii, 12, 17, 23, 29, 66, 91, 97, 103, 119, 120, 136, 137, 142, 143, 146, 153, 157, 159, 189, 199, 204, 205, 216, 219, 231, 232
being born in Sukhāvatī . 43, 163
benefit and ease . 25, 91, 93, 138, 183, 185, 194, 207, 208, 215, 218
　explanation 93
benefiting sentient beings ... 42, 95, 110, 111, 121, 184, 221
benefits belonging to cause .. 43, 154, 155, 224
benefits belonging to fruition
　........ 43, 154, 156, 224, 225
benefits connected with another life 222, 224
benefits connected with seen dharmas 222
benefits seen in a later life ... 43, 148, 154
benefits seen in this life .. 43, 148
beyond-ordinary levels of experience xiv
Bhadravaha .... xvi, 165
bhikṣhu 210, 228
bit-wise commentary xx
bliss .. 24, 71, 74, 178, 231, 239, 244
bodhi tree 25, 31, 91, 97-99, 157, 182, 185, 225
bodhichitta 99, 231
bodhisattva .... x, 231
bodhisatva ...... iv, v, x-xiv, xxiv, xxvii, 1, 3-17, 21-23, 32, 36, 42, 43, 45-48, 51, 52, 54, 55, 64, 65, 67-71, 78-80, 85, 87, 95, 97-99, 101, 103, 105, 107, 109-112, 114, 115, 117-120, 122, 123, 126-128, 132-135, 138-140, 142-146, 149-153, 156, 159-162, 164, 165, 175, 176, 178-180, 184, 185, 187-190, 192-196, 202, 206, 207, 211, 213, 217-222, 224, 226, 231-233, 237, 241
bodhisatva level .. x, xiv, xxiv, 46, 79, 151
bodhisatva levels 23, 67, 71, 110, 120, 122, 128, 164, 196
bodhisatva mahāsatva ... 5, 7, 8, 17, 23, 36, 54, 219
bodhisatva mahāsatva Samantabhadra . 5, 7, 8, 17, 23, 36, 54
bodhisatva sons . x, xi, 9, 70, 117, 143, 144, 160
bodhisatva training 46
bodhisatvas of the same lot .. 42, 114, 115, 192
bodhisatva's conduct ... x-xii, 48, 51, 133, 175, 194, 217, 220
bodies by which the prostration will be done 62

Brahma's speech 127
branches of sound . 28, 127, 198, 200
breadth of merely a hair . 27, 124
buddha sons .. 24, 25, 27, 69, 84, 85, 97, 117, 121-123, 143, 185, 195
buddha speech . 28, 42, 121, 127-130, 195, 198-200
buddha-field
   description 99
buddhas as many as atoms 70
buddhas at the enlightenment
   stage 25, 86, 185
buddhas at the stage 28, 135
buddha-fields .. 4-6, 9-23, 36, 54, 62, 63, 68, 92, 98, 117, 121, 122, 125, 134, 135, 141, 144, 145, 151, 174, 176, 178, 185, 195, 196, 217, 223
buddha's wisdom . 160, 182, 197, 201, 202
bundle 3
case marker ... 66, 130, 200, 201
Changkya Rolpa'i Dorje . xix, 135
chief of the sons 29, 143, 219, 220
chief of the sons of all the
   conquerors 29, 143, 219
classical Indian culture 75
clinging 5, 95, 188, 231
colophon 47, 50, 56
commendation 10, 24, 71, 74, 162, 176
commentaries on the prayer .. iii, xvii-xix
commentary of Śhākyamitra .. 51
company of other bodhisatvas
   .... 114, 192
complete emancipation .. 4, 5, 17, 28, 133, 202
   become-illusory 133
definition 120
complete emancipations .. 23, 27, 119-121, 133, 194, 204, 219
complete purity . 5, 6, 11, 21, 23, 28, 127, 128, 212, 220, 231
complexion 155
conclusion ... xiii, xx, 42, 45, 95, 146, 147, 184, 219
conclusion to the divisions .. 146
conduct of a bodhisatva .. v, x-xiii, 45-48, 51, 52, 64, 68, 107, 112, 115, 118, 119, 139, 143, 145, 161, 233
conduct of enlightenment ... 106, 109, 139, 152, 186, 195, 230
conducts of body, speech, and
   mind 115
conducts of enlightenment ... 26, 102, 103, 155, 186
confess 83
confession 82-84
connecting with being uncloaked
   .... 42, 95, 108, 184, 189
connecting with bodhisatvas of
   same lot 95, 184
conquerors ... 24-31, 62, 63, 65-69, 71, 72, 74, 75, 77, 79, 80, 84, 97, 104-106, 116-118, 127, 129, 130, 134, 142, 143, 149, 162, 175-180, 185, 187, 193, 194, 198-201, 219, 220, 223, 226
conscious decision to remain
   within samsara 109
continuative phrase linker 122, 147
control over karma 215, 216
core bodhisatva teaching 109
critical edition of the prayer . xxiii
cyclic existence . xi, 231, 236, 239
daughters of the family 213
death transfers and births 26, 102

explained 103
dedication
  explanation 93
  fictional and superfactual ... 94
dedication of merit .. xi, 43, 166
dedication verses 43
delineation of training following
  .... 42, 95, 142, 184
descend to buddhahood .. 25, 96
descriptive name 51
desire gods and humans 60
dharmadhātu .. 5, 9, 14, 70, 176,
  193, 232
dharmadhātus 4, 7, 8, 10-12,
  24, 69, 71
dharmakāya 235, 237
dharmatā 176, 212, 232
dhyāna 216, 232
diacritical marks .... ii, xxviii
difference between prostrate and
  homage 53
Dignāga .... xvi, 165, 221
direct perception . 15, 24, 27, 31,
  62, 63, 66-68, 71, 110, 116, 117,
  123, 125, 161, 163, 175, 193,
  204, 226
discipline conduct . 26, 105, 106,
  187, 188
  definition 105
discipline type of conduct ... 105
discriminating wisdom 131
Division 1: Thought 42, 96
Division 10: Gaining an unending
  store 42, 119
Division 11: Entering ... 42, 121
Division 12: Forces 42, 137
Division 13: Accomplishing . 42,
  139
Division 14: Activities ... 42, 140
Division 15: Delineation of
  training following 42, 142

Division 16: Conclusion . 42, 146
Division 2: Not forgetting
  enlightenment mind ... 42, 101
Division 3: Connecting with being
  uncloaked 42, 108
Division 4: Benefiting sentient
  beings 42, 110
Division 5: Armour 42, 112
Division 6: Connecting with
  bodhisatvas of the same lot
  .... 42, 114
Division 7: Acting to please
  virtuous friends 42, 115
Division 8: Having made the
  tathāgata's visible 42
Division 9: Wholly holding the
  holy dharma 42, 118
divisions of the prayer 42, 95
domain of the buddhas' wisdom
  204
domains ... 28, 42, 121, 133, 202
downfall 213
dualistic rational mind 131
Dza Patrul xxi
Dzogchen .... iii, xii, xx, xxi, 170
Dzogchen Monastery ... xxi, 170
early commentaries 58
Eastern Tibet xxi
eighty illustrative signs 155
emancipation .. 4, 5, 17, 28, 120,
  121, 133, 202, 236
emptiness . 70, 94, 110, 133, 161,
  197, 204, 234, 237, 247
end of every sentient 30, 147
end of karma and affliction 30, 147
end of space 30, 147, 222
end of the prayer ... xii, 165, 222
Endurance World ... 13, 16, 232
English .. iii, v-ix, xiii-xv, xix-xxvi,
  xxviii, xxix, 3, 48-52, 54-56, 58,
  59, 61, 64-66, 68, 70, 74, 75, 80,

81, 86, 87, 89, 96, 97, 99,
  103-105, 108, 109, 111, 116,
  119, 122, 126-128, 137,
  140-142, 147, 155, 181, 188,
  190, 194, 200, 203, 206, 214,
  226, 241, 243, 244, 246, 248,
  249
English translation . . . vi, viii, xx,
  65, 86, 128, 226
enlightened conduct 228
enlightenment conduct . . . 26, 27,
  29, 96, 105, 113, 118, 121-124,
  126, 141-143, 146, 153, 156,
  161, 191, 194-196, 218, 219,
  225
enlightenment mind . . 17, 18, 26,
  42, 80, 95, 99, 101, 104, 106-108,
  110, 138, 143, 161, 179, 180, 184,
  186-189, 207-210, 213, 230-232,
  234, 242
entering . . . . x-xii, 22, 23, 27, 28,
  42, 47, 91, 95, 100, 103, 113, 119,
  121, 123, 126, 127, 129, 132-135,
  184, 195, 198, 200, 202-205, 215,
  218, 232
entering into all future aeons
  . . . . 28, 42, 132, 202
entering into entering aeons
  . . . . 121, 195, 202
entering into going before the
  tathāgatas . . . 42, 121, 195, 204
entering into manifesting a
  buddha-field 42, 121, 134
entering into producing a manifest
  buddha-field 195
entering into the buddha speech
  . . . . 42, 121, 127, 195
entering into their domain . . 195
entering into their domains . . 42,
  121, 133
entering into turning the
  tathāgatas' wheel of dharma
  . . . . 42, 121
entering into viewing the buddha-
  fields—two types . 42, 121, 195
entering into viewing the
  tathāgatas . . . 42, 121, 195, 202
Entering the Bodhisatva's Conduct xii
entering the buddha speech . 127
entering their domain 202
epithet for the buddhas 90
equipoise on emptiness 94
European languages . viii, ix, xix,
  xxiv
evil 31, 57, 80, 81, 107, 153,
  172, 174, 179, 183, 211, 214, 215,
  224, 233
evil deeds . 31, 107, 153, 211, 224
evil deeds of the five immediates
  . . . . 31, 153
example of a lotus 109
example of sun and moon . . . 109
excellent conduct . . . v, xi, xii, 24,
  26, 27, 29-32, 34, 36, 46, 51, 52,
  55, 62-68, 77, 80, 96, 101,
  104-107, 109, 112, 115, 118,
  119, 138-140, 142, 143, 145,
  148, 150, 152, 154, 157, 158,
  162, 166, 167, 171, 172, 175,
  179, 184, 187, 189, 191, 193,
  194, 207, 217, 218, 221,
  223-226, 228, 233
  meaning unsurpassed offering
  80
excellent conduct of a bodhisatva
  . . . . v, xi, xii, 46, 51, 52, 64, 68,
  107, 112, 115, 118, 119, 143, 145,
  233
excellent conduct of
  enlightenment 106, 109
excellent conduct prayer . 24, 30-
  32, 62, 64-66, 150, 154, 166, 167,

256 INDEX

.... 184, 223, 224, 228
excellent dedications 29, 144, 220
experience of bodhisatvahood . 47
experienced as a seen reality . 214
explanation of guardian 90
explanation of ma chags pa ... 89
explanations of the prayer . iii, vi-ix, xv, 148
extra-perception 129
extreme torment 111, 190
faith in supreme enlightenment
.... 30, 149, 223
fathomless .. 144, 176, 177, 185, 188, 198, 233
fictional .. 94, 95, 161, 187, 230, 233, 234, 242
fictional and superfactual ... 94, 95, 234
fictional enlightenment mind
.... 161, 187, 230
fictional truth 234, 242
fictional truth enlightenment mind 234, 242
field
  pure and impure 98
field arrangements 28, 134, 135, 203
field arrangements of other buddhas 135
field atoms ... 24, 25, 62, 63, 91, 174, 175, 183
field realm 235
fields ... 4-6, 9-23, 25, 27-30, 36, 54, 62, 63, 68, 92, 97, 98, 117, 121-126, 134, 135, 140, 141, 144, 145, 149, 151, 172, 174, 176, 178, 183, 185, 195-198, 203, 217, 219, 220, 223, 235
fifth buddha of this era x
final end of space ... 30, 147, 222
finest clothes 24, 75, 178
finest flowers 24, 75, 178
finest garlands 24, 75, 178
finest incense 24, 75, 178
five important prayers ..... iii, x
five paths 110, 135, 235
floaters 197, 235
force of laying aside evil 214
force of loving kindnesses 28, 137
force of rational mind ... 28, 32, 129, 130, 164, 201
force of reliance 210
forces .. 24, 28, 29, 42, 62-68, 77, 80, 95, 137-140, 175, 179, 184, 206, 207, 209, 215-218
forces of affliction 29, 139
forces of antidote 139
forces of conduct 28, 137
forces of enlightenment 29, 137, 140
forces of excellent conduct .. 24, 29, 62-66, 139, 140, 217
forces of excellent conduct prayer
.... 24, 62, 64, 65
forces of faith 24, 77, 80, 179
forces of faith in excellent conduct
.... 24, 77
forces of karma 29, 139, 209
forces of māra 29, 139, 217
forces of merit 29, 137
forces of miracles ... 28, 137, 206
forces of the Great Vehicle .. 206
forces of vehicle 28, 137
forces of virtue 64, 66
forces of virtuous karma 216
forces of wisdom 29, 137
foremost instructions 236
four modes of birth 164
framework .. vii, viii, xiv, xv, xviii, xxii, xxiv, xxvi, xxix, 41, 49, 50, 53, 56, 171, 234
fully illuminating ... 27, 118, 194

future births 102, 150
Gaṇḍavyūha Sutra . . . iv, xiii, xvii,
    xxii, xxvi, 3, 34, 36, 45, 46, 48, 53,
    55, 213
gaining an unending store 42,
    95, 119, 184, 194
gaining control over the afflictions
    216
gaining same lot with bodhisatvas
    . . . . 149, 222
gaining the prophecy . 163, 164,
    227
gaol of samsara 142
Gelugpa . . . . xix, 245
gender issues . . . . iv, xxvii
general term . 68, 172, 230, 232,
    233, 238, 239
genitive case marker 66, 130,
    200, 201
gentled
    definition 107
gods of Tuṣhita 210
God's Ear 129
gone in the three times . . 28, 29,
    31, 59, 61, 67, 133, 142, 143, 162,
    180, 187, 202, 219, 226
gone to suchness 60
gone to the other shore 220
good and pleasing maṇḍala . . . 32,
    164, 227
good qualities . . 4, 7, 19, 24, 27,
    30, 61, 71-74, 79, 99, 113, 119,
    120, 144, 146, 155, 161, 177,
    178, 188, 194, 209, 219, 221,
    226, 237, 238
good qualities of all the
    conquerors 24, 71, 79
good qualities of the extra-
    perceptions 209
grammar . . . vi, xvi, xvii, xix, xxi,
    xxv, 48, 58, 59, 62, 63, 66, 72-74,
    86, 90, 119, 125, 130, 139, 156,
    200, 202, 219, 246
great compassion 4, 9, 19, 23,
    107, 194, 234
great enlightenment 93
great type of knowing 201
Great Vehicle . . . . iii, v, x, xii, xiii,
    xv, xvii, xxiii, xxv, 1, 3, 36, 45, 53,
    69, 73, 85, 88, 91-94, 99, 127,
    138, 139, 144, 145, 177,
    206-208, 216, 223, 230,
    232-238, 241, 247
guardian buddhas . . 88, 136, 183
guardians of the world 182,
    196, 205
guru . . . . xii, 19, 236, 240
having made the tathagatas visible
    116
having manifested tathāgata-hood
    184
heavy karmas 214
hell 13, 150, 154, 214
hidden things 197
high level dedication 162
honoured guest 75
incense . . 10, 24, 75-77, 178, 223
incense powders 76
Indian commentaries . . iii, vi-viii,
    xvi-xviii, xxiii, xxiv, 51, 52, 57, 58,
    66, 67, 73, 74, 86, 89, 91, 95-98,
    103, 105, 106, 124, 128,
    135-137, 146, 158, 160
Indian experts . . . . xviii, 51
Indian masters . . . vi, xvi, xvii, xx,
    xxiii, 78, 129, 165, 221, 243
infinite wisdoms 141
intentional conduct 110, 237
intermediate-level dedication 160
intervening state 151
intransitive verbal action 140, 217
its benefits 43, 57, 148, 172

its divisions 57, 172, 184
its ending 43, 57, 147, 172
Jigmey Lingpa xxi
Jinamitra 32, 34, 36, 56
karma and affliction 30, 147,
  148, 187
Karma Chagmey xviii
karma, affliction, and māra's
  works 26, 108, 189
  defined 108
karmas created in this life ... 148
karmas of evil 214
karmic lot 6, 114, 115, 192
Kāshyapa 211, 212
Kaushika 88
kāya 151, 155, 163, 235, 237, 238
Khumbhandas 106
king of prayers ... 34, 36, 51, 55,
  171, 172, 227, 228
king of trees 98, 99, 205
King Ralpachen 53
kiss of death 108, 190
kshetra 68, 99
lamps ... 7, 24, 25, 28, 75-77, 86,
  87, 89, 135, 136, 178, 181, 183,
  204, 223
lamps of the worlds .. 25, 86, 87,
  89, 181, 183
languages of sentient beings . 106
lay aside 81, 179, 238
laying aside ... 25, 42, 57, 80-84,
  93, 139, 172, 179, 183, 211, 214,
  216
laying aside evil ... 57, 172, 179,
  183, 214
layout and decoration of a field
  134
la-equivalent 200
leader of trees 99
leading bodhi tree ... 25, 31, 97,
  157, 185, 225

leaving behind household life 103
Lesser Vehicle .. 85, 92, 94, 139,
  150, 216, 223, 235, 236, 238
Lesser Vehicle merit 85
limb of accumulation 84
line of the tathāgatas xxvii
lions of men .. 23, 28, 58-61, 133,
  173, 174, 202
  explanation 60
literal meaning ... xv-xvii, 63, 77,
  155, 182
locative case marker 130
Lochen .... xix, 98, 129
Lochen Dharmashrī ..... xix, 98
Lodro Gyatso xxi
Longchen Nyingthig xxi
Mahāyāna .... x, 99, 236
Maitreya ..... x, xi, 46, 199, 237,
  240, 247
Maitreya's Prayer .... x, xi
manifest buddhas .. 181, 204, 205
manifest complete buddhahood
  157
Mañjushrī .. x, 30, 31, 34, 43, 46,
  53, 94, 99, 143, 145, 160, 161,
  221, 226
Mañjushrī's Prayer ...... x, 145
Mañjushrī's pure field 99
māra .. 26, 29, 31, 108, 109, 139,
  155, 157, 174, 189, 190, 205, 209,
  217, 225, 238
  defined 108
māra's works 26, 108, 189
men and women ... xx, xxvii, 70
mental offerings 75
metaphor ... 18, 71, 72, 74, 125,
  141, 177
methods 120, 131, 139, 201,
  216
migrator sentient beings 101, 173
migrators .. 4, 20, 25, 26, 32, 34,

75, 84, 85, 91, 101, 108, 110-112,
  117, 167, 180, 181, 183, 185, 186,
  188, 189, 191, 193, 194, 198, 209,
  210, 216, 218, 224, 227, 228
Mindroling monastery xix
miracle 206, 218
miracles . . 14, 28, 134, 135, 137,
  138, 203, 205, 206, 218, 221
miraculous birth 164
miraculous events and revelations
  47
Mirror Revealing Poetry 111
misunderstandings of Sanskrit
  syntax xxiv
mixed powders equal to Mt. Meru
  . . . . 24, 75
modes of the wheel . 28, 129, 131
monastic life 103
most desirable companions . . 115
Mt. Meru 13, 24, 75, 77, 178
Muni . . . . x, xi, 45, 88, 131, 143,
  144, 159-161, 194
my own commentary . . xxiv, xxvi,
  175, 181, 185, 190, 199, 205, 217,
  226
Nāgārjuna . . . . iv, xvi-xviii, xxiii,
  xxvi, 51, 63, 67, 70, 71, 73, 78,
  79, 81, 88-90, 92, 95, 100, 106,
  108, 110-113, 120-122, 128,
  131, 138-140, 142, 144, 150,
  152, 159, 160, 165, 166,
  170-173, 175, 181-183, 185,
  186, 191, 202, 217, 219-221,
  228, 237
Nāgārjuna's commentary . . . xvii,
  xviii, xxiii, 67, 73, 122, 138, 140,
  142, 144, 171, 185
Nāgas 26, 106, 188, 197
narrative of realization of the sow
  210
new arrangement 52-56

nirmāṇakāya buddha-field . . 151,
  163
nirmāṇakāyas 237
nirvana . 25, 28, 91, 92, 100, 135-
  137, 162, 183, 184, 203-205, 231,
  235, 237, 243, 245
no downfall and no topic of
  downfall 213
noble one . . 34, 53, 99, 129, 143,
  171, 211, 213, 220, 234, 239, 247
*Noble One, Sutra of the Store of the
  Tathāgata* 211
noble ones 71, 211
non-conducive side 175, 186
non-conducive side to be
  abandoned 186
non-dualistic rational mind . 131
non-dualistic wisdom . . 123, 165,
  240
non-topic 213
non-virtue 213
non-virtuous 108, 139, 154,
  189, 209, 210, 212, 214-216
non-virtuous karma 108, 139,
  189, 209, 210, 214-216
not forgetting enlightenment
  mind 42, 95, 101, 184, 188
object of prostration 63
obscuration 4, 5, 18, 43, 99,
  108, 120, 149, 153, 162, 213, 222,
  224, 226, 240, 244
obstacles 66, 108, 111, 139,
  189, 190, 217
ocean
  as poetic device 141
ocean of aeons . 27, 29, 124, 125,
  140, 198, 219
ocean of aspects of the voice 24, 71
ocean of buddhas . . . 27, 29, 124,
  140, 142, 198, 218
ocean of conduct . . 29, 140, 141,

ocean of dharmas .. 29, 140, 141, 218, 218
ocean of fields . 27, 29, 124, 140, 217
ocean of prayers 29, 140, 218
ocean of sentient beings . 29, 140
oceans of unending commendation 24, 71, 176
offering to the tathāgatas ... 57, 172, 184
offerings of gods and men 75
official translation of the prayer .... xvii, xxiii, 54, 165
ointments 7, 24, 75
one instance of speech 199
ones gone to bliss 24, 71, 74, 178, 239
one's own pure field 135
one's spiritual friends 115
ordinarion verses become a renunciant 103
origin of Samantabhadra's Prayer .... iii, xiii, 41, 45
ornament . 5, 6, 10, 28, 111, 112, 130, 134, 191, 201, 203, 240
ornament of inclusion .. 130, 201
Ornament of Manifest Realizations 240
ornamentation .. 10, 28, 134, 203
ornamentation of conquerors' fields 28, 134
other shore activity 43, 162
padding term 200, 202
Padma Karpo Translation Committee . i, ii, xi, xxviii, 242, 243, 245-247
Padmāvatī 217
palms joined together ... 25, 91, 92, 183
papaṃ 233

pāramitā of generosity 220
pāramitā of patience 110
pāramitās . 26, 107, 180, 189, 207
parinirvāṇa 91, 92
passage into nirvana .. 25, 91, 183
path of seeing 237
phrase linker 122, 128, 130, 140, 142, 147, 200, 220
physical offerings 75
places of the buddhas 133
poetic device .. 59, 111, 126, 206
power of a bodhisatva's samādhi 178
prajñā . 15, 19, 27, 29, 53, 79, 97, 110, 119, 120, 137, 138, 141, 161, 194, 208, 218, 235, 239
Prajñāpāramitā sutras 15, 110, 161
Prajñāpāramitā teachings 97, 235
Prajñās 120
pratyekabuddhas 25, 84, 85, 150, 225
prayer has sixteen sub-divisions 95
prayer of enlightenment 156
prayer of excellent conduct .. 31, 157, 158, 166, 225
prayers for enlightenment conduct 143
prayers for excellent conduct 63, 65
prayers of aspiration ...... xi, xii
prayer's place in Tibetan Buddhist practice .... iii, xii
problems with the extracts ... iii, xv, 41, 49
problems with the Tibetan arrangement 41, 50
process of craving 187
profound dharma dispels all downfalls 211
prophecy for one's future buddhahood 164

prostration ... 41, 50, 53, 57, 58, 61-63, 68, 69, 71, 79, 80, 92, 171, 172, 174-176
prostration done with mind .. 69
prostration through body 41, 58, 62
prostration through body, speech, and mind 41, 58
prostration through mind . 41, 69
prostration through speech ... 41, 62, 71
prostration to the tathāgatas .. 57, 172
pure field of Samantabhadra .. 47
pure levels 135
pure realm ...... xi, 43, 152, 163
rational mind ... 28, 32, 129-131, 164, 165, 201, 239
realization 54, 79, 133, 141, 182, 210, 230, 236, 240
referenced 240
referencing 240
refuge 152, 210, 240
regiments of māras 225
rejoicing .. 25, 42, 57, 84, 85, 93, 172, 180, 183
  definition 84
  story from the sutras 85
rejoicing in merit 57, 172
remember my births 26, 102, 186
  importance of explained ... 102
requesting the tathāgatas to remain 57, 172
respect and honour 96
roots of merit 57, 162, 172
Russian translations ...... viii, ix
saṃsāra
  Sanskrit definition 119
sake of others 153, 206, 228
samādhi . 16, 135, 178, 208, 209, 218

samādhis . 16, 27, 119, 120, 194, 204, 219, 241
Samantabhadra ... i, iii-v, vii-xiv, xvii, xix, xxii, xxiii, xxvi, 1, 3, 5-9, 12-17, 21-23, 30, 31, 33-36, 39, 41, 43, 45-49, 51, 52, 54, 64-68, 70, 72, 93, 94, 99, 124, 125, 134, 135, 143-145, 148, 150, 152, 153, 155, 157, 158, 160, 161, 163, 167, 169, 171, 172, 184, 196, 202, 206, 219, 220, 222, 224-226, 228, 230, 231, 243, 247
primal guardian x
Samantabhadra's Prayer .. i, iii-v, vii, viii, x-xiv, xvii, xix, xxvi, 33, 35, 36, 39, 41, 45, 48, 51, 52, 64-68, 72, 93, 124, 125, 145, 167, 169, 230, 231, 243, 247
Samantabhadra's pure field ... 99
same expertise 144
same lot ... 42, 43, 95, 114, 115, 149, 152, 184, 192, 222
  definition 114
samsara ... xi, 18, 60, 86, 90, 93, 100, 101, 109-112, 117, 119, 136, 142, 151, 155, 162, 173, 180, 183, 191, 192, 197, 205, 210, 215, 218, 221, 231, 234, 235, 237, 238, 240-242, 244
samsaric mind .. 67, 89, 182, 239
samsaric type of dedication ... 95
Sanskrit .... iv, xvi-xix, xxii, xxiv, xxviii, 3, 32, 36, 51, 54, 58, 59, 61, 72, 74, 80, 86, 90, 91, 97, 99, 103, 107, 108, 113, 119, 124, 126, 130, 141, 146, 151, 155, 171, 172, 177, 181, 188, 190, 191, 202, 206, 230-234, 236-244
Sanskrit texts 3
satva and sattva 231, 241

seeing the tathāgatas 43, 149, 222
seen dharmas 148, 222
seen in this life 43, 148
seen reality 214
sentient beings .... xii, 4-6, 8-15, 17, 19-23, 25, 29, 31, 32, 42, 60, 68, 83, 85, 86, 88, 90, 92-97, 99-101, 106, 110-113, 117-121, 127, 130-132, 138, 140-142, 147, 156, 157, 163, 164, 166, 173, 179, 184, 186, 191, 194, 201, 205-210, 212, 214-216, 221, 225, 227, 232, 234, 236, 238, 241, 244
seven limbs of accumulation .. 57
seven major editions of *The Translated Word* ...... xxii, 243
seven types of śhrāvakas 85
sixty aspects of intonation 73, 127
small and medium karmas ... 214
small cymbals ... 24, 75, 178, 223
son of the gods 210, 217
sons of the family 213
special intention 9, 99, 186, 209, 241
special miracle 206, 218
special miracle of total expression 218
speech of a single tathāgata . 199, 200
speech of the god Brahmā 73
spiritual friends . 3, 4, 19, 21, 32, 36, 48, 56, 115, 193, 223
spiritual teacher 116
stainless and totally pure 105
structure of the prayer 57, 95
style of being of a bodhisatva . 46
Subhuti 36, 213
succession of lives 214
Sudhana ... iv, xiii, xiv, xxii, xxiii, xxvi, 1, 3, 6, 8, 12, 15-17, 21,

45-49, 54, 134, 135
Sudhana's journey 45, 46
suffering of the bad migrations 26, 110, 190
Sukhāvatī .. x, xi, 31, 43, 99, 151, 163, 164, 167, 185, 217, 226
Sukhāvatī Prayer .... x, xi
superfactual ... 94, 95, 161, 230, 234, 242
superfactual enlightenment mind 161, 230
superfactual truth 234, 242
superfactual truth enlightenment mind 234, 242
superfice 242
superficies 187, 242
superior merits 30, 149, 223
supplication . 87, 88, 91, 92, 182, 183
supplication to the buddhas .. 91
supporting kinsmen to the migrators 193
supports for study iv, xi, xxviii, 245
supreme oil lamps ... 24, 75, 178
supreme parasols 24, 75, 178
supreme scents 24, 75
Surendrabodhi 32, 34, 36, 56
surpassed offerings 75
sustained in goodness .. 30, 152, 153, 224
sutra .. ii, iv, v, vii, viii, xi, xiii, xiv, xvii, xxii-xxvi, xxviii, xxix, 1, 3, 15, 32, 34, 36, 37, 45-49, 51, 53-56, 60, 73, 74, 80, 85, 87, 93, 96, 99, 103, 110, 127, 129, 145, 151, 154, 161, 167, 180, 194, 199, 210, 211, 213, 242, 243, 247
Sutra of Completely Cleaning Obscurations of Karma 210
Sutra of the Householder Uncouth

.... 103, 247
Sutra of the Recollection of the Noble Three Jewels 74, 87, 93, 242, 247
Sutra Petitioned by Noble One Upāli 213
syntax .. xvi, xvii, xix, xxi, xxiv, 58, 59, 61, 62, 74, 124, 125, 181
Tāranātha xviii
tathāgata family line 69
ten non-virtuous actions 212
ten topics 57, 95, 172
Tenpa'i Wangchuk ... iv, xii, xiii, xx, xxi, xxvi, 50, 71, 76, 91, 98, 110, 113, 152, 166, 185, 221, 247
Tenpa'i Wangchuk's commentary .. 65, 73, 75, 97, 121, 126, 129, 133, 134, 138, 144, 149, 158, 186, 190
tenth bodhisatva level ..... x, xiv, xxiv, 46
tenth-level bodhisatvas 127
tīrthika .. 31, 155, 156, 212, 225, 243
the actual prayer . 42, 57, 95, 101
the best of excellent displays . 24, 75
the bodhisatva path .. x, 110, 114, 123, 128, 142, 180
the end of the prayer .... xii, 165, 222
the five immediates 31, 153, 154, 214
the five immediates explanation 154
the four forces of antidote ... 139
the four māras 139
the god Indra 88
the immediates ... 212, 214, 224
the importance of Samantabhadra's Prayer ... iii, x
the origin of Samantabhadra's Prayer .... iii, xiii, 41, 45
the prayer is an extract ... iii, xiv, 41, 49
the prayer itself ... 37, 52, 54, 57
the preamble 41, 53
the seven limbs .. 41, 57, 58, 127
the story of Sudhana's journey 45
the Tibetan arrangement 41, 49, 50, 52-55, 64
the title given is a Tibetan invention 41, 51
The Translated Treatises 243
The Translated Word .... xxii-xxv, 3, 120, 124, 125, 134, 165, 243
the twelve deeds .. 92, 136, 137, 156, 183
the undefiled state 25, 86
the unsurpassed wheel 25, 86, 88, 182
third of the five bodhisatva paths 117
third of the four limitless ones 96
thirteen benefits 149
thirty-two major marks 155
this king of dedications . 30, 149, 223
thoroughly virtuous excellent conduct 30, 145
three bad migrations 111, 209, 223
Three Hundred 213
Three Jewels 60, 74, 87, 93, 210, 211, 240, 242, 247
three modes of turning the wheel 131
three types of armour 112
three Vehicles 236
three worlds ... 31, 155, 156, 225
explanation 156
Tibetan arrangement .... xv, 41, 49-55, 64

Tibetan arrangement of the prayer 53
Tibetan commentaries ... iii, vii, viii, xvii-xxi, xxiv, xxv, 37, 50, 57, 67, 71, 86, 89, 95, 100, 109, 128, 158
Tibetan experts . ix, xviii, 90, 241
Tibetan explanations of the prayer vii
title .. vii, 41, 50-53, 64, 158, 171, 236
Topic 1: Prostrations 41, 58
Topic 10: Its benefits 43, 148
Topic 2: Offerings 41, 75
Topic 3: Laying Aside 42, 80
Topic 5: Urging 42, 86
Topic 6: Supplicating 42, 91
Topic 7: Dedication 42, 93
Topic 9: Its ending 43, 147
topics .. xxviii, 41, 42, 57, 58, 95, 132, 172, 184, 213
topics eight to ten, the actual prayer 42, 95
total knowledge of the dharma 118
transformations .. 15, 17, 20, 23, 30, 146, 197, 221
transmission .... ix, xxi, 141
trifles of virtue 93
truly complete buddha ... 92-94, 102, 137, 153, 157, 159, 227, 231-233, 236
turn the wheel of dharma ... 11, 57, 86-88, 130, 172, 181, 184
twelve branches of the excellent speech 194
twelve deeds of enlightenment 136, 156
two main parts to the prayer .. 57
two types of prostration 92
types of karma 108, 139, 189, 209
types of offering 75

Śhākyamitra ..... xvi, 51, 64, 69, 102, 110, 111, 128, 142, 144, 152, 153, 165, 166
Śhākyamuni Buddha ... x, xi, 45, 88, 131, 143, 144, 159-161, 194
Śhāntideva .... x-xii
Śhāriputra 151
śhrāvaka . 85, 150, 151, 159, 177, 187, 206, 223, 225
śhrāvaka arhats 85
śhrāvakas' types 85
uncorrupted and faultless ... 26, 105, 187, 188
under the control of not knowing 31, 153, 224
unending .. 24, 27, 28, 42, 70-74, 87, 92, 93, 95, 119, 120, 127, 129, 130, 141, 176-178, 184, 194, 201, 202, 242, 247
unending store .. 27, 42, 95, 119, 120, 184, 194
unending voices of speech 28, 129
unfathomable . 128, 151, 177, 233
Unfathomable Light 151
unfluctuating karmas .. 139, 189, 216
universes xi
unobstructed and unmixed .. 203
unsatisfactoriness .. 32, 102, 167, 240, 243, 244
unsurpassed offering . 42, 77, 80, 178, 179
unsurpassed offerings ... 75, 79, 80, 184
uprooting non-virtuous karma
   through realizing emptiness 210
   through the force of antidote 209
   through the force of reliance 210
urging 25, 42, 57, 86-89, 93, 116, 136, 172, 181, 183
urging to turn the wheel of

dharma 57, 172, 181, 184
utterly express 19, 72
utterly prostrate .. 24, 62, 68, 174
Vairochana .... xxiv, 9, 14, 16, 47, 54-56
Vajra Vehicle 88, 236
Vajrasatva 241
vanishing of obscuration . 43, 162
Vasubhandu .... xvi, 165
verses of dedication 57, 159
verses of prostration 58
viewing the fields 123, 126
virtuous and unfluctuating karmas
.... 139, 189
virtuous karma ... 108, 139, 189, 209, 210, 214-216
voice 23, 24, 28, 71-74, 107, 127, 198
voice of a buddha 73
Western translators ... 53, 59, 72, 89, 90, 97, 103, 125, 136, 176, 177, 241
wheel of dharma . 11, 42, 57, 86-88, 121, 129-131, 136, 137, 172, 181, 182, 184, 195, 200, 204, 225
whole dedication of the roots of merit 57, 172
whole meaning of the prayer 162
wholly ending karmic obscuration
.... 43, 149, 153, 222
wholly holding merits that are special 43, 149, 222
wholly holding the holy dharma
.... 42, 95, 118, 184
wisdom .. 8, 9, 15, 16, 18, 19, 21, 29, 31, 66, 67, 87, 88, 103, 112, 119, 120, 123, 129, 131-133, 137, 138, 140, 141, 144, 155, 157, 160, 165, 176, 180-182, 191, 194-197, 201-205, 207, 208, 218, 225, 227, 239, 240, 242, 244, 247
wisdom mind 181, 195, 242
wisdom type of knowing 201, 203
word ordering 128
world realms . 7-9, 12-14, 16, 21-23, 36, 54, 156, 182, 185, 196, 204, 205
worldly merit 85, 180
worlds of the ten directions . 23, 25, 58-60, 86, 96, 174, 181
yakṣhas 106, 188
Yeshe De .. vi, xvii, xx, xxiii, xxiv, 32, 34, 36, 51, 54, 56, 58, 61, 64, 65, 79, 86, 89, 90, 98, 101, 112, 128, 132, 135, 151, 152, 156, 158, 163, 165, 221
Yeshe De's commentary .... viii, xviii, xxiv, 51, 66, 67, 98, 124, 146
Yeshe De's Tibetan commentary
.... vii

www.ingramcontent.com/pod-product-compliance
Lightning Source LLC
Chambersburg PA
CBHW021835220426
43663CB00005B/251